"For years we've been saying that counting matters in debates about lesbian and gay issues. Now Gary Gates and Jason Ost have used the biggest and best dataset available on same-sex couples to show why in this remarkable book. In addition to being incredibly useful for researchers, policymakers, businesspeople, and activists, *The Gay and Lesbian Atlas* has some fun surprises tucked inside its rankings that will challenge many stereotypes."

    • *M. V. Lee Badgett, University of Massachusetts Amherst and Institute for Gay and Lesbian Strategic Studies*

"Gates and Ost have used the numbers to tell a powerful story about same-sex couples and their families in America. *The Gay and Lesbian Atlas* will be indispensable for policymakers, marketers, and educators."

    • *Bob Witeck and Wes Combs, marketing communications experts and founders of Witeck-Combs Communications*

"The main purpose of *The Gay and Lesbian Atlas* is to explore the regional diversity in gay and lesbian living arrangements, but it provides much, much more. We not only learn about the geographic patterns of gay and lesbian households but also gain insight into this population's racial and ethnic diversity, age distribution, and socioeconomic variation."

    • *Susan M. Bianchi, Professor of Sociology and Director, Maryland Population Research Center, University of Maryland*

"Landmark advances in civil rights protections for gays and lesbians are attributable in large part to the courage of individuals who chose to 'come out' and be visible. With the data in *The Gay and Lesbian Atlas*, we can now demonstrate to America the truth about our lives as committed partners and parents. Once Americans discover they know gay and lesbian families, they will increasingly support equal protections for those families. *The Gay and Lesbian Atlas* is a timely and powerful tool in telling that story."

    • *U.S. Congresswoman Tammy Baldwin*

Gary J. Gates
&
Jason Ost

The Gay & Lesbian Atlas

Brooks – Cork Library
Shelton State
Community College

THE URBAN INSTITUTE PRESS
Washington, D.C.

THE URBAN INSTITUTE PRESS
2100 M Street, N.W.
Washington, D.C. 20037

Library of Congress Cataloging in Publication Data

Gates, Gary J.
   The gay and lesbian atlas / Gary J. Gates and Jason Ost.
      p. cm.
   Includes bibliographical references and index.
   ISBN 0-87766-721-7 (alk. paper)
  1. Gays—United States—Statistics. 2. United States—Population—
Statistics. I. Ost, Jason. II. Title.
   HQ76.3.U5G355 2004
   306.76'6'0973—dc22

                                           2004002065

Printed in the United States of America
10 09 08 07 06 05 04   1 2 3 4 5

THE URBAN INSTITUTE is a nonprofit, nonpartisan policy research and educational organization established in Washington, D.C., in 1968. Its staff investigates the social, economic, and governance problems confronting the nation and evaluates the public and private means to alleviate them. The Institute disseminates its research findings through publications, its web site, the media, seminars, and forums.

Through work that ranges from broad conceptual studies to administrative and technical assistance, Institute researchers contribute to the stock of knowledge available to guide decisionmaking in the public interest.

To

Mike Beary and Andy Pino

for their unfailing support,

infinite patience, and thoughtful insights.

Contents

Foreword

"But I don't know any gay people."

That impossible thought not only crosses the minds of legislators, but too often, it also crosses their lips.

In educating America about the lives of gays and lesbians, bisexuals, and transgender people, we find time and again that we have been made invisible. While millions more of us live our lives openly and honestly, it is surprising that so many decisionmakers do not yet understand we are truly everywhere. This important and long overdue book is proof.

Simply put, Gary Gates and Jason Ost dispel ignorance with accurate information. Through sound data, crisp graphics, and understandable maps, their analysis explores the population roadmap given us by Census 2000. With all its limitations in accurately counting same-sex households, the U.S. Census has made a historic start to identify who we are and how we live.

Through the census process, an agency of the U.S. government has dared ask same-sex American households to come forward and be counted. The truthfulness of these couples changes the debate for many. From an abstract controversy read about in newspapers or seen in noisy debates on television, instead Americans find ourselves today in an honest discussion about real families, real people, and real lives. These facts will help us dispel stereotypes and present a fuller, more complex, and certainly more accurate picture of the gay and lesbian family in America.

This book makes a timely contribution for many readers including demographers, marketers, urban planners, public health leaders, and political and social scientists. And from my perspective, it is an invaluable resource for all civil rights advocates and our elected officials.

As I write these words, all Americans are coming face to face with the reality of lesbian and gay families around us, like my own. Given the demise of antiquated sodomy laws, more jurisdictions are beginning to offer the protections of domestic partner benefits, civil unions, and even full marriage rights to same-sex couples. Bearing witness makes all the difference. For those who read and apply the knowledge in this book, it promises a fresh, welcome, and valuable light on the lives of same-sex families.

Elizabeth Birch
Executive Director, 1995–2004
Human Rights Campaign, *the nation's largest GLBT advocacy organization*

Acknowledgments

Our thanks go to the many people who made the production of this *Atlas* possible. First and foremost, we thank the more than half a million gay and lesbian couples who took the courageous step to be counted in the 2000 Census.

We are grateful to our colleagues at the Urban Institute, particularly the staffs of the Center on Labor, Human Services, and Population, the Communications Department, and members of the Mapping Users Group, for their assistance and support throughout the development of this book. We also thank Robert Reischauer, Urban Institute president, who provided the encouragement and initial financial support that made this project possible.

The Human Rights Campaign Foundation provided financial support for analyses of Census 2000 that helped to jump-start the development of this project and demonstrated the broad interest in this work.

Martin O'Connell and Jason Fields at the U.S. Census Bureau, along with Seth Sanders at the University of Maryland, Dan Black at Syracuse University, and Lowell Taylor at Carnegie Mellon University, provided invaluable guidance in helping to assess the reliability of the data used in the analyses. We are also grateful to Trudy Suchan at the U.S. Census Bureau for her much-needed advice on the design of the maps.

The Center on Spatially Integrated Social Sciences, especially the instructors and participants at the Population Science and GIS workshop held at Penn State University in May 2003, provided many useful insights into this project.

Robert Witeck and his colleagues at Witeck-Combs Communications offered constant support and assistance. We are also indebted to the two anonymous reviewers who provided detailed, thoughtful, and incredibly useful comments.

Additional thanks go to Lee Badgett, Hetty Barthel, Aaron Belkin, Lisa Bennett, Jeff Cleghorn, Richard Florida, Sharra Greer, Spencer Lieb, Kim Mills, Dan Perez-Lopez, Robert Planansky, Mark Shields, Anthony Silvestre, David Smith, and Freya Sonenstein for helpful insights and encouragement.

CHAPTER ONE

Why Study Gay and Lesbian Location Patterns?

Why Study Gay and Lesbian Location Patterns?

While the words "we are everywhere" can be heard frequently at gay and lesbian political events, Census 2000 provided the first empirical confirmation of this rallying cry. The finding that same-sex unmarried partners were present in 99.3 percent of all counties in the United States (Smith and Gates 2001) was one of the most commonly reported statistics from the release of Census 2000. News that gay and lesbian couples live in nearly every community may not seem all that startling. Yet the census data solidify what was only conjecture among some people. As fact, these data can be used to open minds. When informed that 55 same-sex couples were counted in his hometown in Mississippi, Republican State Sen. Dean Kirby told *The Clarion-Leader* (Jackson, MS), "Surely you jest. Wow! I have never met any of these people."[1]

These census data can open eyes, too. They can dispel stereotypes and present a more accurate picture of gay and lesbian families. Lobbyists from the Human Rights Campaign (HRC), the largest national gay and lesbian political organization, and from other gay/lesbian civil rights groups now regularly use this information to convince congressional representatives that gay and lesbian people live, and most likely vote, in their districts. Elizabeth Birch, then HRC Executive Director, cited the census data in her 2003 testimony before a Senate Judiciary Subcommittee during hearings on a possible constitutional amendment to ban civil marriage for same-sex couples.[2]

Of course, the importance of understanding the location patterns of gay and lesbian couples goes beyond simply acknowledging that they exist. It goes beyond recognition of their political clout. Gay and lesbian service providers, activist organizations, and an increasing number of companies seeking to market to the gay and lesbian population can all benefit from a more precise understanding of the location patterns and demographic characteristics of this population.

Political Awareness

Issues such as civil marriage for same-sex couples, gay and lesbian adoption rights, domestic partner benefits, and hate crime and antidiscrimination statutes (that include sexual orientation) constitute a broad public policy agenda that could be influenced by these new census data. The same-sex marriage issue in particular looms large in the 2004 presidential campaign, as some conservative groups consider banning such contractual unions a higher immediate priority than abortion restrictions.[3] These high-profile debates are marked by an astonishing lack of empirical data. Until now, it was difficult to assess the potential impacts of these policies because so little was known about the gay and lesbian population. That's about to change.

In addition to enlightening policy debate, hard facts on the gay and lesbian population illustrate that it is a sizable voting block and an increasingly visible constituency in many American communities. In the California gubernatorial recall election of 2003, for example, 4 percent of voters identified as gay, lesbian, or bisexual, a figure similar to national polls in the 1996 and 2000 presidential elections.[4] It is probably no coincidence that 8 of the 10 states with the highest concentrations of gay and lesbian couples voted for Al Gore in the 2000 presidential election, and that 14 of the 20 states (and the District of Columbia) with higher-than-average gay and lesbian concentrations also supported the Democratic candidate.

Census 2000 makes it possible to document the extent to which states with high proportions of same-sex couples generally have more favorable laws regarding gay men and lesbians. The data can confirm that 9 of the 12 states that have not passed a "Defense of Marriage Act" restricting marriage to only heterosexual couples are among the 20 states with a gay and lesbian couple concentration above the U.S. average. Similarly, 11 of the 14 states with laws banning discrimination based on sexual orientation are among these same 20 states. Statistically, states with more gay/lesbian-supportive laws have higher concentrations of gay and lesbian couples.[5]

The demographic and geographic analyses of the gay and lesbian community contained in this book offer critical information to inform public policy debates and offer politicians a glimpse at the characteristics of an increasingly important voting constituency.

Providing Public Health Services

Using census data to examine the spatial distribution of gay and lesbian couples can offer important insight into the location patterns of the gay and lesbian community as a whole. The ability to reach this population in certain areas may be critical for public-health workers. While many organizations that provide services or resources to the gay and lesbian community have a good sense of where this population lives in their service area, such estimations often neglect important subgroups of gays and lesbians such as racial and ethnic minorities or people who do not openly identify as gay or lesbian. Evidence of where these populations concentrate could help in reaching these often hard-to-serve groups.

The public health field already has discovered the value of census data. Information on same-sex male couples counted in the 1990 Census was incorporated into the design of the Urban Men's Health Study (Catania et al. 2001), an important survey that provides critical information about HIV risk factors and behaviors among men who have sex with men (MSM). Spencer Lieb, an epidemiologist at the Florida Department of Health, helped with the plan to target prevention and treatment services to HIV-positive MSM in Florida. Lieb compared the location patterns of reported MSM living with HIV/AIDS and census-identified same-sex male unmarried partners within Florida counties and found striking similarities in the location patterns of these two groups, including when the sample was split based on racial/ethnic identification (Lieb et al. 2003).

Lieb's finding has two important ramifications. First, it confirms the ability to reach hard-to-locate populations more efficiently. Many jurisdictions lack good data on the HIV status of residents and often rely on AIDS-incidence data for targeting prevention and treatment programs. Individuals can be infected with HIV, the virus that causes AIDS, for many years before exhibiting any symptoms of the disease necessary for an AIDS diagnosis. Data that count only documented AIDS cases provide potentially decades-old pictures of where any epidemic "hotspots" might exist. The high correlation between HIV-positive MSM location and census same-sex male unmarried partners suggests that census data offer a reasonable and more current proxy for assessing the location clusters of MSM when data on HIV infection are unavailable or viewed as too confidential for release.

The high correlation discovered by Lieb also provides important evidence of the validity of census data in actually representing the location patterns of all gay men. Since the HIV-positive MSM population includes both single and coupled gay men, its strong association with census male couples offers evidence that the broad location patterns of gay-male couples may not differ substantially from the location patterns of gay men in general. This is important because census data only identify gay men who are part of a same-sex couple. The correlation between location patterns of gay men and gay-male couples bodes well for any organization attempting to target resources or services, public health-related or otherwise, toward the gay and lesbian population.

Marketing

An increasing number of companies view the gay and lesbian community, with a buying power estimated at $485 billion (Brown, Washton, and Witeck 2002), as an important component of their overall marketing strategy. While these marketing efforts are not without controversy, they have become increasingly more common, even in "mainstream" media. The success of such television shows as NBC's "Will and Grace" and Bravo's "Queer Eye for the Straight Guy" demonstrates that gay and lesbian subject matter is increasingly acceptable to the general population.

While not a panacea in the gay and lesbian struggle for acceptance, marketing efforts designed to reach this population do offer gay men and lesbians a sense of being included in the broader society. The extent that some of this marketing goes beyond advertising in gay-themed magazines or newspapers into wide-ranging media outlets also demonstrates that gay and lesbian individuals are an important component in American society.

As CEO of Witeck-Combs Communications, Inc., Robert Witeck works with a wide range of companies hoping to target their products to the gay and lesbian population. Witeck states,

> Across America, gays and lesbians hold jobs, own businesses, pay taxes, take vacations, invest in stocks, raise children, and spend money on goods and services. Like everyone else, they save for their education, their retirement, and their pleasure travel too. It's not surprising that corporations have begun to affirm their respect and inclusion of gays and lesbians by adopting fair-minded workplace employment practices—a trend now favored by a majority of the Fortune 500. And by translating this corporate citizenship into marketing strategies, businesses also express how much they value their gay customers and shareholders.[6]

Understanding where to best target gay and lesbian–specific marketing campaigns is critical to these companies, and census data offer a mechanism to focus comprehensive marketing campaigns with a new precision.

Community and Economic Development

One of the most intriguing uses for census data on gay and lesbian location comes from Richard Florida, best-selling author of *The Rise of the Creative Class* (Florida 2002), who argues that creativity constitutes the central driving force for success in today's economy. Florida posits that regions must attract and retain creative and innovative people to secure a promising economic future, and will thrive when individuals with diverse backgrounds and viewpoints can easily interact. Because a concentration of gay/ lesbian couples signals diversity, knowing where they live can prove useful to those communities.

This link between diversity and economic success was first proposed in a Brookings Institution paper (Florida and Gates 2002) exploring the relationship between technology and tolerance. The authors demonstrate a strong link between a thriving tech-oriented economy and diverse populations, including those with high concentrations of gay couples. The presence of a large gay and lesbian population serves as one signal of a high level of community diversity, tolerance, and acceptance for people who are different. This tolerance, the authors find, creates low barriers to entry for all people into the labor market and enables firms to draw from the widest possible mix of creative and innovative employees.

Corporate America and, to a lesser degree, governments are increasingly including gay and lesbian–supportive policies as a way to encourage diversity. Ninety-two Fortune 100 companies ban discrimination based on sexual orientation in their organizations. Further, nearly two-thirds of them offer health benefits to same-sex partners. Governments appear a bit slower to catch on to this trend, as only 14 states and the District of Columbia prohibit discrimination based on sexual orientation in both public and private employment (an additional 11 states prohibit such discrimination in public employment only).[7]

Regional diversity (reflected in part by the visible presence of gay men and lesbians) does not go unnoticed by companies seeking to locate in communities where creative and innovative individuals can flourish. Bill Bishop, reporting on Florida's work for the *Austin American-Statesman,* put it well. He wrote, "Where gay households abound, geeks follow."[8] These geeks can be the engine of success for many regions and corporations responding to their pres-

The presence of a large gay and lesbian population serves as one signal of a high level of community diversity, tolerance, and acceptance for people who are different.

ence. Richard Florida often cites Carley Fiorina, CEO at Hewlett Packard, telling America's governors, "Keep your tax incentives and the like, just give us talent. We will go where the highly skilled people are."[9]

Social Science Research

Census data can reach perhaps their greatest potential in the social science research community. A demographic exploration of gay and lesbian families provides important insights into broader social science theory about family dynamics and economic decisionmaking.

Social science theories on the family acknowledge the importance of fertility and child-rearing behavior on a variety of family decisions. However, most social scientists agree that the decision to have children is part of a cluster of simultaneous decisions including marriage, employment, and location. Lesbians, and even more so gay men, are less likely to have children than other couples and are not able to legally marry in the United States. While no definitive understanding exists of the mechanisms of sexual orientation and gay/lesbian identification, it is commonly understood in the research community that sexual orientation is not chosen. As such, it can be thought of as a randomly occurring event in the population. If this is the case, then the lower probability of child rearing among gay men and lesbians or their inability to marry does not result so much from a constellation of family-related choices, but rather from a random event unrelated to these choices. Thus, gay men and lesbians provide an intriguing social science test case to study how family decision-making processes differ when the probability of hav-

ing children is reduced or when the beneficial effects of marriage are not available.

This case is articulated clearly in a paper by Dan Black, Gary Gates, Seth Sanders, and Lowell Taylor entitled *Why Do Gay Men Live in San Francisco?* (2002). The authors assert that in the absence of children, individuals and households will have higher disposable income and smaller housing requirements. This means that childless households can devote more income toward the purchase of "amenities" and will locate disproportionately in expensive, amenity-rich regions. Because for gay men the child-rearing decision can be thought of as exogenous, or unrelated, to the location decision (since the "random" event of being gay lowers the likelihood of child rearing), they provide the best group from which to test this theory. The results support the theory, finding that gay men tend to locate in more amenity-rich regions of the country.

In addition to children, social science theories about relationship formation and dynamics are often heavily tied to theories of gender roles and expectations. Studying the dynamics of same-sex couples offers a mechanism to explore these issues in the absence of gender differences, again providing insights into broader social science theoretical perspectives.

Selected Findings

Here are some findings from analyses contained in the *Atlas:*

■ Vermont edges out California as the state with the highest concentration of gay and lesbian couples in the nation. California, New York, and Massachusetts rank among the top 10 for both the total number of gay and lesbian couples and the overall concentration of same-sex couples in the state. While Florida does not rank among the top 10 states (it is 11th), three Florida cities (Wilton Manors, Miami Shores, and Key West) make the top 10 list of U.S. cities and towns with the highest concentration of gay and lesbian couples. Among large metropolitan areas, San Francisco, Oakland, Seattle, Fort Lauderdale, and Austin rank highest in same-sex couple concentration.

■ Gay men do not necessarily choose to live in the same communities as their female counterparts, and vice versa. State same-sex male- and female-couple concentration rankings share only five states (Arizona, California, Massachusetts, Vermont, and Washington) between the respective top 10 lists. Only one county (San Francisco County) appears among the top 10 counties for both male and female couples. While San Francisco, Fort Lauderdale, Santa Rosa, Seattle, and New York top the list of metropolitan areas for gay male couples, the top areas for lesbian couples are Santa Rosa, Santa Cruz, Santa Fe, San Francisco, and Oakland.

■ Same-sex couple neighborhoods differ substantially from those of heterosexual married couples, but less so from heterosexual unmarried couples. On average, gay male couples, and to a lesser degree lesbian couples, live in neighborhoods that are more urban, more diverse, have more educated residents, have older housing stock, and have higher crime rates than the neighborhoods heterosexual married couples live in.

■ The one in four gay and lesbian couples with children do not necessarily live near other gay and lesbian couples. Same-sex couples with children tend to live in states and large metropolitan areas with relatively low concentrations of gay

and lesbian couples. Mississippi, South Dakota, Alaska, South Carolina, and Louisiana are where same-sex couples are most likely raising children.

■ Nearly one in five people in a same-sex couple is at least 55 years old. Seniors dominate the gay and lesbian population in the upper Midwest (North Dakota, South Dakota, Montana, and Wyoming). They make up 30 percent or more of each state's gay and lesbian couple population.

■ Areas with large minority communities have the highest concentrations of minority gay and lesbian couples within the broader population and within the gay community. The South dominates the rankings of states by the concentration of African-American couples among all households and among other gay and lesbian couples. Texas metropolitan areas (with their large Hispanic communities) feature prominently in similar rankings by the concentration of Hispanic gay or lesbian couples.

While Census 2000 data on same-sex couples affirm the presence of gay men and lesbians nearly everywhere in the United States, a closer examination of their spatial distribution and demographic characteristics provides important information to the political and public policy communities, public health officials, marketers, community and economic development professionals, and social scientists. Findings from this research can inform a variety of policy debates and provide added value to research on and service delivery to gay men and lesbians.

Census 2000 provides the largest and most geographically representative sample of gay and lesbian families available in the United States today. No other data source permits the exploration of the geographic patterns of this community in greater detail, nor allows for an analysis of such understudied subsets of the gay and lesbian population as couples with children, seniors, and racial and ethnic minorities. Census data also permit comparisons between same-sex couples and their heterosexual counterparts.

The Gay and Lesbian Atlas offers a compelling portrait of gay and lesbian families that both confirms and challenges common anecdotal information about the gay and lesbian community. For example, while it may come as no surprise that San Francisco, Key West, and western Massachusetts all host large gay and lesbian populations, it might surprise some that Houston, Texas contains one of the 10 "gayest" neighborhoods in the country, or that Alaska and New Mexico are among the states with the highest concentration of gay and lesbian coupled seniors in their senior population. The data support the growing anecdotal evidence that increasing numbers of children are being raised by gay and lesbian couples. However, same-sex couples with children frequently live in areas of the country known for more conservative political and cultural views.

This *Atlas* marks a beginning of the exploration of census data to describe the characteristics of gay and lesbian families in the United States. Analyses of more detailed data offer myriad opportunities to construct a rich portrait of the geographic, demographic, and economic characteristics of the gay and lesbian community. These analyses begin to fill an important information gap by providing an empirical perspective to the vibrant policy and intellectual debates affecting the lives of gay men and lesbians that reach into corporate boardrooms, classrooms, and virtually all levels and branches of government across the United States.

Endnotes

1. Clay Harden, "Census: 4,774 gay couples in Miss.," *The Clarion-Leader*, August 22, 2001.

2. See http://www.hrc.org/newsreleases/2003/030904eb _testimony.asp for a transcript of her testimony.

3. See Mike Allen's article "Gay Marriage Looms Large," *Washington Post*, October 25, 2003.

4. California poll results can be found at http://www.washington post.com/wp-srv/politics/replacementballotexitpoll.html. According to the National Gay and Lesbian Task Force, Voter News Service polls indicate that nearly 5 percent of all voters reported being gay or lesbian in the 1996 and 2000 presidential elections (see http:// www.ngltf.org/news/release.cfm?releaseID=568).

5. The gay-supportive laws score is constructed using state laws regarding civil unions, Defense of Marriage Acts, gay/lesbian adoption policies, sexual orientation discrimination statutes, hate crime laws including sexual orientation, and the absence of sodomy laws enacted as of December 2003. The gay/lesbian law score and the gay/lesbian concentration index have a significant statistical correlation of 0.62 ($p < .05$). Interpreting this relationship is not simple. Several factors could contribute to this positive association. Gay and lesbian couples may migrate to states with a more favorable legal climate. However, favorable laws are more likely the consequence of a state's larger and more visible gay and lesbian population. Same-sex couples in states with more favorable laws may also be the most comfortable in reporting their relationship as such on their census form.

6. Author interview of Robert Witeck, March 4, 2003.

7. States that prohibit discrimination based on sexual orientation in both public and private employment (as of December 2003) are California, Connecticut, Hawaii, Maryland, Massachusetts, Minnesota, Nevada, New Hampshire, New Jersey, New Mexico, New York, Rhode Island, Vermont, and Wisconsin. States that prohibit such discrimination in public employment only are Alaska, Arizona, Colorado, Delaware, Illinois, Indiana, Kentucky, Michigan, Montana, Pennsylvania, and Washington.

8. William Bishop, "Technology and Tolerance: Austin Hallmarks," *Austin American-Statesman*, June 25, 2000.

9. Richard Florida, "Pittsburgh, Let's Wake Up and Play," *Pittsburgh Post-Gazette*, June 11, 2000.

CHAPTER TWO

Data and Methods

Data and Methods

Data from Census 2000 are used for the construction of all maps and for the majority of the analyses presented in this book. Of all government data collection processes, none has the weight of this household survey. Census 2000 is the latest decennial census administered by the U.S. Census Bureau for the constitutionally mandated purpose of apportioning congressional seats among the 50 states. In addition to its mandated purpose, the decennial census is also used to determine the appropriate distribution of government funding, draw state legislative districts, evaluate the success of programs, identify populations in need of services, and for a host of other functions (U.S. Census Bureau 2002).

During the census collection period in spring 2000, each housing unit in the 50 states, the District of Columbia, and Puerto Rico received a census questionnaire with six basic questions about each person in the household: name, sex, age, relationship to the householder, Hispanic origin, and race. The householder (the person filling out the census form) was also asked whether the housing unit was rented or owned. These seven questions make up what is commonly called the census "short form."[1]

The specific sources of primary data for the analyses presented in the *Atlas* are as follows:

- Summary File 1 (SF 1): based on short-form questionnaire responses from 100 percent counts of households (including same-sex unmarried partners)
- Summary File 2 (SF 2): based on short-form questionnaire responses from 100 percent counts of households (including same-sex unmarried

partners), broken down by the race/ethnicity of the householder

■ Summary File 3 (SF 3): based on long-form questionnaire responses from one in six households

■ Census Special Tabulation: based on short-form questionnaire responses from 100 percent counts of households as reported in a Census Bureau special tabulation of county-level counts of same-sex unmarried partner households with children under age 18 in the household and counts of individuals within same-sex unmarried partner couples by age

Counting Gay Men and Lesbians in Census 2000

The census does not ask any questions about sexual orientation, sexual behavior, or sexual attraction, three common ways used to identify gay men and lesbians in surveys (see Laumann, Gagnon, and Michael 1994). Rather, census forms include a number of relationship categories to define how individuals in a household are related to the householder. These fall into two broad categories: related persons (including husband/wife, son/daughter, brother/sister, and so on), and unrelated persons. Since 1990, the Census Bureau has included an "unmarried partner" category to describe an unrelated household member's relationship to the householder.[2] If the householder designates another adult of the same sex as his or her unmarried partner, the household counts as a same-sex unmarried-partner household. The actual question from the census form is shown in figure 2.1.

Research comparing 1990 Census data on same-sex unmarried partners and data from other surveys

Figure 2.1. Census 2000 Household Roster

How is this person related to Person 1?
Mark ◯ ONE box.
◯ Husband/wife
◯ Natural-born son/daughter
◯ Adopted son/daughter
◯ Stepson/stepdaughter
◯ Brother/sister
◯ Father/mother
◯ Grandchild
◯ Parent-in-law
◯ Son-in-law/daughter-in-law
◯ Other relative— Print exact relationship.

If NOT RELATED to Person 1:
◯ Roomer, boarder
◯ Housemate, roommate
◯ Unmarried partner
◯ Foster child
◯ Other nonrelative

Source: Census 2000.

provides strong evidence that same-sex unmarried partners counted by the census are by and large gay and lesbian couples (Black et al. 2000).

Differences between 1990 and 2000 Counts

Same-sex unmarried partners were enumerated, or determined in the official count, differently between the 1990 and 2000 Census data collection processes. The main difference stems from the editing, or data cleaning, procedures used by the Census Bureau following data collection.

When information about a person or household is missing or inconsistent, the Census Bureau performs a variety of imputations to make the data both consistent and complete. Consistency edits occur when an obvious inconsistency is present in the data, for example if a 4-year-old male is enumerated as the "husband" of a 35-year-old female. Census might edit this record by either altering the age of the male or changing his status to "child," depending on other information provided by the household. Consistency edits are not flagged in the data, and any records of these edits are internal to the Census Bureau.

It is possible that a gay or lesbian couple could consider themselves "married," based on their own interpretation of that social construct, even though at the time the census was collected, no state government officially recognized marital unions between two people of the same sex (although Vermont recognized a category called "civil unions" that provides many of the same rights as those afforded to married couples). Since no federal or state law recognizes same-sex marriages,[3] if a gay or lesbian householder designates his or her same-sex partner as a "husband/wife," the Census Bureau could not report these households as same-sex married couples.

During the post-collection data editing for the 1990 Census, the Census Bureau treated most same-sex "married" couples as an inconsistency in the sex variable for the "husband/wife," and usually changed the sex as a consistency edit. This means that in data released by the Bureau the couple was counted as a heterosexual married couple.

Due in part to lobbying by demographers and gay and lesbian interest groups, the Census Bureau changed their post-collection data editing procedures in Census 2000 to treat the issue as an inconsistency

in the relationship to householder rather than in the spouse's sex. That is, the "husband/wife" relationship designation was changed as a consistency edit to an "unmarried partner" relationship. Since the sex variables were not changed, the couple was counted as a same-sex unmarried partner couple.[4]

This change in editing procedures constitutes one factor in the dramatic increases in the counts of same-sex unmarried partners between 1990 and 2000. Large-scale publicity efforts made by national gay and lesbian groups along with increased willingness of gay men and lesbians to identify themselves as partners likely also account for the large increases.

Undercount of Same-Sex Unmarried Partners in Census 2000

Despite the changes in the Census Bureau's data-editing procedures, significant undercount issues remain in Census 2000's count of same-sex unmarried partners. There are several potential reasons for this undercount. Concerns about the confidentiality of their responses may have led many gay and lesbian couples to indicate a status that would not provide evidence of the true nature of their relationship.[5] Other couples may have felt that "unmarried partner" or "husband/wife" does not accurately describe their relationship. A study of the undercount of same-sex unmarried partners in Census 2000 indicates that these were the two most common reasons behind why some gay and lesbian couples chose not to designate themselves as unmarried partners (Badgett and Rogers 2003).[6]

Estimate of the Undercount

Estimating the size of any potential undercount in the census data is a challenge. A rough estimate of the severity of the undercount of same-sex unmarried partners in Census 2000 can be made by combining estimates of coupling rates among gay men and lesbians and estimates of the prevalence of gay and lesbian individuals in the United States.

Black et al. (2000) measured same-sex coupling rates for two different definitions of "gay" and "lesbian" in the National Health and Social Life Survey (NHSLS) data—identifying as gay or lesbian and having had exclusively same-sex sexual partners in the last year. The coupling rate for men ranged from 18.4 percent among those who identified as gay to 28.6 percent among those who had exclusively same-sex sexual partners in the last year. The comparable rates for women were 41.6 percent and 43.8 percent. Clearly, these data suggest that coupling behavior may be quite different for gay men and lesbians. Nonetheless, taking the midpoint of these estimates suggests that 23.5 percent of gay men and 42.7 percent of lesbians are coupled.

Prevalence estimates of the proportion of men and women in the United States who are gay or lesbian are more difficult to obtain. The size of these estimates varies tremendously with how homosexuality is defined (attraction, behavior, or identity). In perhaps the most well-respected recent work on the topic, Laumann et al. (1994) find that 2.8 percent of men and 1.4 percent of women self-identify as homosexual. Chapter 3 explores in greater detail how assumptions of various coupling rates among gay men and lesbians along with different levels of an undercount provide estimates of the size of the total gay and lesbian population. Using an undercount of approximately 25 percent yields estimates of the total gay and lesbian population that are most similar to Laumann's 1994 estimates, although the actual undercount could be higher if Laumann's data also undercount gay men and lesbians.

Potential Measurement Error within the Same-Sex Unmarried-Partner Population

While the existence of an undercount is quite likely, an equally relevant issue is the possibility that some portion of same-sex unmarried-partner couples might be incorrectly designated as such due to a miscoding of either the "unmarried partner" relationship status or the sex of one of the partners. There are a number of ways a household could be classified in the census data as a same-sex unmarried partner household even though it is not headed by a gay or lesbian couple.

Sex Miscoding among Heterosexual Married Couples

The largest source of measurement error among the same-sex unmarried partner data from Census 2000 is likely a result of sex miscoding errors among heterosexual couples. It can be assumed that some very small fraction of the population makes an error when completing the census form and possibly miscodes a variety of responses, including the sex of the householder or the householder's "husband/wife" or "unmarried partner." Under Census 2000 editing procedures, all these miscoded couples would be included in the counts of same-sex unmarried partners.

Recall that in 1990, married couples that inadvertently checked the wrong sex for the householder or the "husband/wife" most likely had the sex of the "husband/wife" changed. However, in Census 2000, these sex-miscoded couples are now counted as same-sex unmarried partners. Because the ratio between married couples and same-sex couples is so large (roughly 90 to 1), even a small fraction of sex miscoding among married couples adds a sizable fraction of heterosexual married couples to the same-sex unmarried-partner population, possibly distorting some demographic characteristics, particularly child rearing. While this same error could occur among heterosexual unmarried partners, the smaller ratio between them and same-sex unmarried partners greatly reduces the effects of this form of measurement error on the same-sex couple population.

Ascertaining the extent of sex miscoding is challenging, as the most recent published census study involved the 1970 Census (U.S. Census Bureau 1975). We are grateful to Census Bureau officials, who conducted a detailed internal analysis of Census 2000 data to provide some insights into the possible extent of the measurement error problem among same-sex unmarried-partner couples. Their analyses suggest a sex-miscoding rate no higher than 0.2 percent among heterosexual couples, and even that is likely an upper-bound error rate. Further, they have determined that the sex-miscoding measurement error does not have any significant effect on geographical distribution patterns. As a result, the data used for the construction of all maps and charts in this book concerning geographic distribution of all same-sex couples do not make any corrections for possible measurement error.

However, this form of error could have a much more pronounced effect on data regarding same-sex couples with children under the age of 18, since married couples (the primary source of the measurement error) are much more likely to have children in the home than gay or lesbian couples. These sex-miscoded couples' inadvertent presence among the same-sex unmarried partners could artificially inflate the proportion of same-sex couples with children. The Census Bureau found that 45.6 percent of married couples reported children in their household in Census 2000, compared with 21.8 percent of gay male couples and 32.7 percent of lesbian couples.[7]

This translates to roughly 24.8 million married couples with children and about 162,000 same-sex partners with children; in other words, there are over 150 times as many married couples with children as there are same-sex partners with children. This ratio highlights that even a small sex-miscoding rate of 0.2 percent among the married couples would mean that 49,600 of the 162,000 same-sex unmarried partners with children (or nearly 31 percent) are actually married couples with children.

To at least partially correct for this measurement error, counts in all analyses involving same-sex coupled households with children are adjusted assuming that 0.2 percent of heterosexual couples miscoded the sex of one partner. That is to say, 0.2 percent of married couples with and without children (data on the counts of heterosexual unmarried partners with children were not available) are subtracted from counts of same-sex couples with and without children, respectively. Census Bureau officials concur that the 0.2 percent sex-miscoding rate represents an upper-bound estimate of this error, so calculations for the analyses generate lower-bound estimates of the proportion of same-sex unmarried partners who have children under age 18 present in the household.

Other Sources of Measurement Error

Mistakes in the designation of an unmarried partner could also cause errors. One essentially undetectable form of error (discussed at length in Black et al. 2000) occurs when the person filling out the census form (the householder) does not have a spouse or unmarried partner in the household, but does have a child or other adult in the household living with an unmarried partner. For example, if a female householder classifies the female unmarried partner of her son as an "unmarried partner," then this household

46 percent of married couples reported children in their household in Census 2000, compared with 22 percent of gay male couples and 33 percent of lesbian couples.

would be counted as a female same-sex unmarried-partner, or lesbian, household.

While analysis of 1990 Census data suggests that this type of error has negligible effects on the quality of the data at a national level, it could be more common in analyses of certain communities where extended families are more likely to be living in the home and households are larger. For example, Hispanic and American Indian populations are more likely to have extended families living in the home. Communities with large Hispanic and American Indian populations are therefore more susceptible to this type of error because there are proportionally more households where the error could occur. This form of measurement error would have the greatest effect on analyses of same-sex households with children because households most prone to this form of error (those with larger extended families in them) are also more likely to have children in the home. Short of examining the exact family structure within the home (an exercise only possible with more detailed census data), there is no simple correction for this form of measurement error.

Another form of measurement error could be language-based. Confusion may result when respondents fill out a census form not written in their native language or if the census enumerator translations of terms such as "unmarried partner" and "roommate" in other languages, particularly Spanish, do not have the same meanings as the English version. All households in the 50 states and the District of Columbia received English language forms, regardless of the predominant language spoken in either the household or the neighborhood. However, if a census form was not returned, most likely an enumerator who speaks local native languages would have visited the house and assisted the householder in filling out an English-language form.[8] Since 58 percent of Hispanic households have children under 18 living in them, compared with only 36 percent of all households in the U.S., a measurement error in this population that results in additional mistaken coding of same-sex unmarried-partner households would have a disproportionate effect on statistics involving same-sex couples with children. Unfortunately, we cannot determine the exact nature of any language-related error, nor are we able to estimate the magnitude of such errors.

Reporting figures from regions with larger and more diverse populations helps minimize any disproportionate influence of these uncorrectable measurement-error issues. Therefore, analyses of same-sex couples with children are limited to the nation, states, and large metropolitan areas.

Summary: Who Counts and Who Doesn't?

Despite these measurement-error issues, Census 2000 data on same-sex partners represent the most comprehensive source of data on gay and lesbian couples living in the United States. That said, many members of the gay, lesbian, bisexual, and transgender (GLBT) community are left out of these data. The largest omission is single gay men and lesbians, who form a majority of the GLBT community. Since only about a quarter of gay men and two-fifths of lesbians are coupled at any given time, over half of all gay and lesbian individuals in the United States are not included in census data counting same-sex couples.

Bisexual and transgender individuals will sporadically appear in the data, but cannot be identified as such. When they are part of a same-sex unmarried partner couple, they are counted as a gay or lesbian couple; however, there is no mechanism to separately identify bisexual or transgender individuals using census data. Certainly some men and women who are currently living with an unmarried partner of their same sex identify as bisexual, but since there is no census question about sexual orientation self-identification, it is unknown what portion bisexuals make up among the population of same-sex unmarried partners. Likewise, transgender people may also appear in the same-sex couple population if they are living with an unmarried partner and both individuals report the same sex. In this case, they are counted as part of a gay or lesbian couple, although this is likely a very small portion of the same-sex unmarried partner counts.

Endnotes

1. In addition, one out of every six housing units received a census "long form," which has a much wider array of questions, including questions about individual ancestry, household income, mortgage/rent, length of residence, size of the housing unit, utility bills, and so on.

2. Other relationship categories for unrelated persons are "roomer/boarder," "housemate/roommate," "foster child," and "other nonrelative."

3. In fact, the federal Defense of Marriage Act (DOMA) of 1996 prohibits any federal agency from recognizing a same-sex couple as being married. The Massachusetts Supreme Judicial Court ruled that the state must begin issuing marriage licenses to same-sex couples in May 2004. Marriage licenses issued to same-sex couples in San Francisco in 2004 will likely face multiple court challenges questioning their validity.

4. For more information about differences between the 1990 and 2000 counts of same-sex unmarried partners, see the Census Bureau's "Technical Note on Same-Sex Unmarried Partner Data From the 1990 and 2000 Censuses," at http://www.census.gov/population/www/cen2000/samesex.html.

5. The short form collects the following pieces of identifying information: each household member's name, the exact address of the household, and the householder's telephone number.

6. Another potential source of undercount is gay and lesbian couples who do not live together. The short form instructs you not to list "people who live or stay at another place most of the time." But this undercount issue would also apply to married couples who live apart, and we do not see it as a relevant source of undercount.

7. These statistics refer to the presence of children under the age of 18 who are sons or daughters of the householder. For our adjustments, we used statistics on the presence of children under the age of 18, regardless of the children's relationship to the householder.

8. The Spanish census form distributed in Puerto Rico translates "housemate/roommate" as "compañero(a) de casa/compañero(a) de cuarto" and "unmarried partner" as "compañero(a) no casado(a)." If enumerators used the word "compañero(a)" in both categories, this could have created some confusion in distinguishing between the two relationship types.

CHAPTER THREE

Estimating the Size of the Gay and Lesbian Population

The Census and Estimating
the Size of the Gay and
Lesbian Population

Estimating the Size of the
Gay and Lesbian Population

As with many issues concerning this group, estimating the size of the gay and lesbian population often provokes heated debate. Probably the most quoted, and misleading, figure is the mythical 10 percent. In his path-breaking 1948 book *Sexual Behavior in the Human Male,* Alfred Kinsey wrote, "Ten percent of the males are more or less exclusively homosexual" (Kinsey 1948). But the end of that sentence never really entered the public lexicon: "for at least three years between the ages of 16 and 55." Kinsey also states that 4 percent of white males are exclusively homosexual throughout their lives. While not minimizing the importance of Kinsey's research, it is simply not possible to ascertain a clear incidence rate of gay men and lesbians in the population from his studies. His subjects were all purposefully recruited from many venues, including institutional settings such as prisons and reform schools, rather than drawn from a known sampling frame, and his methods for defining homosexual behavior are therefore subject to bias (see Laumann et al. 1994, 287–90 for a more detailed discussion).

More recently, voter exit polls found that between 4 and 5 percent of voters in the last five national elections identified as gay or lesbian. While voters may constitute a better sample of the U.S. population than Kinsey's prisoners and reform school residents, they are still not representative of the population at large. Nationally representative polls or surveys that ask questions about sexual orientation are remarkably rare given the high-profile public policy debates that affect gay men and lesbians.

Even with a reliable survey of adults, accurately assessing how many people in the United States are gay or lesbian still presents an enormous challenge. There is no consensus definition of who is actually gay or lesbian. Definitions range from counting only those who are "out" and identify as gay or lesbian to including even those who admit to a sexual attraction to others of the same sex, regardless of their sexual behavior. Another definition is to count anyone who reports engaging in sexual activity with others of the same sex. Each of these definitions yields different estimates of the size of the gay and lesbian population. While a thorough examination of the complex interactions among sexual attraction, behavior, and identity, and the challenges posed in measuring these concepts is beyond the scope of this book,[1] work conducted by Black, Gates, Sanders, and Taylor (2000) demonstrates how these definitions can dramatically change the estimates of the size of the gay and lesbian population.

Analyses reported in "Demographics of the Gay and Lesbian Population in the United States: Evidence from Available Systematic Data Sources" in the May 2000 issue of *Demography* consider differing definitions of "gay" and "lesbian" and combine two datasets made up of nationally representative samples of men and women in the United States: the

General Social Survey and the National Health and Social Life Survey. The findings are shown in figure 3.1. Not only do incidence rates vary considerably depending on the definition of "gay" and "lesbian" used, but they also vary considerably by sex.

In general, the more restrictive the definition, the lower the incidence rate. Only 1 percent of women identified as lesbian or bisexual, and just 2.5 percent of men identified as gay or bisexual.[2] However, 3.6 percent of women and nearly 5 percent of men report having had sexual contact with a partner of the same sex since they were age 18. In their book, *The Social Organization of Sexuality*, Laumann and colleagues observe that more than 4 percent of women and more than 6 percent of men report a sexual attraction to people of the same sex (a definition not shown in figure 3.1).

The Census and Estimating the Size of the Gay and Lesbian Population

Despite the difficulties inherent in estimating the size of the gay and lesbian population in the United States, the examination of the possible undercount of same-sex couples provided in chapter 2 showed how counts of same-sex couples can help in estimating the size of the gay and lesbian population if reasonable assumptions about the rate of coupling among gay men and lesbians and the undercount of same-sex couples in the census are made. Table 3.1 demonstrates how estimates of the size of the gay and lesbian population vary under differing assumptions of the magnitude of any undercount.

Assuming no undercount, census figures imply that nearly 4 million Americans are gay or lesbian, or about 2 percent of all adults (1.3 percent of

Nationally representative polls that ask questions about sexual orientation are remarkably rare given the high-profile public policy debates that affect gay men and lesbians.

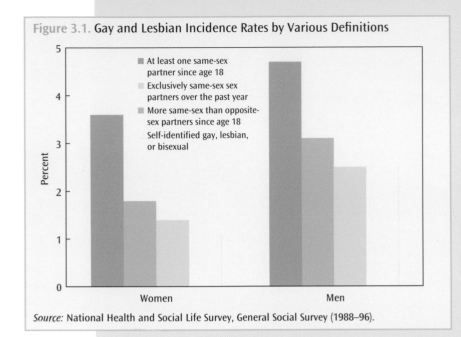

Figure 3.1. Gay and Lesbian Incidence Rates by Various Definitions

Legend:
- At least one same-sex partner since age 18
- Exclusively same-sex sex partners over the past year
- More same-sex than opposite-sex partners since age 18
- Self-identified gay, lesbian, or bisexual

Source: National Health and Social Life Survey, General Social Survey (1988–96).

lation (1.6 percent of women and 3.2 percent of men). If half of all gay and lesbian couples are not present in the census counts, then the estimates suggest that there are nearly 6 million gay and lesbian Americans, about 3 percent of the U.S. adult population (roughly 2 percent of women and 4 percent of men).

Clearly, gay men and lesbians make up a nontrivial portion of the population in the United States. While these calculations suggest that gay men and lesbians represent 2 to 3 percent of the U.S. adult population, a similar analysis on specific regions reveals that the proportions in some areas are substantially higher. For example, the assumptions suggest that 16 to 25 percent of adult men in San Francisco are gay and 10 to 15 percent of the population there is either gay or lesbian. In Hampshire County, Massachusetts, home to Amherst College, 5 to 7.5 percent of women are likely lesbian. Of course, coupling rates could vary by region, affecting these local estimates.

Estimating the size of the gay and lesbian population from census counts of same-sex unmarried partners requires making assumptions about definitions of

women and 2.5 percent of men). If a quarter of all gay and lesbian couples chose not to report themselves as spouses or unmarried partners in the census, then nearly 5 million Americans are gay or lesbian, representing 2.4 percent of the adult popu-

Table 3.1. Incidence Rates of Gay Men and Lesbians in the U.S. Population under Various Undercount Assumptions

	Men	Women	Total
Coupled gay men and lesbians	602,052	586,730	1,188,782
Total adults 18 and over	100,994,367	108,133,727	209,128,094
Estimated total gay men/lesbians assuming 23.5/42.7% coupling	2,561,923	1,374,075	3,935,998
Incidence rate with no undercount	**2.5%**	**1.3%**	**1.9%**
Estimated total gay men/lesbians assuming 23.5/42.7% coupling and 25% undercount	3,202,404	1,717,594	4,919,998
Incidence rate with 25% undercount	**3.2%**	**1.6%**	**2.4%**
Estimated total gay men/lesbians assuming 23.5/42.7% coupling and 50% undercount	3,842,885	2,061,112	5,903,998
Incidence rate with 50% undercount	**3.8%**	**1.9%**	**2.8%**

Source: Authors' calculations based on Census 2000 data.

who is gay and lesbian, coupling rates in a specifically defined gay and lesbian population, and the accuracy of census counts. The estimates garnered from even quite conservative assumptions reveal very high concentrations of gay men and lesbians in some areas of the United States. This finding demonstrates that the most compelling use of census data in studying the demographic patterns of gay and lesbian households in the United States is a study of proportions rather than one of levels. That is to say, estimating specific counts of gay men and lesbians with particular traits like race, age, or presence of children is not the best use of census data. Rather, census data are best used as a tool to explore both how the proportions of coupled gay men and lesbians with various demographic traits differ among states and communities across the nation, and how gay and lesbian households compare to other households. That important observation drives the book's further analyses.

Endnotes

1. See Sell and Petrulio (1996) and Laumann et al. (1994) for good discussions of this issue.

2. This question was only asked on the NHSLS and represents responses from only 22 of 1,921 women and 36 of 1,511 men in this sample.

CHAPTER FOUR

Where Do Gay and Lesbian Couples Live?

Where Do Gay and Lesbian Couples Live?

Put simply, gay and lesbian couples live everywhere. Census 2000 counts same-sex couples in 99 percent of U.S. counties and 97 percent of census tracts (geographic areal units with approximately 2,000 occupied households, regardless of the physical size of the area). However, like the distribution of the U.S. population at large, the distribution of gay and lesbian families is far from uniform across the nation. The analyses that follow explore the location patterns of gay and lesbian couples by comparing these patterns with those of all households and examining different patterns between male and female couples.

The Gay and Lesbian Index

Much of the analysis of gay and lesbian couples' location patterns uses the Gay/Lesbian Index, which serves as a measure of the concentration of gay and lesbian couples among households in a particular geographic region. The index is a ratio of the proportion of same-sex couples living in a region to the proportion of households that are located in a region (a detailed explanation of this calculation can be found in chapter 7). This ratio then measures the over- or underrepresentation of same-sex couples in a geographic area relative to the population. A Gay/Lesbian Index value of 1.0 indicates that a same-sex couple is just as likely as a randomly picked household to locate in a particular region. A value of 2.0 indicates that gay- and lesbian-couple households are twice as likely as the "average" U.S. household to locate in that region, while values less than 1.0 indicate that gay and lesbian couples are less likely than the average household to locate there.

Gay and Lesbian Couple Location Patterns

Not surprisingly, states with large populations tend to be states with large numbers of same-sex couple households. Observe in table 4.1 that the six states with the most households in the United States (California, New York, Texas, Florida, Illinois, and Pennsylvania) are also the six states with the most same-sex couple households. Among the 10 states with the largest number of same-sex couple households, only Massachusetts and Georgia do not rank among the top 10 states in number of households.

This ranking by number of households only tells part of the gay- and lesbian-couple location story, though. The last column in table 4.1 shows that the rankings of states by their Gay/Lesbian Index differ substantially from their rankings simply by size of the gay- and lesbian-couple population. Only three states (California, New York, and Massachusetts)

rank in the top 10 for both the total number of gay and lesbian couples and the Gay/Lesbian Index measure of the overall concentration of same-sex couples in the state.

The 10 states with the highest Gay/Lesbian Index values are shown in table 4.2. Vermont ranks first and is followed by California, Washington, Massachusetts, and Oregon. All states with an Index value above 1.0 are shown in varying shades of red and yellow in the map shown on page 60. Northeast, western, and southwestern states dominate in terms of gay and lesbian couple concentration among households.

County Location Patterns

County-level location patterns (shown in the map on page 61) show high-concentration levels of gay and

Only three states (California, New York, and Massachusetts) rank in the top 10 for both the total number of gay and lesbian couples and the Gay/Lesbian Index.

Table 4.1. Distribution of Gay and Lesbian Couples (Top 10 States) Compared with the Distribution of All Households

	Percentage of all same-sex couple households nationwide	Rank: portion of same-sex couple households nationwide	Percentage of all households nationwide	Rank: portion of all households nationwide	Gay/Lesbian Index	Rank: Gay/Lesbian Index
California	15.5	1	10.9	1	1.42	2
New York	7.8	2	6.7	3	1.17	8
Texas	7.2	3	7.0	2	1.03	17
Florida	6.9	4	6.0	4	1.15	11
Illinois	3.9	5	4.4	6	0.88	26
Pennsylvania	3.6	6	4.5	5	0.78	34
Georgia	3.2	7	2.9	11	1.14	12
Ohio	3.2	8	4.2	7	0.75	38
Massachusetts	2.9	9	2.3	13	1.24	4
New Jersey	2.8	10	2.9	10	0.96	21

Source: Authors' calculations based on Census 2000 data.

Table 4.2. Gay/Lesbian Index: Top 10 States

Rank	State	Gay/Lesbian Index
1	Vermont	1.43
2	California	1.42
3	Washington	1.24
4	Massachusetts	1.24
5	Oregon	1.19
6	New Mexico	1.18
7	Nevada	1.17
8	New York	1.17
9	Maine	1.16
10	Arizona	1.15

Source: Authors' calculations based on Census 2000 data.

Gay and lesbian couples are more than three times as likely as the average American household to live in the San Francisco metropolitan area.

Midwest with high concentrations of gay and lesbian couples. The top 10 counties ranked by a county-level Gay/Lesbian Index are San Francisco County (California), Monroe County (Key West, Florida), Hampshire County (Amherst, Massachusetts), Washington D.C.,[1] DeKalb County (Atlanta, Georgia), New York County (Manhattan, New York City, New York), Arlington County (Virginia, D.C. metropolitan area), Suffolk County (Boston, Massachusetts), Sonoma County (California), and Denver County (Colorado). Gay and lesbian couples are more than twice as likely as the average American household to locate in any of these counties.

Gay and lesbian couples are more than three times as likely as the average American household to live in the San Francisco metropolitan area (see table 4.3), which ranks first among all metropolitan statistical areas (MSAs) in the Gay/Lesbian Index.[2] Rank-

lesbian couples along nearly the entire California coast, in southern Florida, and throughout New England. Similar to the state-level map, county-level location patterns show only a few counties in the

Table 4.3. Gay/Lesbian Index: Top 10 Metropolitan Statistical Areas, by Population Groupings

Rank	Population > 500K (103 MSAs)	Gay/Lesbian Index	Overall rank	Population 200K–500K (106 MSAs)	Gay/Lesbian Index	Overall rank	Population ≤ 200K (122 MSAs)	Gay/Lesbian Index	Overall rank
1	San Francisco, CA	3.11	1	Santa Rosa, CA	2.19	2	Santa Fe, NM	1.89	4
2	Oakland, CA	1.76	5	Santa Cruz-Watsonville, CA	1.91	3	Burlington, VT	1.50	9
3	Seattle-Bellevue-Everett, WA	1.68	6	Portland, ME	1.61	8	Bloomington, IN	1.31	25
4	Fort Lauderdale, FL	1.62	7	Madison, WI	1.41	13	Iowa City, IA	1.26	32
5	Austin-San Marcos, TX	1.47	10	Asheville, NC	1.36	20	Barnstable-Yarmouth, MA	1.24	35
6	New York, NY	1.47	11	Salinas, CA	1.33	23	Yolo, CA	1.18	45
7	Los Angeles-Long Beach, CA	1.43	12	Eugene-Springfield, OR	1.30	26	Medford-Ashland, OR	1.16	46
8	Albuquerque, NM	1.40	14	Boulder-Longmont, CO	1.26	31	Corvallis, OR	1.11	58
9	Atlanta, GA	1.40	15	Olympia, WA	1.24	34	Lawrence, KS	1.10	59
10	Jersey City, NJ	1.38	16	Reno, NV	1.23	37	Flagstaff, AZ-UT	1.09	61

Source: Authors' calculations based on Census 2000 data.
Note: Total MSAs surveyed was 331.

ings of MSAs by population size demonstrate that metropolitan areas in nearly every region of the country have relatively large concentrations of lesbian and gay couples. Note that "university" towns like Madison, Wisconsin; Boulder, Colorado; and Bloomington, Indiana, are common among small and medium-sized MSAs.

Even though San Francisco ranks highest in gay- and lesbian-couple concentration at both the county and MSA level, it is not actually the "gayest" town in America.[3] That distinction goes to Provincetown, Massachusetts, a Cape Cod mecca for gay and lesbian tourists. Same-sex couples are 22 times more likely than the average household to live in Provincetown, where over one in eight households is a gay or lesbian couple. The top 10 cities or towns, along with their Gay/Lesbian Index values, are shown in table 4.4 (the city of San Francisco ranks 11th with a Gay/Lesbian Index of 4.79).

The proportion of lesbian and gay couples in some communities far exceeds the national average of nearly one in a hundred households. This is also true of many neighborhoods. More than 100 neighborhoods (defined roughly as ZIP Codes) in the United States have gay- and lesbian-couple concentrations that exceed one in fifty households. These neighborhoods can be found in 52 different cities located in 18 states and the District of Columbia, and include 10 neighborhoods in San Francisco, nine in Atlanta, six in Seattle, and five each in New York and Portland, Oregon. The top 10 ZIP Codes, ranked by their Gay/Lesbian Index values, are shown in table 4.5, with Provincetown and the Castro neighborhood in San Francisco topping the list.

Location Patterns Differ between Gay Male and Lesbian Couples

Thus far, the analysis has explored the location patterns of gay and lesbian couples as a group. However, demographic studies suggest that gay men differ substantially from lesbians across at least two important categories that would affect location decisions: income and child rearing. Several studies find

Table 4.4. Gay/Lesbian Index: Top 10 Cities or Towns with at least 50 Gay or Lesbian Couples

City/Town	Gay/Lesbian Index
Provincetown, MA	22.72
Guerneville, CA	13.91
Wilton Manors, FL	9.63
West Hollywood, CA	7.38
Palm Springs, CA	7.20
Miami Shores, FL	5.82
Decatur, GA	5.64
Key West, FL	5.53
Northampton, MA	5.35
North Druid Hills, GA	5.05

Source: Authors' calculations based on Census 2000 data.

Table 4.5. Gay/Lesbian Index: Top 10 ZIP Codes with at least 50 Gay or Lesbian Couples

Rank	ZIP Code	Neighborhood/City	Gay/Lesbian Index
1	02657	Provincetown, MA	23.39
2	94114	Castro, San Francisco, CA	20.07
3	95446	Guerneville, CA	12.93
4	94131	Twin Peaks, San Francisco, CA	12.12
5	90069	West Hollywood, CA	10.06
6	33305	Oakland Park/Fort Lauderdale, FL	8.93
7	94117	Haight Ashbury, San Francisco, CA	8.10
8	10011	Chelsea, New York, NY	8.06
9	02118	Roxbury, Boston, MA	8.01
10	77006	Montrose, Houston, TX	7.93

Source: Authors' calculations based on Census 2000 data.

that gay men have higher average earnings than lesbians, and that lesbians are more likely than gay men to have children (Badgett 1995, 2001; Black et al. 2000). Analyses show that in Census 2000, women in same-sex unmarried partnerships have median incomes of approximately $24,000, while their male counterparts have incomes of $27,000. Lesbian couples are also more likely to have children living in the home (Simmons and O'Connell 2003). With this in mind, the analysis continues with an exploration of how the location patterns of same-sex couples differ by the sex of the couple.

Same-sex male and female couples share only five states (California, Washington, Arizona, Massachusetts, and Vermont) among their respective top 10 states ranked by Gay Male or Lesbian Index values calculated for each (table 4.6). While New Mexico, Oregon, Maine, New Hampshire, and Colorado complete the top 10 list for female couples, the list of top 10 states for gay-male couples is rounded out by Nevada, Florida, New York, Georgia, and Delaware.

The difference in location patterns is even more apparent at the county level, where only San Fran-

cisco County appears in the top 10 counties for both male and female couples (table 4.7). Note that, with the exception of Monroe County, Florida, the top 10 counties for gay-male couples all contain a large city within their borders.

Lesbian couples are less urban than their gay-male counterparts, as the top 10 counties for lesbian couples are much less urbanized than the top 10 counties for gay men. While 57 percent of gay-male couples live in central counties of metropolitan areas with a population of more than one million, only 50 percent of lesbian couples live in these counties. Conversely, 28 percent of lesbian couples live in metropolitan areas with populations between 250,000 and one million, while only 25 percent of gay-male couples reside in these areas. It is possible that lesbian couples may have lower earnings in part because they choose to live in less urban areas that offer lower-paying job options. Because lesbian couples have lower earnings than gay-male couples and are more likely to have children, they likely have less disposable income to devote to housing and other living expenses. The relatively high cost of living and

Same-sex male and female couples share only five states among their respective top 10 states.

Table 4.6. **Top 10 States by Gay Male and Lesbian Indices**

Rank	Gay Male Index top 10 states	Gay Male Index	Lesbian Index rank	Lesbian Index top 10 states	Lesbian Index	Gay Male Index rank
1	California	1.52	5	Vermont	1.75	10
2	Nevada	1.28	17	New Mexico	1.37	16
3	Florida	1.27	21	Oregon	1.37	13
4	New York	1.22	13	Massachusetts	1.34	9
5	Georgia	1.20	15	California	1.33	1
6	Washington	1.18	7	Maine	1.32	14
7	Arizona	1.16	10	Washington	1.30	6
8	Delaware	1.15	16	New Hampshire	1.17	25
9	Massachusetts	1.14	4	Colorado	1.17	17
10	Vermont	1.11	1	Arizona	1.14	7

Source: Authors' calculations based on Census 2000 data.

Table 4.7. Top 10 Counties by Gay Male and Lesbian Indices

Rank	Gay Male Index top 10 counties	Gay Male Index	Lesbian Index rank	Lesbian Index top 10 counties	Lesbian Index	Gay Male Index rank
1	San Francisco County, CA	6.96	5	Hampshire County, MA	4.64	811
2	Monroe County, FL	3.89	53	Franklin County, MA	3.09	330
3	District of Columbia, DC	3.80	130	Tompkins County, NY	2.69	286
4	New York County, NY	3.40	185	Sonoma County, CA	2.58	29
5	Arlington County, VA	3.28	297	San Francisco County, CA	2.57	1
6	Suffolk County, MA	2.72	51	Orange County, VT	2.53	197
7	DeKalb County, GA	2.64	13	Santa Cruz County, CA	2.47	106
8	Alexandria City, VA	2.62	194	Santa Fe County, NM	2.42	34
9	Fulton County, GA	2.61	266	Multnomah County, OR	2.38	26
10	Denver County, CO	2.49	35	Windham County, VT	2.35	148

Source: Authors' calculations based on Census 2000 data.

expensive housing costs associated with larger metropolitan areas may be less attractive to many lesbian couples.

Comparing location differences between gay-male and lesbian couples among metropolitan areas and cities and towns continues to highlight the pattern of men locating in more urbanized areas than women (table 4.8). New York, San Francisco, and Los Angeles are all in the top 10 MSAs for gay-male couples, while smaller metropolitan areas such as Santa Rosa, California; Santa Cruz, California; Santa Fe, New Mexico; and Burlington, Vermont, rank high among female couples. While Provincetown, Massachusetts, and Guerneville, California, rank first and second on both the male- and female-couple top 10 list for cities and towns, the remaining cities on the lists are quite different. Eight of the top 10 cities for coupled gay men are in either California or southern Florida, while the same list for coupled lesbians includes communities in seven different states.

Another interesting difference between male and female same-sex couples is how much each group concentrates or clusters. Note that the highest index values for lesbian couples always fall below the highest values for gay-male couples. Female couples do not tend to cluster as prominently as male couples. This is most obvious when looking at ZIP Code–level neighborhoods. The neighborhood with the highest concentration of gay-male couples, San Francisco's Castro district, has a Gay Male Index value of 32.41. Nearly one in 10 households in this neighborhood is a gay-male couple. In the Provincetown ZIP Code of 02657, which ranks first with a Lesbian Index value of 18.01, only one in 20 households is a lesbian couple.

Having established unique location patterns between gay-male and lesbian couples, the analysis continues with an examination of location differences across different couple types, specifically heterosexual married couples and same-sex and different-sex unmarried partners.

Table 4.8. Top 10 Metropolitan Statistical Areas, Cities/Towns, and ZIP Codes, by Gay Male and Lesbian Indices

Gay male couples	Gay Male Index	Lesbian couples	Lesbian Index
Top 10 Metropolitan Statistical Areas			
San Francisco, CA	4.14	Santa Rosa, CA	2.58
Fort Lauderdale, FL	2.02	Santa Cruz-Watsonville, CA	2.47
Santa Rosa, CA	1.80	Santa Fe, NM	2.19
Seattle-Bellevue-Everett, WA	1.70	San Francisco, CA	2.06
New York, NY	1.65	Oakland, CA	1.94
Jersey City, NJ	1.63	Burlington, VT	1.94
Los Angeles-Long Beach, CA	1.62	Portland, ME	1.88
Santa Fe, NM	1.60	Springfield, MA	1.87
Oakland, CA	1.58	Corvallis, OR	1.79
Miami, FL	1.57	Madison, WI	1.77
Top 10 cities and towns			
Provincetown, MA	28.22	Provincetown, MA	17.08
Guerneville, CA	17.25	Guerneville, CA	10.49
Wilton Manors, FL	16.40	Northampton, MA	9.62
West Hollywood, CA	12.82	Decatur, GA	6.65
Palm Springs, CA	12.64	Vashon, WA	5.83
Miami Shores, FL	9.26	Eldorado at Santa Fe, NM	5.31
Key West, FL	8.46	Takoma Park, MD	5.06
North Druid Hills, GA	7.40	Easthampton, MA	4.67
Laguna Beach, CA	7.12	Gulfport, FL	4.14
San Francisco, CA	6.96	Scottdale, GA	4.03
Top 10 neighborhoods (ZIP Code)			
Castro, San Francisco, CA (94114)	32.41	Provincetown, MA (02657)	18.01
Provincetown, MA (02657)	28.61	Florence/Northampton, MA (01062)	10.23
Twin Peaks, San Francisco, CA (94131)	17.95	Florence/Northampton, MA (01060)	9.25
West Hollywood, CA (90069)	17.83	Guerneville, CA (95446)	8.67
Guerneville, CA (95446)	17.06	Jamaica Plain, MA (02130)	7.72
Oakland Park/Ft. Lauderdale, FL (33305)	14.89	Decatur, GA (30030)	7.53
Roxbury, Boston, MA (02118)	14.06	Castro, San Francisco, CA (94114)	7.40
Dallas, TX (75219)	13.57	Oakland/Piedmont, CA (94602)	7.12
Chelsea, New York, NY (10011)	13.30	Berkeley, CA (94702)	7.12
Haight Ashbury, San Francisco, CA (94117)	13.17	Mission District, San Francisco, CA (94110)	6.49

Source: Authors' calculations based on Census 2000 data.

Endnotes

1. For purposes of census enumeration, the District of Columbia is included as a state, a county, and a city. In this book, Washington, D.C., is shown in both county and city/metropolitan-area rankings, but not among state rankings. As D.C. residents and taxpayers, the authors are cognizant of worthy local aspirations toward statehood and congressional representation for the District. However, for purposes of this *Atlas*, the wholly urban nature of D.C. makes for a somewhat unfair comparison between it and the 50 states.

2. All discussions and rankings of metropolitan areas refer to all census-defined Metropolitan Statistical Areas (MSAs) and Primary Metropolitan Statistical Areas (PMSAs). For ease of discussion, text and tables refer to simply metro areas or MSAs.

3. Cities, towns, and other Census Designated Places differ from MSAs, which nearly always extend beyond the "political" boundaries of a city. Cities and towns reflect the actual political jurisdictions, and only those jurisdictions with 50 or more same-sex unmarried partner couples are included in this ranking.

CHAPTER FIVE

Comparing Location Patterns across Different Couple Types

Comparing Location Patterns across Different Couple Types

Gay- and lesbian-couple location choices differ substantially from the choices of heterosexual married couples, but less so from heterosexual unmarried couples. None of the top 10 states ranked by their Gay/Lesbian Index values are among the top 10 of a similarly constructed index for heterosexual married couples (table 5.1). In general, as the concentration of married couples increases, the concentration of same-sex couples decreases.[1] However, this negative association is not true between location patterns of same-sex and different-sex unmarried partners.[2]

Rather than simply reviewing differences among lists of counties or towns with high concentrations of different types of couples, the comparative analysis that follows constructs four "typical" neighborhoods occupied by the following couple types:

- Same-sex male couple (gay male)

- Same-sex female couple (lesbian)

- Heterosexual unmarried-partner couple

- Heterosexual married couple

To construct these four composite neighborhoods, the proportion of each couple type living in a ZIP Code in the United States is used as a weighting factor to calculate the "weighted average" of a variety of neighborhood characteristics.[3] Specifically, the analysis explores the following characteristics:

- *Urbanicity:* The probability that the neighborhood is part of an urban area.

- *Diversity:* The proportion of the neighborhood that is nonwhite, non-English speaking, and foreign-born.

Table 5.1. State-Level Concentration Indices for Gay/Lesbian and Heterosexual Married and Unmarried Partners

State	Gay/Lesbian Index	Gay/Lesbian Index rank	Heterosexual Married Couple Index	Married Couple Index rank	Heterosexual Unmarried Partner Index	Unmarried Partner Index rank
Vermont	1.43	1	1.02	23	1.45	2
California	1.42	2	0.99	40	1.11	14
Washington	1.24	3	1.01	28	1.18	10
Massachusetts	1.24	4	0.95	47	1.01	26
Oregon	1.19	5	1.01	31	1.23	7
New Mexico	1.18	6	0.98	42	1.24	6
Nevada	1.17	7	0.96	46	1.41	4
New York	1.17	8	0.90	50	1.01	24
Maine	1.16	9	1.02	25	1.44	3
Arizona	1.15	10	1.00	32	1.20	8

Source: Authors' calculations based on Census 2000 data.

- *Educational attainment:* The proportion of adults in the neighborhood with a college degree.

- *Income:* Median household income and median individual incomes for all adults and for men and women in the neighborhood.

- *Housing characteristics:* Median house value and percent of households in the neighborhood that were built prior to 1939, have three or more bedrooms, and are owner-occupied.

- *Crime:* Incidence of violent and all crime per 1,000 population (at the county level).

- *Household composition:* Percentage of married couples, heterosexual unmarried-partner couples, and same-sex unmarried-partner couples among all households in the neighborhood.

Constructing these "typical," or composite, neighborhoods offers a unique way to compare the average demographic characteristics of places where each of the four couple types lives. For reference purposes, all analyses also show the comparable figure for the entire country.

Urbanicity

Same-sex couples have the highest probability of living in an urban area among the different couple types (see figure 5.1). A gay-male couple's neighborhood is more likely to be urban than that of a lesbian couple, and both are more likely to be urban than the neighborhoods of either a heterosexual unmarried-partner or a married couple. This higher propensity toward urban areas no doubt influences many other demographic differences to be explored.

Diversity

Gay and lesbian couples, particularly gay-male couples, live in areas with more heterogeneous pop-

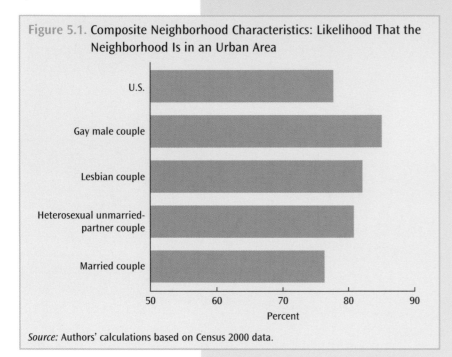

Figure 5.1. Composite Neighborhood Characteristics: Likelihood That the Neighborhood Is in an Urban Area

Source: Authors' calculations based on Census 2000 data.

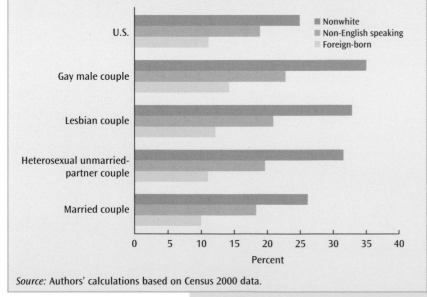

Figure 5.2. Composite Neighborhood Characteristics: Proportions Nonwhite, Non-English Speaking, and Foreign-Born

Source: Authors' calculations based on Census 2000 data.

ulations. As shown in figure 5.2, gay-male and lesbian couple neighborhoods have higher rates of nonwhite, foreign-born, and non-English speaking populations than the national average and than heterosexual unmarried-partner or married couple neighborhoods. This attraction to diverse areas is consistent with census findings that same-sex couples are about twice as likely as married couples to be of mixed race or ethnicity (Simmons and O'Connell 2003).

Educational Attainment

Most demographic analyses indicate relatively high levels of educational attainment among gay men and lesbians (Badgett 2001; Black et al. 2000). Similarly, the typical gay-male and lesbian couple neighborhood has a higher proportion of college graduates (among adults age 25 and older) than the U.S. average or than the typical heterosexual unmarried-partner and married couple neighborhood (figure 5.3). Note that while the married couple neighborhood is the lowest among the couple types in terms of urbanicity and diversity, it does have a higher proportion of college graduates than both the national average and the composite heterosexual unmarried-partner couple neighborhood.

Income

Education is so strongly linked to income that one might expect the pattern of household incomes in neighborhoods to mirror that of educational attainment. However, figure 5.4 shows that the typical married couple neighborhood has the highest median household income among the four composite neighborhoods. Notably, the neighborhoods for all couple types have a median household income above the U.S. median household income. Since couples most likely live in areas with relatively higher concentrations of other couples (of any type), it is not surprising that median household incomes are higher, as more households have two incomes.

An examination of individual earnings for all people over age 16 and for men and women (shown in figure 5.5) shows a somewhat different pattern. The married couple neighborhood has about the same median individual earnings as the gay-male and lesbian couple neighborhoods, with lower median earnings observed in the heterosexual unmarried-

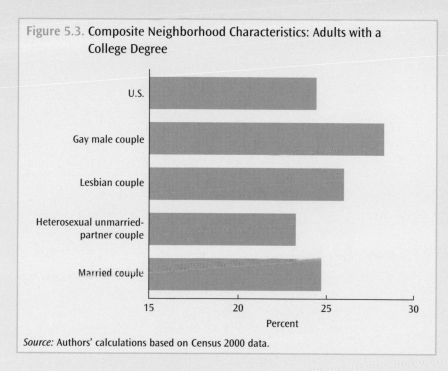

Figure 5.3. Composite Neighborhood Characteristics: Adults with a College Degree

Source: Authors' calculations based on Census 2000 data.

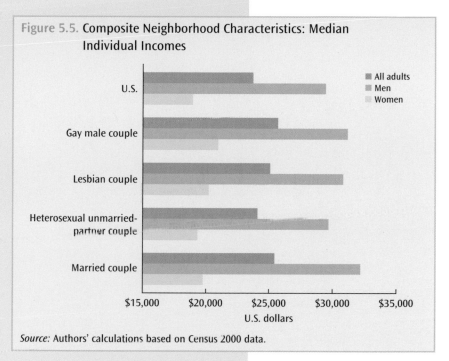

Figure 5.5. Composite Neighborhood Characteristics: Median Individual Incomes

Source: Authors' calculations based on Census 2000 data.

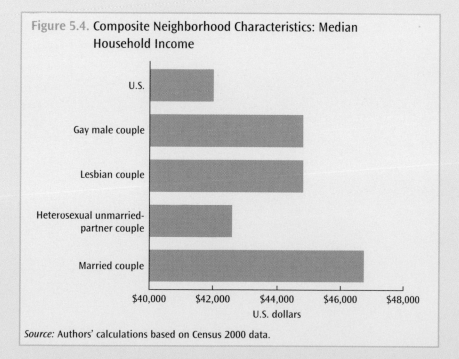

Figure 5.4. Composite Neighborhood Characteristics: Median Household Income

Source: Authors' calculations based on Census 2000 data.

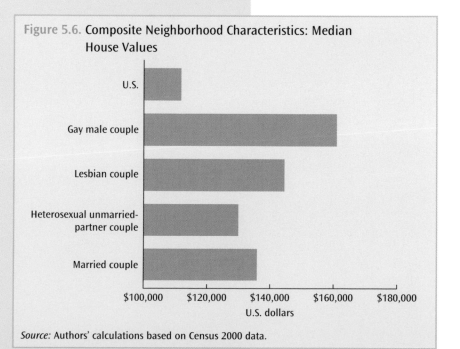

Figure 5.6. Composite Neighborhood Characteristics: Median House Values

Source: Authors' calculations based on Census 2000 data.

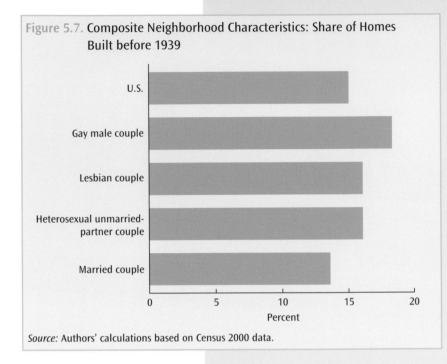

Figure 5.7. Composite Neighborhood Characteristics: Share of Homes Built before 1939

Percent

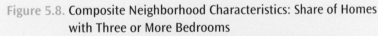

Source: Authors' calculations based on Census 2000 data.

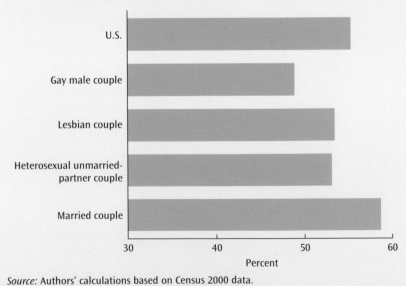

Figure 5.8. Composite Neighborhood Characteristics: Share of Homes with Three or More Bedrooms

Percent

Source: Authors' calculations based on Census 2000 data.

partner couple neighborhood. The unusually high level of household earnings observed in the typical married couple neighborhood is being driven in large part by high male earnings. This is consistent with numerous studies showing that married men are the highest wage earners in the nation.

Housing Characteristics

An exploration of housing characteristics in gay and lesbian neighborhoods demonstrates the extent to which gay-male couples, in particular, cluster in expensive and older inner-city neighborhoods. The median house value in the average gay-male couple neighborhood exceeds the national median house value by 44 percent—$160,000 compared with $110,000 (figure 5.6). The typical lesbian couple neighborhood has the next highest median house value, followed by the heterosexual married couple and unmarried-partner neighborhoods.

While the gay-male couple neighborhood homes might be expensive, it is not because they are new construction. The gay-male couple neighborhood has the oldest housing stock among the four composite neighborhoods. Married couples live in neighborhoods with the lowest portions of homes being built before 1939, even lower than the national average (figure 5.7).

Not only does the gay-male couple neighborhood have older homes, these homes tend to be smaller. The typical gay-male couple neighborhood is the only one where less than 50 percent of the homes have at least three bedrooms (figure 5.8). The gay-male couple neighborhood also has the lowest home ownership rates, while the married couple neighborhood has the highest level of ownership (figure 5.9).

Crime

The composite gay-male couple county has the highest levels of both overall crime and violent crime (figure 5.10).[4] This is not surprising given that, of any couple type, gay men are the least likely to have children. Married couples, the most likely to have children, live in communities with the lowest crime rates, even below the national averages.

Like Attracts Like?

Not surprisingly, all couples show evidence of locating in neighborhoods with high concentrations of couples like them. Figures 5.11–5.13 explore the extent to which specific couple types choose neighborhoods with high concentrations of similar couples. This behavior is most striking among gay-male couples, which tend to cluster more heavily than any of the other couple types. The gay-male neighborhood has a prevalence of gay-male couples nearly three times higher than their prevalence in the married couple neighborhood (figure 5.11). Conversely, the prevalence of married couples in the gay-male neighborhood is not nearly so different—47 percent in the gay-male neighborhood compared with 56 percent in the married couple neighborhood (figure 5.12). While the prevalence of lesbian couples in the lesbian couple neighborhood exceeds that in the other neighborhoods, the magnitude of the differences is not nearly as dramatic as that for the gay-male couple concentration. The prevalence of heterosexual unmarried-partner couples is fairly similar across each of the composite neighborhoods (figure 5.13).

Gentrification

The characteristics that distinguish gay and lesbian neighborhoods from the typical neighborhoods of other couples are consistent with the often-observed propensity for gay men and lesbians to move to less-desirable neighborhoods within urban areas and gentrify their surroundings. With a low probability of having children, gay-male couples, and to a lesser extent their lesbian counterparts, are more likely to live in diverse urban neighborhoods with older, smaller, and more expensive housing stock, lower levels of home ownership, higher levels of education among residents, and higher crime rates. Without children, they have more disposable income to invest in their homes and do not require as much space as other families.[5] In time,

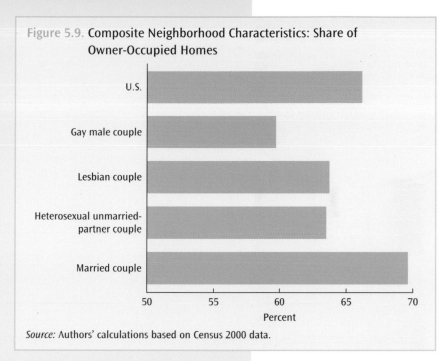

Figure 5.9. Composite Neighborhood Characteristics: Share of Owner-Occupied Homes

Source: Authors' calculations based on Census 2000 data.

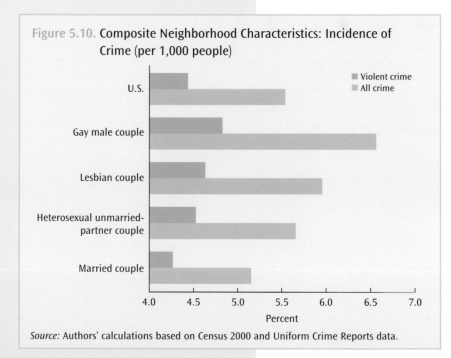

Figure 5.10. Composite Neighborhood Characteristics: Incidence of Crime (per 1,000 people)

Source: Authors' calculations based on Census 2000 and Uniform Crime Reports data.

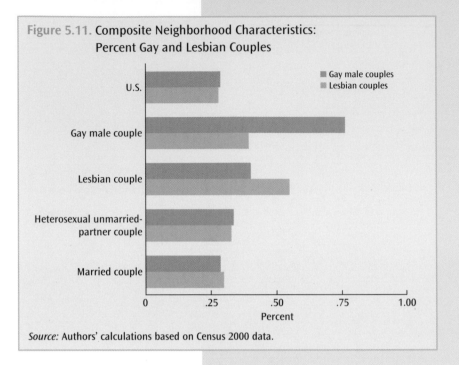

Figure 5.11. Composite Neighborhood Characteristics: Percent Gay and Lesbian Couples

Source: Authors' calculations based on Census 2000 data.

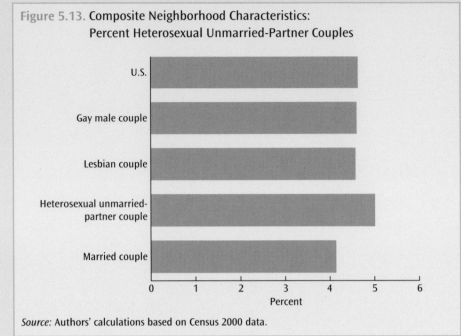

Figure 5.13. Composite Neighborhood Characteristics: Percent Heterosexual Unmarried-Partner Couples

Source: Authors' calculations based on Census 2000 data.

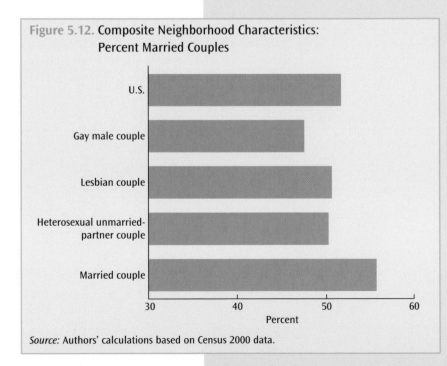

Figure 5.12. Composite Neighborhood Characteristics: Percent Married Couples

Source: Authors' calculations based on Census 2000 data.

the additional money and subsequent renewal can begin to alter the neighborhood.

Economic- and community-development agencies are increasingly aware of this gentrification phenomenon. Erin Miller, from Live Baltimore Marketing Center, acknowledges that the first advertising campaign in 20 years promoting Baltimore neighborhoods to young professional Washington, D.C., residents specifically targeted gay and lesbian couples and singles. The campaign ran in the *Washington Blade*, the District of Columbia's gay and lesbian newspaper, and included posters in the Dupont Circle metro stop, the center of the District's most visible gay neighborhood.[6]

A May 2003 story on National Public Radio described how a leading real estate development agency in Detroit, the Farbman Group, has targeted gay men and lesbians for its efforts to populate inner-city loft apartments. David Farbman, president of the organization, said, "The gay community tends to have the guts to go into an area as pioneers before the masses arrive. I think that the gay community also has the tendencies to actually go out and put their money where their mouth is and invest in the city around them" (NPR 2003). Urban governments and developers have caught on to the idea that given their lower rates of child rearing, gay men and lesbians can devote higher levels of their household resources to tax-boosting property enhancement without placing much demand on costly city services like public schools.

So far, the analyses have explored traits among all gay and lesbian couples. One benefit of census data is the ability to explore unique demographic and geographic traits of important subpopulations within same-sex couples. To that end, the *Atlas* continues with an examination of location patterns among gay and lesbian couples with children, seniors, and racial/ethnic minorities.

Endnotes

1. The Gay/Lesbian Index and the Married Couple Index at the state level have a Pearson correlation coefficient of –0.78, significant at the $p < .001$ level. The negative correlation holds at the county (–0.34), MSA (–0.31), and census tract (–0.23) levels.

2. The Gay/Lesbian Index and the Heterosexual Unmarried Partner Index are only weakly correlated at 0.33. This relatively weak positive association holds at the county (0.29), MSA (0.24), and census tract (0.16) levels.

3. For example, suppose there are only two ZIP Codes in the United States, and 25 percent of lesbian couples live in ZIP Code One and 75 percent live in ZIP Code Two. If ZIP Code One has a poverty rate of 5 families per 100 households and ZIP Code Two has a poverty rate of 8 families per 100 households, then the poverty rate of the "typical" neighborhood that a lesbian couple lives in would be $(5 \times 0.25) + (8 \times 0.75)$, or 7 families per 100 households.

4. Crime data are not easily available at the ZIP Code level, so a county-level composite is constructed for this analysis in the same fashion as the ZIP Code–level composite neighborhoods.

5. Higher disposable income is not the same as higher income. Evidence suggests that gay men's individual earnings are not on average any higher than other men and are substantially lower than the earnings of married men (Badgett 1995, 2001; Black et al. 2000).

6. Scott Calvert, "City Ads Moving on DC Dwellers," *Baltimore Sun,* April 25, 2002.

CHAPTER SIX

Other Demographic Characteristics

Other Demographic Characteristics

Census 2000 data offer insight into the location patterns of important subsets of the gay and lesbian population. It is possible to estimate both the number and location patterns of same-sex couples with children, as well as the location patterns of gay and lesbian seniors and gay and lesbian racial and ethnic minorities.

How Many Gay and Lesbian Couples Have Children?

The public decisions of such high-profile gay men and lesbians as comedian Rosie O'Donnell, singer Melissa Etheridge, and writer/columnist Dan Savage to have children with their same-sex partners have focused attention on the growing trend of gay men and lesbians raising children. Increased access to adoption, along with advances in reproductive technology—artificial insemination, egg donation and in-vitro fertilization, and surrogate mothering—provide a variety of ways for same-sex couples to become parents. As this happens, family law courts around the country are forced to reconsider what precisely it means to be a parent and a family under the law, and adapt policies concerning adoption and child custody and support to the realities of these "nontraditional" families. In 2002, courts in Delaware and Pennsylvania ordered lesbians to pay child support to their ex-partners with whom they were raising children.[1] According to the Human Rights Campaign, seven states and the District of Columbia legally recognize second-parent adoption (allowing another adult to assume parental responsibility for a child without the biological parent losing that right), and courts in 16 other states have permitted such arrangements.[2]

Measuring the Presence of Children in Same-Sex Unmarried-Partner Households

The growing public interest in the rate of child rearing among same-sex couples is evidenced in the U.S. Census Bureau report, "Married-Couple and

Unmarried-Partner Households: 2000" (Simmons and O'Connell 2003). This report marks the first time that the Census Bureau officially released statistics about the rate of child rearing among same-sex unmarried-partner households. The census report (which addresses other demographic characteristics) states that one in five male same-sex couples and one in three female same-sex couples report having children under 18 living in the household. Chapter 2 explained why a potential measurement error involving sex miscoding among heterosexual couples could mean that the census figures overstate the actual rate of child rearing among gay and lesbian couples. Figures in this analysis are adjusted to compensate for this form of measurement error and will differ somewhat from figures reported by the Census Bureau.

Even with these adjustments, the analysis of same-sex couples with children at smaller geographic levels, such as counties, suggests there might be additional measurement error that disproportionately affects counts of same-sex couples with children. In ranking counties containing at least 50 same-sex couples with children by the proportion of same-sex couples that have children in the household, seven of the top 10 counties are either along the U.S.-Mexico border or home to American Indian reservations. While it may be possible that Hispanic and American Indian gay and lesbian couples are much more likely to have children than other gay and lesbian couples, this finding could also be evidence of additional measurement-error problems that particularly affect counts of unmarried partners with children.

Estimates of Child Rearing among Gay and Lesbian Couples

An estimated one in four same-sex couple households (27.5 percent) report children under age 18 living in the home, compared with just over one in three (36 percent) households in the United States reporting the presence of children in Census 2000. Put another way, a gay or lesbian couple heads 3.5 of every 1,000 households with children. On average, there are two children present in all households with children under the age of 18. Analysis of the 1-Percent Public Use Microdata Sample (PUMS) of Census 2000 shows that this figure holds true in same-sex couple households as well, so adjusted census figures suggest that there are more than a quarter-million children living in households headed by a same-sex couple. Of course, this figure substantially underestimates the total number of children with gay or lesbian parents. Single gay men and lesbians are not reflected in the census, and therefore this analysis cannot determine how many of them are raising children. Further, census figures only reflect coresidential parents. Children who do not live with their gay or lesbian parents cannot be counted in the census.

Location Patterns of Gay and Lesbian Couples with Children

Three different rankings of gay and lesbian child rearing are shown in table 6.1: the concentration of same-sex couples with children among all households, among households with children, and among other same-sex couples. Each ranking offers a different perspective on the prevalence of gay and lesbian families with children.

The concentration of same-sex couples with children among all households provides an indication of where one is most likely to find a gay or lesbian couple raising a child. Obviously, states with higher proportions of gay and lesbian couples in the population will tend to rank higher in this category. So it is not

Table 6.1. State and Large Metropolitan Area Rankings by Gay and Lesbian Households with Children under 18

Rank	By rate of gay and lesbian couples with children per 1,000 households		By rate of gay and lesbian couples with children per 1,000 households with children		By proportion of gay and lesbian couples with children, among all gay and lesbian couples	
	States					
1	California	1.82	Vermont	5.14	Mississippi	41.3%
2	New Mexico	1.74	Nevada	4.88	South Dakota	39.7%
3	Vermont	1.73	California	4.58	Alaska	38.1%
4	Nevada	1.72	New Mexico	4.52	South Carolina	36.3%
5	Alaska	1.66	Arizona	4.49	Louisiana	35.0%
6	Texas	1.63	New York	4.43	Alabama	34.9%
7	Arizona	1.59	Florida	4.10	Texas	34.6%
8	New York	1.55	Massachusetts	4.07	Kansas	33.5%
9	Georgia	1.51	Texas	3.97	Utah	33.1%
10	Louisiana	1.50	South Carolina	3.88	Arizona	32.8%
	Large metropolitan areas					
1	New York, NY	2.02	San Francisco, CA	6.17	San Antonio, TX	36.5%
2	Los Angeles-Long Beach, CA	2.00	New York, NY	5.86	Bergen-Passaic, NJ	34.5%
3	Oakland, CA	1.97	Oakland, CA	5.28	Memphis, TN	33.8%
4	Miami, FL	1.97	Miami, FL	5.06	Houston, TX	33.2%
5	Houston, TX	1.85	Las Vegas, NV	4.95	Fort Worth-Arlington, TX	32.6%
6	Riverside-San Bernardino, CA	1.85	Los Angeles-Long Beach, CA	4.86	Newark, NJ	32.4%
7	Las Vegas, NV	1.71	Austin-San Marcos, TX	4.38	Riverside-San Bernardino, CA	32.2%
8	San Francisco, CA	1.62	Phoenix-Mesa, AZ	4.36	Nassau-Suffolk, NY	31.8%
9	New Orleans, LA	1.60	Houston, TX	4.31	Norfolk-Virginia Beach-Newport News, VA	31.4%
10	Phoenix-Mesa, AZ	1.58	Boston, MA	4.25	Orange County, CA	30.5%

Source: Authors' calculations based on adjusted Census 2000 data.
Note: Large metropolitan areas are those with populations of more than one million people.

Same-sex couples who live in areas where couples are more likely to have children may simply reflect those values and are also more likely to have children.

surprising to find such states as California, New Mexico, Vermont, and Nevada among the top five, given that all rank among the top 10 states in proportion of gay and lesbian couples in the population. However, the top-10 rankings of Alaska, Texas, and Louisiana are in contrast to their "middle of the pack" rankings (22, 17, and 23, respectively) in the overall concentration of same-sex couples in the pop-ulation and their low rankings in terms of a gay and lesbian–supportive legal climate. It may be that same-sex couples who live in areas where all couples are more likely to have children (often more socially conservative communities) simply reflect these values and are also more likely to have children. It also could be that gay and lesbian couples with children move near other couples with children (and the better child-oriented amenities such as schools and parks that likely go with them) rather than locating near other gay and lesbian couples.

New York, Los Angeles, Oakland, and Miami rank as the large metropolitan areas with the highest concentration of gay and lesbian couples with children in the population. All four metropolitan areas have rates of gay- and lesbian-coupled households with children that are nearly twice the national average. With the exception of San Francisco, the remaining metropolitan areas among the top 10 rank no higher than 19th (among 61 large metropolitan areas) in overall gay- and lesbian-couple concentration.

Vermont, Nevada, California, New Mexico, and Arizona rank highest in concentration of same-sex couples with children among all households with children. Texas and South Carolina are notable among the top 10 states in this ranking, as they do not rank nearly as high in the overall concentration of gay and lesbian couples in the population. Gay and lesbian couples with children are most prevalent among households with children in the Bay Area of California, where San Francisco and Oakland are ranked first and third, respectively. New York, Miami, and Las Vegas round out the top five in this category. Among these large metropolitan areas, Las Vegas, Phoenix, and Houston rank in the top 10 for this category but do not rank among the top 20 in terms of the concentration of same-sex couples in the population.

States and large metropolitan areas with relatively low concentrations of gay and lesbian couples in the population tend to be areas where same-sex couples are more likely to have children in the household. High-ranking states such as Mississippi, South Dakota, Alaska, South Carolina, and Louisiana, and metropolitan areas such as San Antonio, Texas; Bergen-Passaic, New Jersey; Memphis, Tennessee; Houston, Texas; and Fort Worth, Texas, do not have extraordinarily high proportions of gay and lesbian couples in the population. Yet, more than a third of the gay and lesbian couples in these areas are raising children. Further, among both states and large metropolitan areas, the percentage of gay and lesbian couples with children rises as the proportion of all households with children rises in a region.[3] Conversely, the portion of same-sex couples with children goes down as the concentration of gay and lesbian couples rises in a region.[4]

Location Patterns of Gay and Lesbian Seniors

Increasing numbers of gay men and lesbians are joining the ranks of the elderly population. Nearly one in five people in a same-sex couple is at least 55 years old. In response to this growing population, *Time* magazine reports that at least a dozen developers are proposing gay retirement villages across the country, including sites in Florida, California, Massachusetts, and New Mexico (Cole 2003). Despite these efforts, the relatively recent acknowledgment of gay and lesbian seniors has exposed enormous gaps in the assistance and support offered to this group. In their report, "Outing Age," Cahill, South, and Spade (2000) document the extent to which senior-targeted service systems—financial services, health care, housing and nursing homes, and kinship care (caring for grandchildren or other minor-aged relatives whose parents are absent)—have limited understanding of the unique needs and concerns of gay and lesbian seniors. This is particularly true in regions with relatively small and nonvocal gay and lesbian populations.

Rankings of the concentration of same-sex coupled seniors among adults, other seniors, and other same-sex coupled individuals are shown for states, metropolitan areas, and counties in table 6.2. While

Table 6.2. State, Metropolitan Statistical Area, and County Rankings by Proportions of Same-Sex Coupled Seniors

Rank	By rate of gay and lesbian coupled seniors per 1,000 adults		By rate of gay and lesbian coupled seniors per 1,000 seniors		By proportion of coupled seniors among all gay and lesbian coupled persons	
States						
1	Vermont	1.63	Vermont	5.59	North Dakota	48%
2	Florida	1.56	Alaska	5.17	South Dakota	43%
3	New Mexico	1.41	New Mexico	4.99	Montana	31%
4	North Dakota	1.40	California	4.87	Wyoming	30%
5	Maine	1.39	Wyoming	4.80	West Virginia	29%
6	Wyoming	1.35	North Dakota	4.56	Nebraska	29%
7	South Dakota	1.30	Hawaii	4.43	Iowa	27%
8	Hawaii	1.29	Maine	4.42	Arkansas	26%
9	New York	1.28	Florida	4.41	Mississippi	26%
10	Alabama	1.24	New York	4.41	Idaho	26%
Metropolitan Statistical Areas						
1	Barnstable-Yarmouth, MA	3.12	Santa Rosa, CA	8.77	Punta Gorda, FL	43%
2	Santa Rosa, CA	2.48	San Francisco, CA	8.47	Barnstable-Yarmouth, MA	41%
3	San Francisco, CA	2.31	Santa Fe, NM	7.84	Sarasota-Bradenton, FL	36%
4	Sarasota-Bradenton, FL	2.30	Barnstable-Yarmouth, MA	6.99	Naples, FL	35%
5	Santa Fe, NM	2.20	Fort Lauderdale, FL	6.43	Ocala, FL	35%
6	Fort Myers-Cape Coral, FL	2.09	Santa Cruz-Watsonville, CA	6.11	Johnstown, PA	35%
7	Fort Lauderdale, FL	2.06	Riverside-San Bernardino, CA	5.69	Fort Myers-Cape Coral, FL	34%
8	West Palm Beach-Boca Raton, FL	2.00	Burlington, VT	5.61	Fort Pierce-Port St. Lucie, FL	34%
9	Naples, FL	1.94	Goldsboro, NC	5.61	Danville, VA	34%
10	Punta Gorda, FL	1.84	New York, NY	5.48	Bismarck, ND	34%
Counties with more than 50 same-sex coupled seniors						
1	Monroe County, FL	4.24	Monroe County, FL	12.97	Curry County, OR	55%
2	La Paz County, AZ	4.11	San Francisco County, CA	12.22	Marshall County, KY	54%
3	Nye County, NV	3.83	Montgomery County, KY	10.06	Franklin County, IL	53%
4	Northampton County, NC	3.29	Taos County, NM	9.23	Vilas County, WI	50%
5	Curry County, OR	3.22	Nye County, NV	8.91	La Paz County, AZ	49%
6	San Francisco County, CA	3.16	Sonoma County, CA	8.77	Hernando County, FL	49%
7	Barnstable County, MA	3.11	Northampton County, NC	8.75	Medina County, TX	48%
8	Vilas County, WI	3.00	New York County, NY	8.57	Elk County, PA	48%
9	Montgomery County, KY	2.95	Santa Fe County, NM	8.56	Hopkins County, TX	47%
10	Taos County, NM	2.87	Orleans County, VT	8.16	Oneida County, WI	47%

Source: Authors' calculations based on Census 2000 data.
Note: Seniors are those age 55 and older.

States such as Vermont, Florida, New Mexico, Maine, and New York have high concentrations of same-sex couples in general, and also rank highly among states with high proportions of same-sex coupled seniors.

such states as North Dakota and Wyoming have relatively small concentrations of same-sex couples in the population, they actually have high concentrations of same-sex coupled seniors. Both states rank in the top 10 for the concentration of same-sex coupled seniors among the adult population, the senior population, and other same-sex coupled individuals. States such as Vermont, Florida, New Mexico, Maine, and New York have high concentrations of same-sex couples in general, and also rank highly among states with high proportions of same-sex coupled seniors. These states are among the top 10 in rankings of gay and lesbian senior concentration in the population and among other seniors.

The states with high proportions of seniors within the coupled gay and lesbian population are dominated by states with relatively old populations, such as West Virginia, Iowa, Arkansas, South Dakota, North Dakota, and Montana, which all rank in the top 10 in the proportion of seniors among all adults. However, Wyoming, Nebraska, Mississippi, and Idaho have high proportions of seniors among same-sex couples, but not particularly high proportions of seniors among adults.

Barnstable-Yarmouth, Massachusetts, stands out among metropolitan areas, ranking among the top 10 in each measure of coupled gay and lesbian seniors. In addition, Florida is clearly not only a retirement destination for heterosexual couples. Eight Florida metropolitan areas—Sarasota, Ft. Myers, Ft. Lauderdale, West Palm Beach, Naples, Punta Gorda, Ocala, and Ft. Pierce—appear in at least one of the top 10 lists, and five appear in two lists. Similar to the state rankings, metropolitan areas with high proportions of seniors among all gay and lesbian couples are also areas with high concentrations of seniors in the adult population in general. Among the top 10 metropolitan areas ranked by the concentration

of same-sex coupled seniors among all same-sex couples, only Bismarck, North Dakota, is not among the top 20 metropolitan areas ranked by the percentage of seniors in the adult population.

Monroe County, Florida (containing Key West), ranks highest among counties in terms of the concentration of coupled gay and lesbian seniors within both the adult and senior populations.[5] Five other counties are among the top 10 in both these rankings: Nye County, Nevada; Northampton County, North Carolina; San Francisco County, California; Montgomery County, Kentucky; and Taos County, New Mexico. Curry County, Oregon, ranks first in the concentration of seniors among individuals in a same-sex couple.

Location Patterns of Gay and Lesbian Racial and Ethnic Minorities

More than a quarter of the same-sex couples in the United States include a racial or ethnic minority. Two patterns emerge from the rankings of states and metropolitan areas by various measures of the concentration of African American and Hispanic gay and lesbian couples (shown in table 6.3):[6]

■ Areas with large minority communities tend to have higher concentrations of minority gay and lesbian couples, both in the population and among gay and lesbian couples.
■ Areas with large gay and lesbian populations tend to have higher rates of gay and lesbian couples within minority communities.

In the case of African Americans, the South dominates the rankings of states and metropolitan areas by the concentration of African American couples among all households and among other gay and lesbian couples. Mississippi, Louisiana, South Carolina,

Table 6.3. State and Metropolitan Statistical Area Rankings by Race and Ethnicity in Same-Sex Coupled Households

	African American Gay and Lesbian Households		
Rank	By rate of African American gay and lesbian coupled households per 1,000 households	By rate of African American gay and lesbian coupled households per 1,000 African American households	By proportion of African American gay and lesbian coupled households among all gay and lesbian coupled households
States			
1	Mississippi 1.68	Vermont 14.29	Mississippi 37%
2	Louisiana 1.50	New Hampshire 7.31	South Carolina 29%
3	South Carolina 1.44	Utah 7.03	Louisiana 28%
4	Georgia 1.42	Maine 6.93	Alabama 26%
5	Maryland 1.38	Idaho 6.78	Maryland 24%
6	Alabama 1.22	North Dakota 6.69	Georgia 22%
7	North Carolina 0.99	Rhode Island 6.32	North Carolina 19%
8	Delaware 0.97	Massachusetts 6.27	Arkansas 16%
9	Virginia 0.84	Oregon 6.17	Virginia 16%
10	New York 0.83	California 6.17	Delaware 16%
Metropolitan Statistical Areas with more than 50 African American gay or lesbian couples			
1	Sumter, SC 2.62	San Francisco, CA 10.57	Sumter, SC 59%
2	Albany, GA 2.28	Jersey City, NJ 7.96	Pine Bluff, AR 57%
3	Pine Bluff, AR 2.03	Newburgh, NY 7.66	Albany, GA 50%
4	Rocky Mount, NC 2.00	Fresno, CA 7.63	Rocky Mount, NC 47%
5	Florence, SC 1.93	Oakland, CA 7.61	Florence, SC 43%
6	Memphis, TN 1.87	Seattle-Bellevue-Everett, WA 7.24	Macon, GA 41%
7	Macon, GA 1.84	West Palm Beach-Boca Raton, FL 6.79	Montgomery, AL 41%
8	New Orleans, LA 1.81	Boston, MA 6.63	Columbus, GA 40%
9	Montgomery, AL 1.81	Sarasota-Bradenton, FL 6.62	Goldsboro, NC 38%
10	Columbus, GA 1.78	Houma, LA 6.59	Jackson, MS 38%

Metropolitan areas such as San Francisco, Jersey City, Oakland, Seattle, and Boston have high concentrations of African American same-sex couples both in the population and among African American households.

Georgia, Maryland, Alabama, North Carolina, and Virginia are in the top 10 of both rankings. Similarly, all top-10 metropolitan areas in both rankings are in the South.

New England states such as Vermont, New Hampshire, Maine, Rhode Island, and Massachu-setts, along with Oregon and California on the west coast, rank among the top 10 states in the concentration of African American same-sex couples among other African American households. Each of these states also has a relatively high concentration of same-sex couples in the broader population. On the

Table 6.3. (*continued*)

Hispanic Gay and Lesbian Households

Rank	By rate of Hispanic gay and lesbian coupled households per 1,000 households		By rate of Hispanic gay and lesbian coupled households per 1,000 Hispanic households		By proportion of Hispanic gay and lesbian coupled households among all gay and lesbian coupled households	
	States					
1	New Mexico	2.28	Georgia	10.92	New Mexico	34%
2	California	1.78	South Carolina	10.92	Texas	28%
3	Texas	1.63	North Carolina	10.69	California	22%
4	Arizona	1.37	Alabama	10.40	Arizona	21%
5	Nevada	1.13	Mississippi	9.36	Nevada	17%
6	Florida	0.98	Maine	9.29	Florida	15%
7	New York	0.94	Washington	9.19	New Jersey	15%
8	Colorado	0.87	Delaware	9.19	Colorado	14%
9	New Jersey	0.80	Arkansas	9.07	New York	14%
10	Illinois	0.68	Kentucky	9.01	Illinois	14%
	Metropolitan Statistical Areas with more than 50 Hispanic gay or lesbian couples					
1	McAllen, TX	5.32	San Francisco, CA	15.25	Laredo, TX	94%
2	Laredo, TX	5.18	Madison, WI	14.11	McAllen, TX	87%
3	Brownsville, TX	4.87	Birmingham, AL	13.09	Brownsville, TX	85%
4	Miami, FL	3.85	Santa Rosa, CA	12.23	El Paso, TX	75%
5	El Paso, TX	3.54	Seattle, WA	12.16	Las Cruces, NM	54%
6	Visalia, CA	3.12	Indianapolis, IN	11.99	Corpus Christi, TX	52%
7	Las Cruces, NM	3.07	Atlanta, GA	11.73	Miami, FL	51%
8	Santa Fe, NM	2.92	Raleigh-Durham-Chapel Hill, NC	11.46	Yuma, AZ	50%
9	Salinas, CA	2.64	Santa Cruz-Watsonville, CA	11.37	Visalia, CA	49%
10	San Antonio, TX	2.61	Greensboro, NC	10.98	San Antonio, TX	49%

Source: Authors' calculations based on Census 2000 data.

other hand, the remaining three top-10 states in this ranking—Utah, Idaho, and North Dakota—all have relatively low concentrations of both racial/ethnic minorities and same-sex couples. Metropolitan areas such as San Francisco, Jersey City, Oakland, Seattle, and Boston have high concentrations of African American same-sex couples both in the population and among African American households. While Newburgh, New York; Fresno, California; West Palm Beach, Florida; and Sarasota, Florida, also follow this general pattern, Houma, Louisiana, serves as a notable exception; it does not have a particularly high concentration of same-sex couples in the population, yet ranks highly in the concentration of same-sex couples in the African American community.

The top 10 states ranked by the concentration of Hispanic gay and lesbian households among all households and among other same-sex couples are exactly the same, although the rankings vary slightly. Note that high-ranking states such as New Mexico, Texas, California, Arizona, and Nevada all have large Hispanic populations. Texas metropolitan areas (with their large Hispanic communities) feature prominently in the same rankings by metropolitan areas. McAllen, Laredo, El Paso, and San Antonio appear in both top 10 lists, as do Miami, Florida; Visalia, California; and Las Cruces, New Mexico.

States with high concentrations of same-sex couples among all Hispanic households are mostly in the South, with Georgia, South Carolina, North Carolina, Alabama, and Mississippi ranked as the top five. Interestingly, this ranking does not really follow the pattern observed before, where states with high concentrations of same-sex couples in the population also tend to have high concentrations of same-sex couples among minority households. However, the pattern is more evident among Hispanics in metropolitan areas, where cities like San Francisco, Madison, Santa Rosa, Seattle, Atlanta, and Santa Cruz rank among the top 10. All have high concentrations of same-sex couples in the population. Like in the state rankings, several southern cities also rank highly, including Birmingham, Raleigh/Durham/Chapel Hill, and Greensboro.

So far, this *Atlas* has described the geographic and demographic patterns of gay and lesbian couples primarily with tables and charts. While this can certainly be informative, the visual display of location patterns of same-sex couples through maps offers perhaps the most compelling use of census data. The *Atlas* continues with maps of gay and lesbian couple concentration within all 50 states and 25 major cities.

Endnotes

1. Joan Biskupic, "Same-Sex Couples Redefining Family Law in the US," *USA Today,* February 17, 2003, http://www.usatoday.com/news/nation/2003-02-17-cover-samesex_x.htm.

2. See http://www.hrc.org/familynet.

3. The Pearson correlation coefficient comparing the percentage of same-sex unmarried partner households with children and the percentage of households with children is 0.53 among states and 0.66 among large metropolitan areas. Both are significant at the $p < .001$ level.

4. The Pearson correlation coefficient comparing the percentage of same-sex unmarried-partner households with children and the percentage of same-sex unmarried-partner households in the population is −0.35 among states and −0.50 among large metropolitan areas. Both are significant at the $p < .001$ level.

5. County rankings include only counties reporting at least 50 same-sex coupled seniors.

6. Analyses of the location patterns of gay and lesbian racial and ethnic minorities use the Census Bureau's Summary File 2 (SF 2). This file provides data on same-sex unmarried partners by the race and ethnicity of the householder. Thus, the discussion of gay and lesbian racial and ethnic minorities is actually one of households headed by a gay or lesbian couple in which the householder is a racial or ethnic minority. For ease of discussion the texts refers to these households as an "African-American couple" or a "Hispanic couple." Census data on all African-American and Hispanic households is also from SF 2 to yield some level of comparability.

States with high concentrations of same-sex couples among all Hispanic households are mostly in the South.

Maps

Maps

While census data on same-sex unmarried partners provide valuable information about those couples' demographic and household characteristics, the data's obvious spatial component served as the genesis of this book. Census data on the number of reported same-sex unmarried partners are available at every dimension of census-defined geography, from the national level to the block level. This wide array of geographic aggregations provides many options for analyzing and displaying the data.

Understanding the methods used to display the data is critical for proper analysis and inference about the characteristics of gay and lesbian location patterns. Readers should note that the maps display the *concentration* of gay and lesbian couples, not the *population*. Areas where same-sex couples are highly concentrated may not always be areas with high population density. The decision to display the relative concentration of gay and lesbian couples means the reader can quickly assess where gay and lesbian couples constitute the highest proportion of households within the region shown on the map.

It is critical to emphasize that *the concentrations shown on each map are relative only to the area shown on the map*. At one scale, an area may appear to have a very low concentration of gay and lesbian couples, while at a larger or smaller scale the same area may appear to have a very high concentration. This is because concentration is relative to the area shown.

For example, in the context of a national county-level map, Cook County, Illinois (which includes Chicago) has a high concentration of gay-male couples (figure 7.1). However, a tract-level state map reveals that the same county has areas of low, mod-

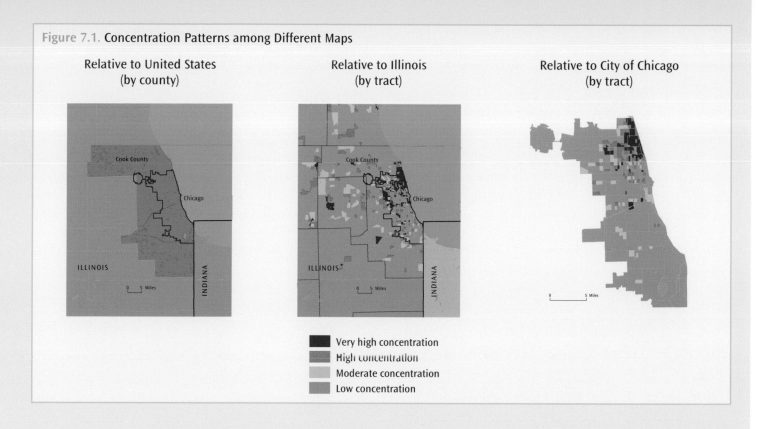

Figure 7.1. Concentration Patterns among Different Maps

Relative to United States
(by county)

Relative to Illinois
(by tract)

Relative to City of Chicago
(by tract)

Very high concentration
High concentration
Moderate concentration
Low concentration

erate, high, and very high concentration of gay-male couples. These tracts are only compared with other tracts in the state, so new patterns of concentration emerge. Note that the counties surrounding Chicago have pockets of very high concentration, though those counties appear to have a low concentration on the national map. When looking just within the city limits of Chicago, a different pattern emerges than was evident in the state map. Some South Chicago tracts appear highly concentrated when compared with the distribution of gay-male couples throughout Illinois, but when compared with the distribution of couples throughout the city, the northside tracts in and around Boystown overwhelm them.

In addition to maps, figures and tables showing a variety of state- or city-level characteristics of same-sex couples—including overall concentration, lists of highly concentrated areas, the prevalence of couples with children, and racial/ethnic and age characteristics—are provided for each state and a select group of cities. The map reference tools that precede both the state and city map sections provide detailed explanations of all elements presented in the analyses.

The United States map depicting concentrations of same-sex unmarried partners (see page 60) begins to provide information about basic location patterns of gay and lesbian couples at a national scale and encourages consideration of a variety of interesting questions. Do the location patterns of gay and lesbian couples appear to be correlated with gay-friendly state policies? Are there major urban areas with surprisingly low concentrations of gay and lesbian couples? Or, conversely, are there suburban or rural areas with unexpectedly high concentrations of same-sex couples?

The location pattern of gay and lesbian couples within each state also tells an interesting story. For instance, an area in Pennsylvania may appear to have a low concentration of same-sex couples when measured against the national distribution of same-sex couples; however, the same area may have a high concentration of gay and lesbian couples when compared with the distribution of only those gay and lesbian couples living in Pennsylvania. The state maps can also be displayed at a larger scale than a national map, providing a greater resolution with which to study location patterns.

Viewing the relative concentrations at the state level sparks questions about topics unable to be studied on a national scale. In the current era of federal-to-state fiscal and program devolution, there may be a greater interest in how gay and lesbian couples are geographically distributed throughout a state rather than throughout the nation. Although there is an ongoing national debate about many gay and lesbian issues, much of the policy that affects the daily lives of gay men and lesbians is legislated and decided at the state level. It is therefore relevant to study the concentrations of same-sex couples within each state.

Further, gay men and lesbians are commonly thought to cluster in large cities, and analysis of census data on same-sex couples in some ways supports this view. Given the large portion of the nation's population that is urban, and the even larger portion of the nation's gay and lesbian population that is urban, it makes sense to map gay and lesbian couples' loca-

tion patterns within large cities. Seeing same-sex couples' location patterns at the city scale gives the advantage of seeing the true variation of the citywide distribution at the census tract level (tracts are census-defined areas designed to contain roughly 2,000 households, regardless of the physical size of the area).

For many readers of this book, the city maps may be the most interesting and useful of all the maps. The clusters of same-sex couples within a local area are important from the service provision, community planning, and marketing points of view. The existence of "gay ghettos," or areas that have a traditionally high concentration of gay men and lesbians, can be confirmed in some cases, discovered in others.

A fundamental area of inquiry also served by all the maps is the difference in gay male and lesbian location patterns. For each city and state map, two smaller maps compare the separate geographic distributions of male and female same-sex couples. These maps highlight the differences between male- and female-couple location patterns and promote serious thought about the reasons behind those differences.

Map Methodology

The data displayed by the maps and included in the tables, charts, and rankings are primarily based on the Gay/Lesbian, Gay Male, and Lesbian Indices (commonly referred to as the Index). The Index is used in place of counts or proportions of same-sex couples because it offers a more intuitive sense of where gay and lesbian couples are over- or underrepresented.

Since areas with high population numbers are likely areas with high numbers of gay and lesbian couples, simple counts of same-sex unmarried partners convey limited information about the true location patterns of gay and lesbian couples relative to the general population. The proportion of households headed by a same-sex couple gives a somewhat better sense of gay and lesbian couples' location patterns, but suffers from a lack of intuitive comparability across various census geographic units, such as counties and census tracts.

The Index measures where gay and lesbian couples live *relative to* the general population, and thus captures whether gay and lesbian couples are over- or underrepresented in a particular geographic region.

The Index is calculated using the total number of households (AU_{HH}), the number of households headed by a male same-sex unmarried-partner couple (AU_{Gay}), and the number of households headed by a female same-sex unmarried-partner couple ($AU_{Lesbian}$) for each areal unit in a given map.[1] These numbers are then summed over the entire geographic area of interest (e.g., the state or city being mapped), giving a total count of households (T_{HH}), male same-sex unmarried-partner households (T_{Gay}), and female same-sex unmarried-partner households ($T_{Lesbian}$) in the state or city. Three indices are then calculated for each areal unit:

$$INDEX_{Gay} = \frac{AU_{Gay}/T_{Gay}}{AU_{HH}/T_{HH}}$$

$$INDEX_{Lesbian} = \frac{AU_{Lesbian}/T_{Lesbian}}{AU_{HH}/T_{HH}}$$

$$INDEX_{Gay/Lesbian} = \frac{(AU_{Gay}+AU_{Lesbian})/(T_{Gay}+T_{Lesbian})}{AU_{HH}/T_{HH}}$$

These indices can all be interpreted the same way. Since each index is a ratio of proportions, a value of 1.00 indicates that the proportions are the same. In this case, it means a gay and/or lesbian couple is just as likely to be in that areal unit as any other household. Any value over 1.00 indicates that gay and/or lesbian couples are more concentrated, or overrepresented, in that areal unit than the population in the area shown by the map. For example, a Gay/Lesbian Index value of 2.00 for a specific place means that gay and lesbian couples are twice as likely as the typical households from the area shown to live in that location. Any value below 1.00 indicates that gay and/or lesbian couples are less concentrated in that areal unit than the population in the area shown.

Each map consists of four main colors: green, yellow, orange, and red. Areal units with index values of 1.00 or less are green. Thus, the green areas on a map show where gay and/or lesbian couples are equally or underrepresented. Areal units with index values greater than 1.00 are split into three relatively equal groups based on their index values. The bottom third of these overrepresented areal units are yellow (moderate concentration), the next third is orange (high concentration), and the top third of these overrepresented areal units is red (very high concentration). Blue represents water, while areal units that are colorless have no person-level census data in Summary File 2.[2]

On the county-level state maps (labeled "by county"), any county with fewer than 10 gay-male or lesbian couples is colored green because we consider this count too small to provide accurate analysis (see chapter 2's section on data caveats). Again, this applies only to the two smaller county-level state maps on each state's layout.

All maps in this atlas were created using ArcView GIS 3.2 and ArcMap™ 8.3 software.[3] The state, county, tract, and ZIP Code Tabulation Area (ZCTA) boundary files were downloaded directly from the Census Bureau's web site.[4] The water boundary files were obtained from Geolytics's StreetCD 2000. The data for the maps come from the Census Bureau's Census 2000 Summary File 2.

Selection of Cities

Maps and demographic characteristics of same-sex couples are shown for 25 large American cities. The 25 cities selected include the 20 cities with the highest number of same-sex couples along with five additional cities chosen to reflect better geographic diversity or acknowledge a particularly high concentration of gay and lesbian couples. The 20 cities with the highest number of same-sex unmarried partner couples (in order) are New York, Los Angeles, Chicago, San Francisco, Houston, Dallas, Seattle, San Diego, Philadelphia, Phoenix, Washington (D.C.), Boston, Portland (Oregon), Denver, Atlanta, Oakland, Minneapolis/St. Paul, Columbus (Ohio),

Miami/Fort Lauderdale, and Austin. Of the five additional cities selected, Orlando and New Orleans both rank among the 20 cities with the highest concentration of gay and lesbian couples. Nashville, Kansas City, and Albuquerque provide a broader geographic balance to the cities selected.

Endnotes

1. U.S. census data are publicly released only after they have been aggregated to arbitrarily drawn areal units. The most common areal unit in spatial analyses involving census data is the census tract. We often use census tracts as the areal units in our maps (maps labeled "by tract"), but also use counties as areal units in some state-level maps (maps labeled "by county") and our national maps.

2. Summary File 2 data could be missing for two reasons: no population in the areal unit, or data were suppressed by the Census Bureau for confidentiality reasons.

3. Copyright ESRI, Inc. 1992–99 (ArcView GIS 3.2); copyright ESRI, Inc. 1999–2002 (ArcMap™ 8.3).

4. See http://www.census.gov/geo/www/cob/bdy_files.html.

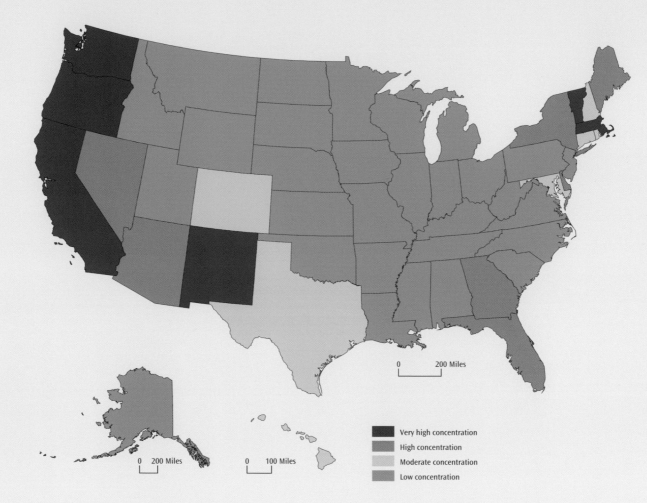

STATE-LEVEL CONCENTRATION OF SAME-SEX COUPLES

Very high concentration
High concentration
Moderate concentration
Low concentration

60

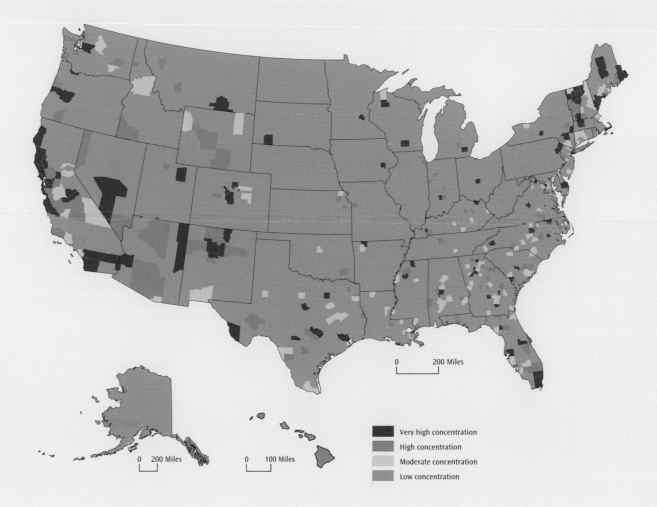

0   200 Miles

0   200 Miles

0   100 Miles

Very high concentration
High concentration
Moderate concentration
Low concentration

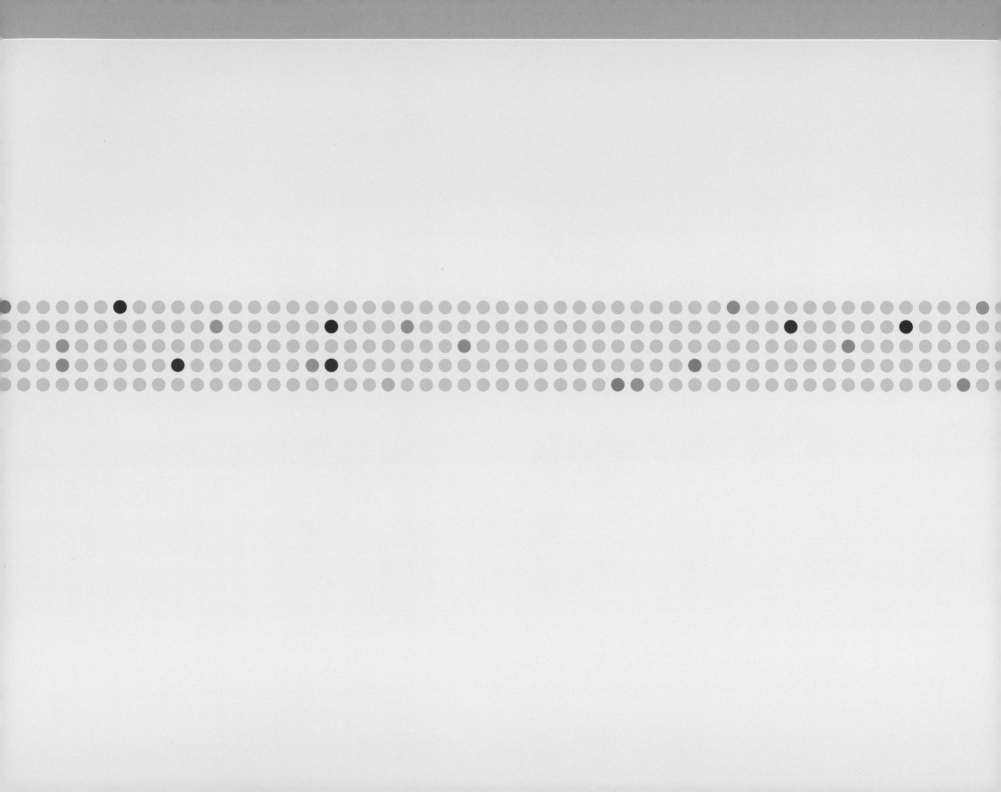

Seattle
WASHINGTON
Portland
OREGON
IDAHO
Boise

MONTANA
Billings

NORTH DAKOTA
Fargo
MINNESOTA
Minneapolis
St. Paul

WYOMING
Cheyenne

SOUTH DAKOTA
Sioux Falls

WISCONSIN
Milwaukee
MICHIGAN
Detroit

San Francisco
NEVADA
Salt Lake City
UTAH

CALIFORNIA

Las Vegas

Los Angeles

ARIZONA

Phoenix

Albuquerque

NEW MEXICO

NEBRASKA
Omaha

IOWA
Des Moines

Chicago
ILLINOIS
INDIANA
Indianapolis

Columbus
OHIO

Denver
COLORADO

KANSAS
Wichita

MISSOURI

Kansas City

Lexington
KENTUCKY

VIRGINIA

NORTH CAROLINA
Charlotte

Charleston

Oklahoma City
OKLAHOMA

ARKANSAS

Little Rock

Nashville
TENNESSEE

Memphis

SOUTH CAROLINA
Columbia

Atlanta

Birmingham

TEXAS

Dallas

MISSISSIPPI

ALABAMA

GEORGIA

Austin
Houston

LOUISIANA
Jackson

New Orleans

Jacksonville

FLORIDA

Fort Lauderdale
Miami

Burlington
VERMONT

MAINE

Portland
Manchester NEW HAMPSHIRE
Boston MASSACHUSETTS

NEW YORK

Providence RHODE ISLAND
Bridgeport CONNECTICUT
New York
Newark NEW JERSEY

PENNSYLVANIA
Philadelphia

Wilmington DELAWARE
Baltimore MARYLAND
Washington DISTRICT OF COLUMBIA

Virginia Beach

0   200 Miles

ALASKA

Anchorage

0   200 Miles

HAWAII
Honolulu

0   100 Miles

How to Read the State Maps

1 The large state map presents same-sex unmarried partner concentration at the census tract level. Tracts are designed to all contain a similar number of housing units, so rural tracts tend to be much larger than urban tracts. The different colors indicate the relative concentration of same-sex couples in tracts within the state only.

2 This legend defines the corresponding concentration level for each color on the map. Note that these concentrations are relative only to the state displayed. Any areal unit with an Index value of 1.0 or less is colored green. In addition, any tract on the tract-level state map with 10 or fewer gay and lesbian couples is colored green out of concern for the validity of these data. Similarly, counties on the separate Gay Male and Lesbian county-level state maps with 10 or fewer gay male or lesbian couples, respectively, are colored green. Areas with Index values greater than 1.0—i.e., areas with an overrepresentation of same-sex couples—were divided into three roughly equal groups, varying in color from yellow (moderate concentration) to red (very high concentration).

3 The two smaller state maps present separate county-level concentrations for same-sex male and female couples. The different colors indicate the relative concentration of male or female couples in counties within the state only.

4 These indices indicate the state-level concentration of all same-sex couples, male couples, and female couples, relative to the United States.

5 These statistics compare demographic characteristics of the same-sex couple population in the state with the state's general population. The Gay/Lesbian Rank column gives that state's rank among the 50 states for each same-sex couple population measure. Ranks are high to low, meaning a state ranked number one has the highest percentage for that characteristic.

6 This chart shows the distribution of all people counted as same-sex couples among five age categories: 18 to 24; 25 to 34; 35 to 44; 45 to 54; and 55 and older, based on U.S. Census tabulations.

7 This chart shows the share of all same-sex couple households in the state that are headed by a white householder, a black householder, a Hispanic householder, or a householder of some other race/ethnicity.

8 These numbers indicate where the state ranks among the 50 states based on its Gay/Lesbian Index, Gay Male Index, Lesbian Index, and Gay/Lesbian-Supportive Laws values. The Gay/Lesbian-Supportive Laws value was determined by an author calculation of gay-friendly and gay-unfriendly laws in each state, as reported by the Human Rights Campaign in December 2003.

9 There are 331 metropolitan statistical areas (MSAs) and primary metropolitan statistical areas (PMSAs) in the United States. Gay/Lesbian Index values were calculated for each of the 331 MSAs and PMSAs, and each was given a ranking from 1 to 331. A rank of one means the MSA or PMSA has the highest Gay/Lesbian Index in the nation among all MSAs and PMSAs. This table shows the top five MSAs and PMSAs in the state and the national ranking of each. National rankings for each MSA and PMSA based on separate Gay Male and Lesbian Indices are also shown. In states with less than five MSAs and PMSAs, all MSAs and PMSAs in the state are listed.

10 This table shows the top five communities in each state based on the Gay/Lesbian Index, and their national ranking among the 1,360 U.S. cities and towns with 50 or more same-sex couples. National rankings based on separate Gay Male and Lesbian Indices for each community are also shown. In states with less than five communities with 50 or more same-sex couples, all communities meeting that threshold are listed.

11 This chart shows the share of all same-sex couple households in the state with at least one child under the age of 18 present, based on U.S. Census tabulations.

12 In some cases, a city's metropolitan area includes counties from a neighboring state or states. Any MSA or PMSA containing at least one county in the state of interest is considered for the rank of top state metropolitan areas, so some metropolitan areas might appear on multiple state pages. An asterisk indicates MSAs or PMSAs containing counties in more than one state.

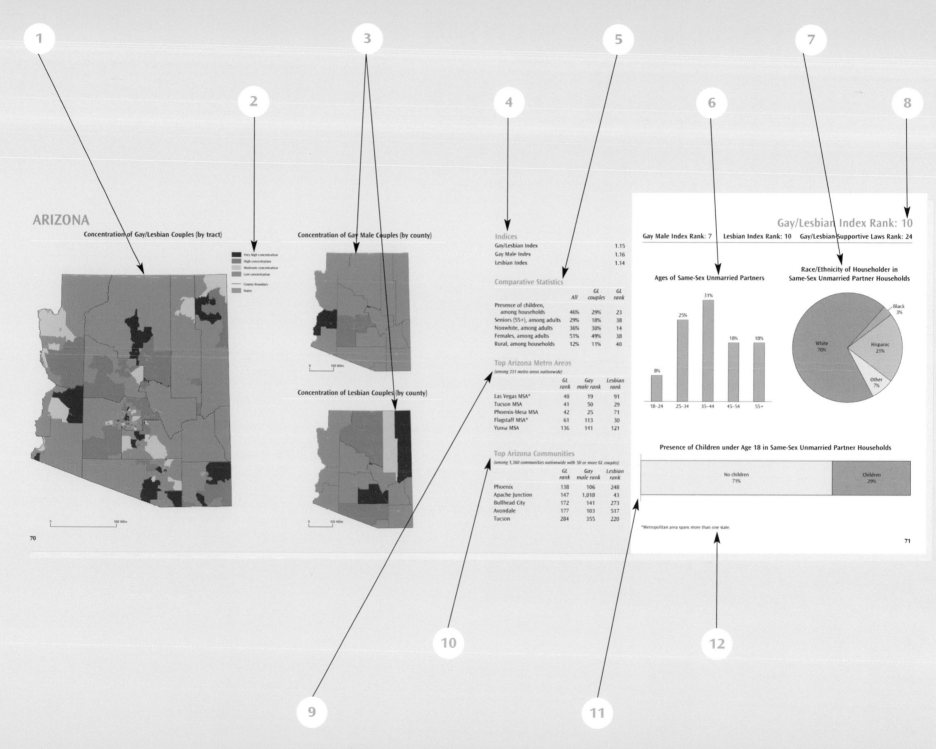

ARIZONA

Concentration of Gay/Lesbian Couples (by tract)

Very high concentration
High concentration
Moderate concentration
Low concentration
County boundary
Water

Concentration of Gay Male Couples (by county)

Concentration of Lesbian Couples (by county)

0   100 Miles

Indices

Gay/Lesbian Index	1.15
Gay Male Index	1.16
Lesbian Index	1.14

Comparative Statistics

	All	GL couples	GL rank
Presence of children, among households	46%	29%	23
Seniors (55+), among adults	29%	18%	38
Nonwhite, among adults	36%	30%	14
Females, among adults	51%	49%	38
Rural, among households	12%	11%	40

Top Arizona Metro Areas
(among 331 metro areas nationwide)

	GL rank	Gay male rank	Lesbian rank
Las Vegas MSA*	40	19	91
Tucson MSA	41	50	29
Phoenix-Mesa MSA	42	25	71
Flagstaff MSA*	61	113	30
Yuma MSA	136	141	121

Top Arizona Communities
(among 1,360 communities nationwide with 50 or more GL couples)

	GL rank	Gay male rank	Lesbian rank
Phoenix	138	106	248
Apache Junction	147	1,018	43
Bullhead City	172	141	273
Avondale	177	103	517
Tucson	284	355	220

Gay/Lesbian Index Rank: 10

Gay Male Index Rank: 7   Lesbian Index Rank: 10   Gay/Lesbian-Supportive Laws Rank: 24

Ages of Same-Sex Unmarried Partners

18–24: 8%
25–34: 25%
35–44: 31%
45–54: 18%
55+: 18%

Race/Ethnicity of Householder in
Same-Sex Unmarried Partner Households

White 70%
Hispanic 21%
Other 7%
Black 3%

Presence of Children under Age 18 in Same-Sex Unmarried Partner Households

No children 71%
Children 29%

*Metropolitan area spans more than one state.

70

71

ALABAMA

Concentration of Gay/Lesbian Couples (by tract)

Very high concentration
High concentration
Moderate concentration
Low concentration
County boundary
Water

0   50 Miles

Concentration of Gay Male Couples (by county)

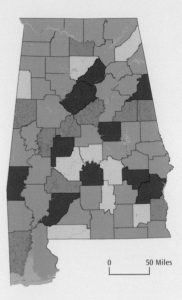

0   50 Miles

Concentration of Lesbian Couples (by county)

0   50 Miles

Gay Male Index Rank: 28   **Lesbian Index Rank: 31**   **Gay/Lesbian-Supportive Laws Rank: 43**

Indices

Gay/Lesbian Index	0.83
Gay Male Index	0.80
Lesbian Index	0.85

Comparative Statistics

	All	GL couples	GL rank
Presence of children, among households	46%	35%	6
Seniors (55+), among adults	30%	26%	6
Nonwhite, among adults	30%	31%	12
Females, among adults	53%	51%	29
Rural, among households	45%	43%	10

Top Alabama Metro Areas

(among 331 metro areas nationwide)

	GL rank	Gay male rank	Lesbian rank
Birmingham MSA	106	62	142
Mobile MSA	129	108	136
Dothan MSA	170	137	206
Tuscaloosa MSA	176	206	138
Montgomery MSA	196	148	241

Top Alabama Communities

(among 1,360 communities nationwide with 50 or more GL couples)

	GL rank	Gay male rank	Lesbian rank
Birmingham	252	194	378
Homewood	512	302	857
Prichard	541	1,019	211
Phenix City	705	601	756
Gadsden	787	997	502

Ages of Same-Sex Unmarried Partners

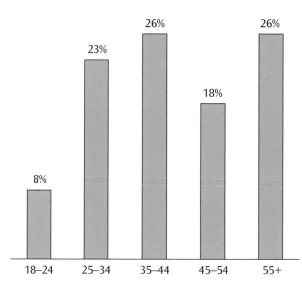

Race/Ethnicity of Householder in Same-Sex Unmarried Partner Households

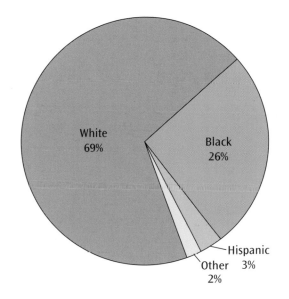

Presence of Children under Age 18 in Same-Sex Unmarried Partner Households

No children 65%   Children 35%

ALASKA

Concentration of Gay/Lesbian Couples (by tract)

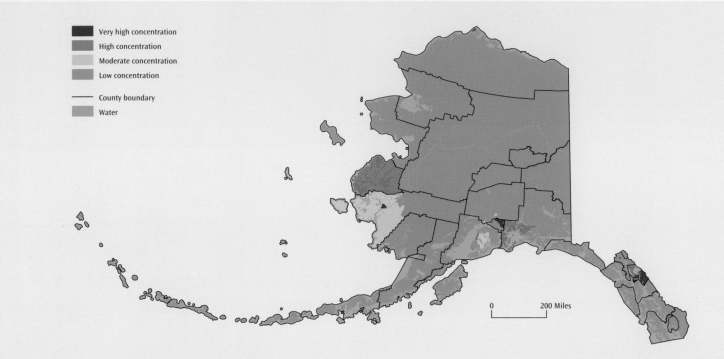

Very high concentration
High concentration
Moderate concentration
Low concentration

County boundary
Water

0   200 Miles

Concentration of Gay Male Couples (by county)

0   200 Miles

Concentration of Lesbian Couples (by county)

0   200 Miles

Indices

Gay/Lesbian Index	0.94
Gay Male Index	0.76
Lesbian Index	1.13

Comparative Statistics

	All	GL couples	GL rank
Presence of children, among households	57%	38%	3
Seniors (55+), among adults	18%	16%	47
Nonwhite, among adults	32%	26%	18
Females, among adults	48%	59%	2
Rural, among households	34%	31%	17

Top Alaska Metro Areas

(among 331 metro areas nationwide)

	GL rank	Gay male rank	Lesbian rank
Anchorage MSA	90	117	67

Top Alaska Communities

(among 1,360 communities nationwide with 50 or more GL couples)

	GL rank	Gay male rank	Lesbian rank
Juneau	222	853	76
Anchorage	688	777	540
Fairbanks	982	1,342	410

Ages of Same-Sex Unmarried Partners

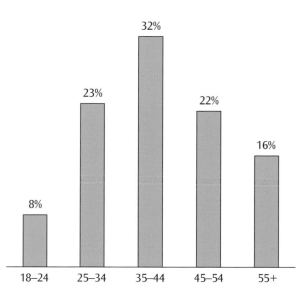

Race/Ethnicity of Householder in Same-Sex Unmarried Partner Households

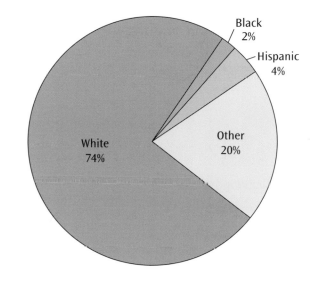

Presence of Children under Age 18 in Same-Sex Unmarried Partner Households

No children 62%   Children 38%

ARIZONA

Concentration of Gay/Lesbian Couples (by tract)

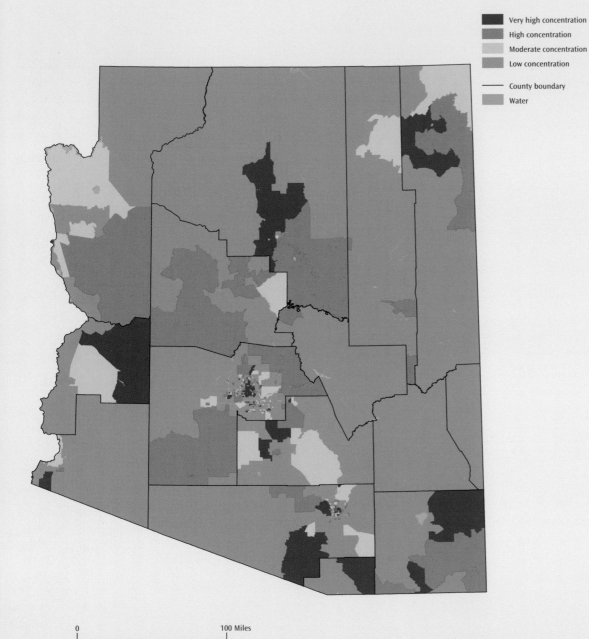

Very high concentration
High concentration
Moderate concentration
Low concentration
County boundary
Water

0   100 Miles

Concentration of Gay Male Couples (by county)

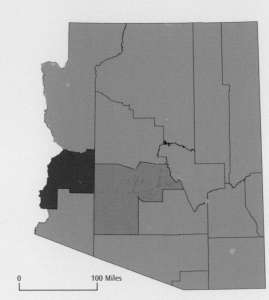

0   100 Miles

Concentration of Lesbian Couples (by county)

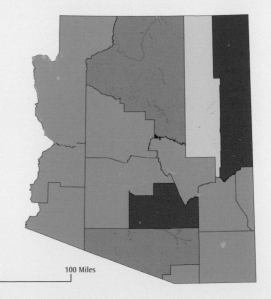

0   100 Miles

Indices

Gay/Lesbian Index	1.15
Gay Male Index	1.16
Lesbian Index	1.14

Comparative Statistics

	All	GL couples	GL rank
Presence of children, among households	46%	29%	23
Seniors (55+), among adults	29%	18%	38
Nonwhite, among adults	36%	30%	14
Females, among adults	51%	49%	38
Rural, among households	12%	11%	40

Top Arizona Metro Areas

(among 331 metro areas nationwide)

	GL rank	Gay male rank	Lesbian rank
Las Vegas MSA*	40	19	91
Tucson MSA	41	50	29
Phoenix-Mesa MSA	42	25	71
Flagstaff MSA*	61	113	30
Yuma MSA	136	141	121

Top Arizona Communities

(among 1,360 communities nationwide with 50 or more GL couples)

	GL rank	Gay male rank	Lesbian rank
Phoenix	138	106	248
Apache Junction	147	1,018	43
Bullhead City	172	141	273
Avondale	177	103	517
Tucson	284	355	220

Gay/Lesbian Index Rank: 10

Gay Male Index Rank: 7   Lesbian Index Rank: 10   Gay/Lesbian-Supportive Laws Rank: 24

Ages of Same-Sex Unmarried Partners

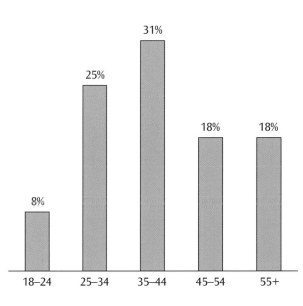

Race/Ethnicity of Householder in Same-Sex Unmarried Partner Households

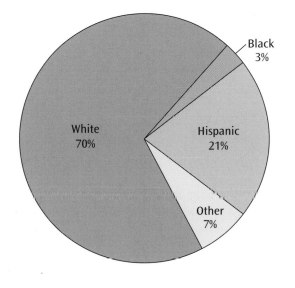

Presence of Children under Age 18 in Same-Sex Unmarried Partner Households

No children 71%   Children 29%

* Metropolitan area spans more than one state.

71

ARKANSAS

Concentration of Gay/Lesbian Couples (by tract)

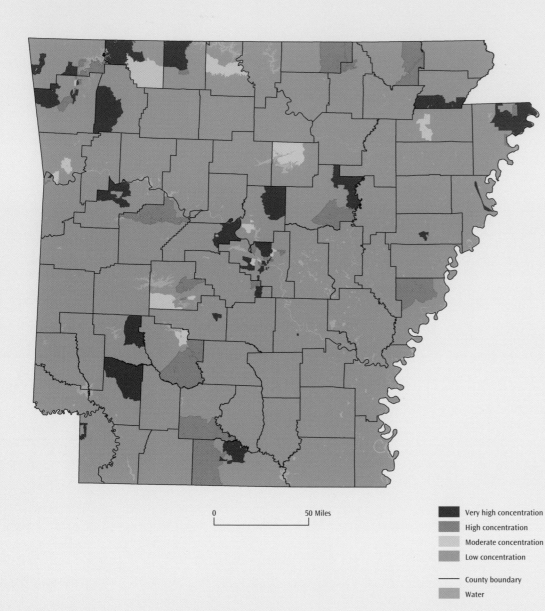

Concentration of Gay Male Couples (by county)

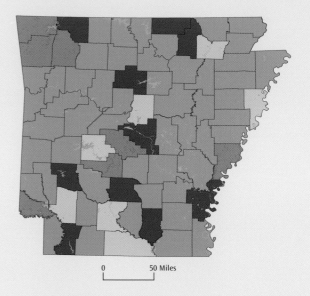

0   50 Miles

Concentration of Lesbian Couples (by county)

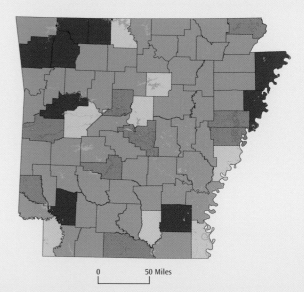

0   50 Miles

0   50 Miles

Very high concentration
High concentration
Moderate concentration
Low concentration

County boundary
Water

Indices

Gay/Lesbian Index	0.75
Gay Male Index	0.73
Lesbian Index	0.77

Comparative Statistics

	All	GL couples	GL rank
Presence of children, among households	45%	33%	10
Seniors (55+), among adults	32%	25%	7
Nonwhite, among adults	21%	23%	22
Females, among adults	52%	51%	30
Rural, among households	47%	45%	7

Top Arkansas Metro Areas

(among 331 metro areas nationwide)

	GL rank	Gay male rank	Lesbian rank
Memphis MSA*	125	90	144
Fayetteville-Springdale-Rogers MSA	161	127	192
Little Rock-North Little Rock MSA	164	121	205
Fort Smith MSA*	246	235	252
Texarkana MSA*	253	253	237

Top Arkansas Communities

(among 1,360 communities nationwide with 50 or more GL couples)

	GL rank	Gay male rank	Lesbian rank
Fayetteville	525	441	619
Little Rock	568	413	730
West Memphis	615	599	583
Springdale	671	773	503
Rogers	971	754	1,117

Gay Male Index Rank: 38   Lesbian Index Rank: 39   Gay/Lesbian-Supportive Laws Rank: 40

Ages of Same-Sex Unmarried Partners

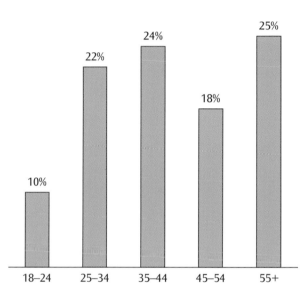

18–24	25–34	35–44	45–54	55+
10%	22%	24%	18%	25%

Race/Ethnicity of Householder in Same-Sex Unmarried Partner Households

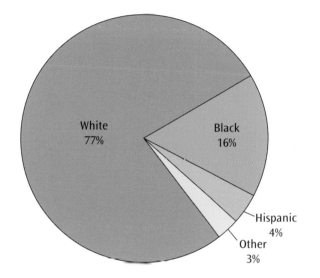

White 77%
Black 16%
Hispanic 4%
Other 3%

Presence of Children under Age 18 in Same-Sex Unmarried Partner Households

No children 67%   Children 33%

* Metropolitan area spans more than one state.

CALIFORNIA

Concentration of Gay/Lesbian Couples (by tract)

Very high concentration
High concentration
Moderate concentration
Low concentration

County boundary
Water

0   100 Miles

Concentration of Gay Male Couples (by county)

0   100 Miles

Concentration of Lesbian Couples (by county)

0   100 Miles

Indices

Gay/Lesbian Index	1.42
Gay Male Index	1.52
Lesbian Index	1.33

Comparative Statistics

	All	GL couples	GL rank
Presence of children, among households	54%	26%	32
Seniors (55+), among adults	25%	16%	44
Nonwhite, among adults	53%	37%	5
Females, among adults	51%	46%	48
Rural, among households	6%	5%	50

Top California Metro Areas

(among 331 metro areas nationwide)

	GL rank	Gay male rank	Lesbian rank
San Francisco PMSA	1	1	4
Santa Rosa PMSA	2	3	1
Santa Cruz-Watsonville PMSA	3	17	2
Oakland PMSA	5	9	5
Los Angeles-Long Beach PMSA	12	7	38

Top California Communities

(among 1,360 communities nationwide with 50 or more GL couples)

	GL rank	Gay male rank	Lesbian rank
Guerneville	2	2	2
West Hollywood	4	4	111
Palm Springs	5	5	157
San Francisco	11	10	41
Laguna Beach	12	9	46

Gay Male Index Rank: 1   Lesbian Index Rank: 5   Gay/Lesbian-Supportive Laws Rank: 2

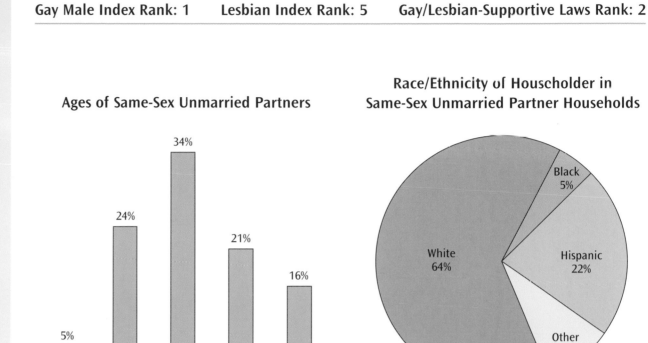

Ages of Same-Sex Unmarried Partners

- 18–24: 5%
- 25–34: 24%
- 35–44: 34%
- 45–54: 21%
- 55+: 16%

Race/Ethnicity of Householder in Same-Sex Unmarried Partner Households

- White 64%
- Hispanic 22%
- Other 9%
- Black 5%

Presence of Children under Age 18 in Same-Sex Unmarried Partner Households

- No children 74%
- Children 26%

COLORADO

Concentration of Gay/Lesbian Couples (by tract)

Very high concentration
High concentration
Moderate concentration
Low concentration

County boundary
Water

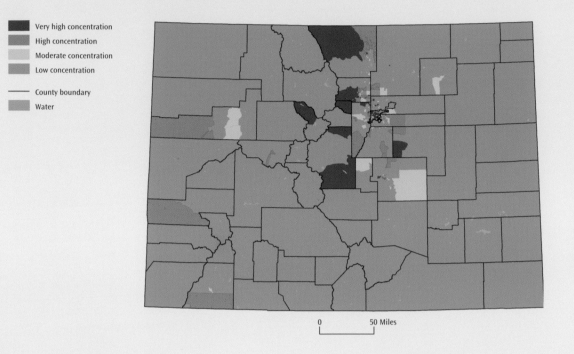

0   50 Miles

Concentration of Gay Male Couples (by county)

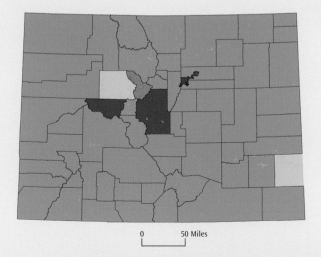

0   50 Miles

Concentration of Lesbian Couples (by county)

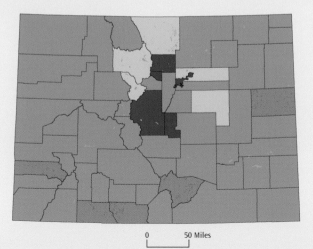

0   50 Miles

Indices

Gay/Lesbian Index	1.07
Gay Male Index	0.98
Lesbian Index	1.17

Comparative Statistics

	All	GL couples	GL rank
Presence of children, among households	49%	22%	48
Seniors (55+), among adults	24%	13%	50
Nonwhite, among adults	26%	22%	24
Females, among adults	50%	54%	8
Rural, among households	16%	13%	38

Top Colorado Metro Areas

(among 331 metro areas nationwide)

	GL rank	Gay male rank	Lesbian rank
Denver PMSA	28	24	31
Boulder-Longmont PMSA	31	123	14
Fort Collins-Loveland MSA	135	280	40
Greeley PMSA	144	182	111
Colorado Springs MSA	191	261	120

Top Colorado Communities

(among 1,360 communities nationwide with 50 or more GL couples)

	GL rank	Gay male rank	Lesbian rank
Denver	59	50	99
Lafayette	140	1,287	35
Boulder	230	589	110
Louisville	306	1,205	77
Wheat Ridge	509	499	499

Gay Male Index Rank: 17   Lesbian Index Rank: 9   Gay/Lesbian-Supportive Laws Rank: 24

Ages of Same-Sex Unmarried Partners

- 18–24: 7%
- 25–34: 26%
- 35–44: 34%
- 45–54: 20%
- 55+: 13%

Race/Ethnicity of Householder in Same-Sex Unmarried Partner Households

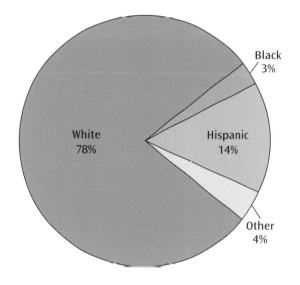

- White 78%
- Hispanic 14%
- Black 3%
- Other 4%

Presence of Children under Age 18 in Same-Sex Unmarried Partner Households

- No children 78%
- Children 22%

CONNECTICUT

Concentration of Gay/Lesbian Couples (by tract)

Very high concentration
High concentration
Moderate concentration
Low concentration
County boundary
Water

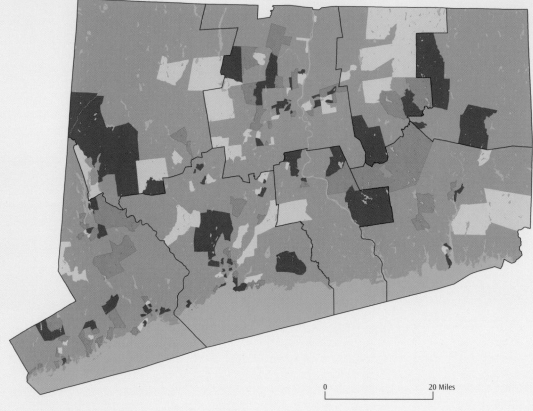

0   20 Miles

Concentration of Gay Male Couples (by county)

0   20 Miles

Concentration of Lesbian Couples (by county)

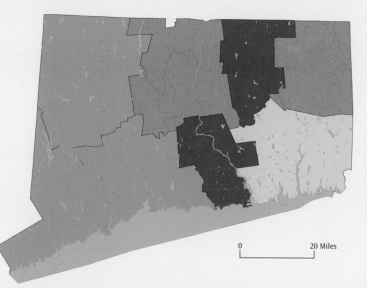

0   20 Miles

Indices

Gay/Lesbian Index	1.01
Gay Male Index	0.96
Lesbian Index	1.05

Comparative Statistics

	All	GL couples	GL rank
Presence of children, among households	47%	25%	36
Seniors (55+), among adults	30%	21%	24
Nonwhite, among adults	23%	20%	25
Females, among adults	52%	52%	24
Rural, among households	12%	13%	37

Top Connecticut Metro Areas

(among 331 metro areas nationwide)

	GL rank	Gay male rank	Lesbian rank
Danbury PMSA	52	31	96
New Haven-Meriden PMSA	68	68	80
Hartford MSA	71	88	56
Stamford-Norwalk PMSA	77	35	173
Worcester PMSA*	108	125	88

Top Connecticut Communities

(among 1,360 communities nationwide with 50 or more GL couples)

	GL rank	Gay male rank	Lesbian rank
Hartford	233	217	276
West Hartford	250	191	392
New Haven	271	230	346
New London	296	505	172
Norwalk	327	220	561

Ages of Same-Sex Unmarried Partners

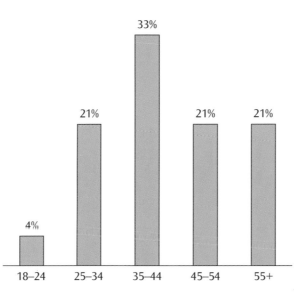

Race/Ethnicity of Householder in Same-Sex Unmarried Partner Households

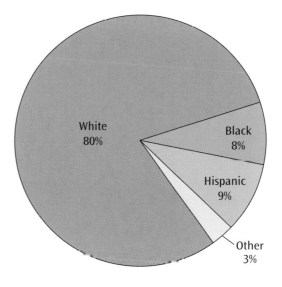

Presence of Children under Age 18 in Same-Sex Unmarried Partner Households

No children 75% | Children 25%

* Metropolitan area spans more than one state.

DELAWARE

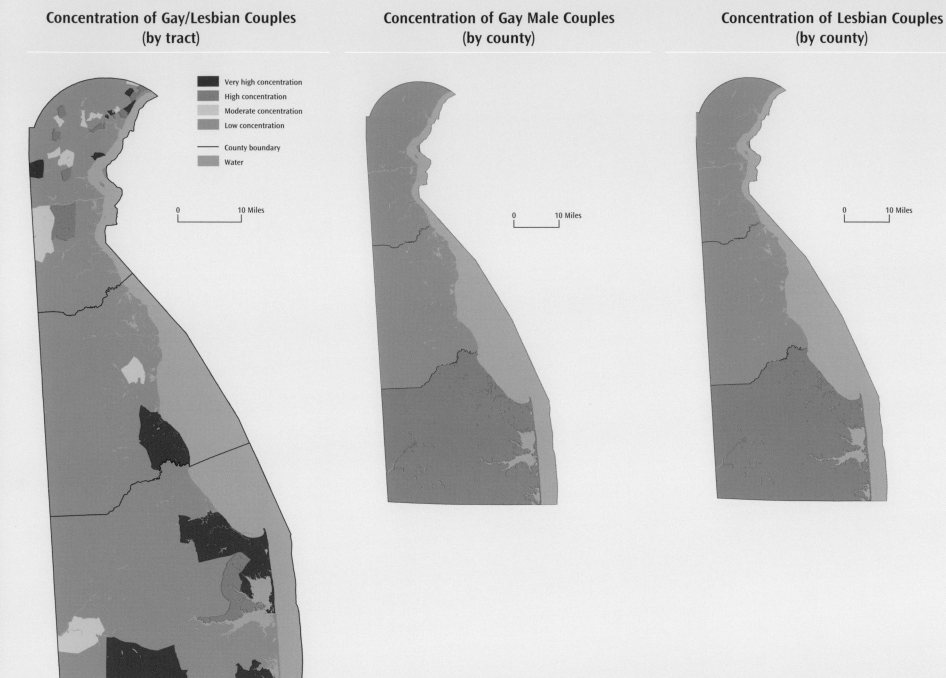

**Concentration of Gay/Lesbian Couples
(by tract)**

Very high concentration
High concentration
Moderate concentration
Low concentration

County boundary
Water

0   10 Miles

**Concentration of Gay Male Couples
(by county)**

0   10 Miles

**Concentration of Lesbian Couples
(by county)**

0   10 Miles

Gay Male Index Rank: 8   **Lesbian Index Rank: 16**   **Gay/Lesbian-Supportive Laws Rank: 20**

Indices

Gay/Lesbian Index	1.11
Gay Male Index	1.15
Lesbian Index	1.07

Comparative Statistics

	All	GL couples	GL rank
Presence of children, among households	46%	25%	38
Seniors (55+), among adults	29%	20%	31
Nonwhite, among adults	28%	23%	21
Females, among adults	52%	48%	44
Rural, among households	20%	21%	30

Top Delaware Metro Areas

(among 331 metro areas nationwide)

	GL rank	Gay male rank	Lesbian rank
Wilmington-Newark PMSA*	84	65	104
Dover MSA	200	176	215

Top Delaware Communities

(among 1,360 communities nationwide with 50 or more GL couples)

	GL rank	Gay male rank	Lesbian rank
Wilmington	263	215	355
Dover	1,077	846	1,205

Ages of Same-Sex Unmarried Partners

Age	Percent
18–24	6%
25–34	21%
35–44	31%
45–54	22%
55+	20%

Race/Ethnicity of Householder in Same-Sex Unmarried Partner Households

White 77%
Black 16%
Hispanic 5%
Other 3%

Presence of Children under Age 18 in Same-Sex Unmarried Partner Households

No children 75%   Children 25%

* Metropolitan area spans more than one state.

FLORIDA

Concentration of Gay/Lesbian Couples (by tract)

Concentration of Gay Male Couples (by county)

Concentration of Lesbian Couples (by county)

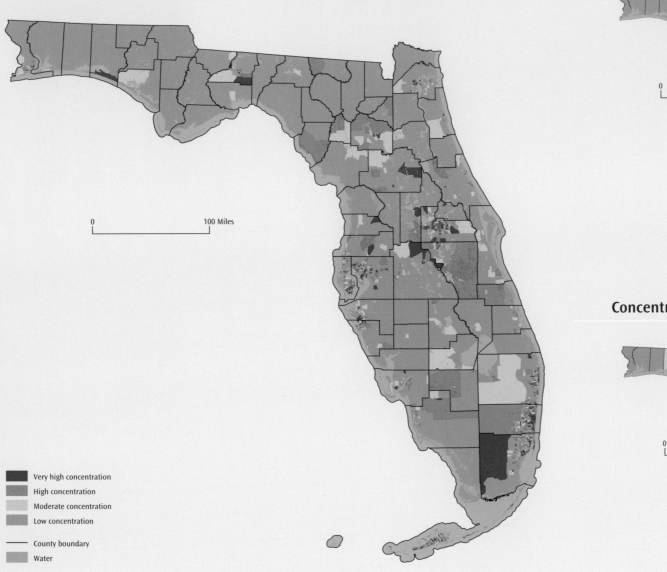

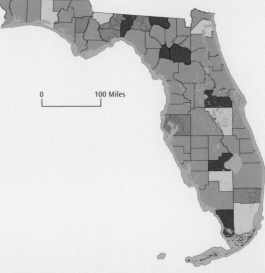

Very high concentration

High concentration

Moderate concentration

Low concentration

County boundary

Water

Indices

Gay/Lesbian Index	1.15
Gay Male Index	1.27
Lesbian Index	1.02

Comparative Statistics

	All	GL couples	GL rank
Presence of children, among households	41%	24%	41
Seniors (55+), among adults	35%	24%	14
Nonwhite, among adults	35%	28%	17
Females, among adults	52%	44%	50
Rural, among households	11%	8%	45

Top Florida Metro Areas

(among 331 metro areas nationwide)

	GL rank	Gay male rank	Lesbian rank
Fort Lauderdale PMSA	7	2	46
Miami PMSA	21	10	74
Orlando MSA	30	15	79
Tampa-St. Petersburg-Clearwater MSA	43	27	72
West Palm Beach-Boca Raton MSA	49	22	124

Top Florida Communities

(among 1,360 communities nationwide with 50 or more GL couples)

	GL rank	Gay male rank	Lesbian rank
Wilton Manors	3	3	33
Miami Shores	6	6	50
Key West	8	7	42
Oakland Park	13	12	75
Gulfport	22	30	9

Ages of Same-Sex Unmarried Partners

Race/Ethnicity of Householder in Same-Sex Unmarried Partner Households

Presence of Children under Age 18 in Same-Sex Unmarried Partner Households

No children 76%   Children 24%

GEORGIA

Concentration of Gay/Lesbian Couples (by tract)

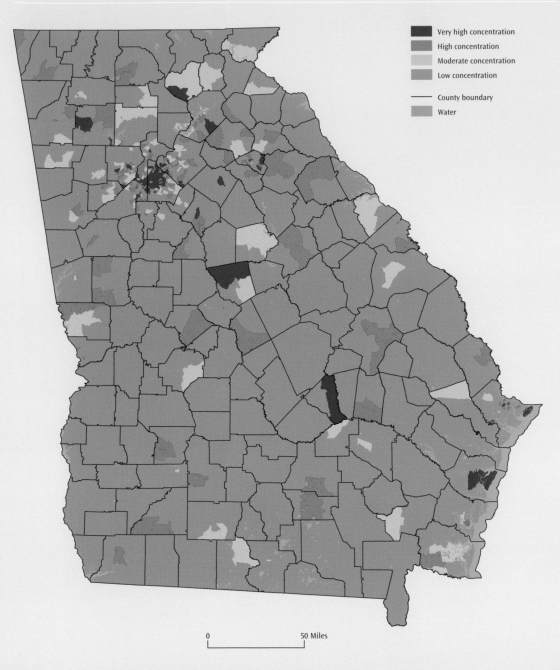

Very high concentration
High concentration
Moderate concentration
Low concentration
County boundary
Water

0   50 Miles

Concentration of Gay Male Couples (by county)

0   50 Miles

Concentration of Lesbian Couples (by county)

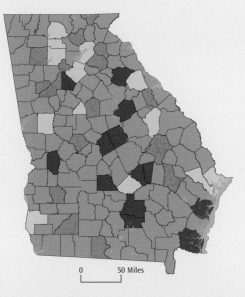

0   50 Miles

Indices

Gay/Lesbian Index	1.14
Gay Male Index	1.20
Lesbian Index	1.08

Comparative Statistics

	All	GL couples	GL rank
Presence of children, among households	50%	28%	28
Seniors (55+), among adults	24%	15%	48
Nonwhite, among adults	37%	31%	13
Females, among adults	52%	47%	47
Rural, among households	28%	22%	29

Top Georgia Metro Areas

(among 331 metro areas nationwide)

	GL rank	Gay male rank	Lesbian rank
Atlanta MSA	15	11	37
Savannah MSA	57	41	89
Athens MSA	64	38	114
Augusta-Aiken MSA*	149	128	170
Chattanooga MSA*	171	132	211

Top Georgia Communities

(among 1,360 communities nationwide with 50 or more GL couples)

	GL rank	Gay male rank	Lesbian rank
Decatur	7	17	4
North Druid Hills	10	8	36
Druid Hills	15	16	17
Scottdale	21	24	10
North Decatur	24	31	12

Gay Male Index Rank: 5   Lesbian Index Rank: 15   Gay/Lesbian-Supportive Laws Rank: 32

Ages of Same-Sex Unmarried Partners

- 18–24: 8%
- 25–34: 28%
- 35–44: 32%
- 45–54: 18%
- 55+: 15%

Race/Ethnicity of Householder in Same-Sex Unmarried Partner Households

- White 69%
- Black 22%
- Hispanic 6%
- Other 3%

Presence of Children under Age 18 in Same-Sex Unmarried Partner Households

- No children 72%
- Children 28%

* Metropolitan area spans more than one state.

HAWAII

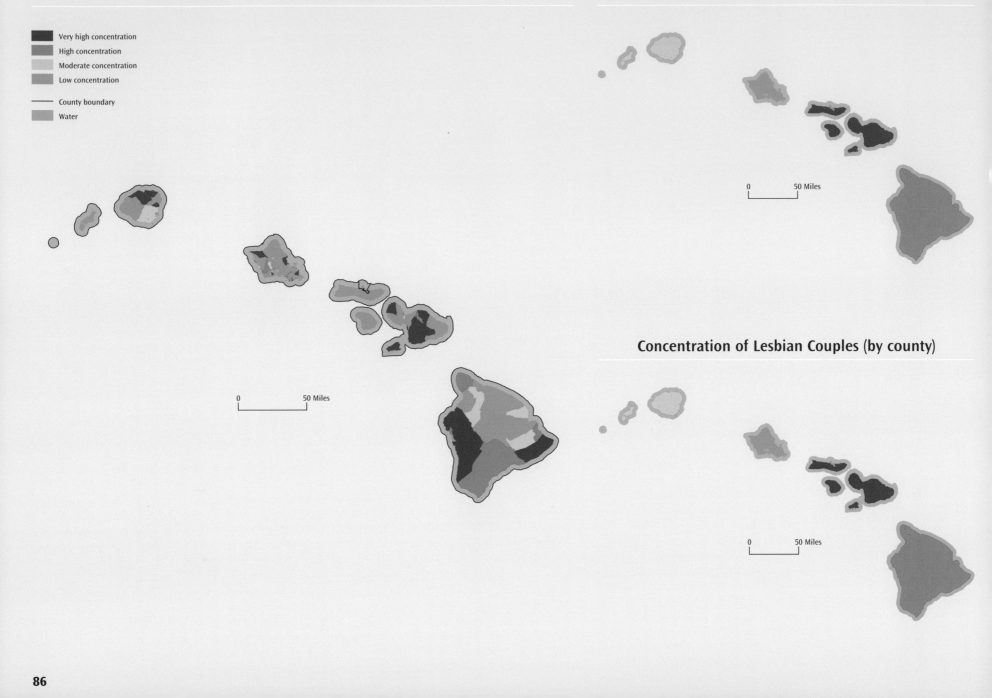

Concentration of Gay/Lesbian Couples (by tract)

- Very high concentration
- High concentration
- Moderate concentration
- Low concentration
- County boundary
- Water

0   50 Miles

Concentration of Gay Male Couples (by county)

0   50 Miles

Concentration of Lesbian Couples (by county)

0   50 Miles

Indices

Gay/Lesbian Index	1.05
Gay Male Index	1.07
Lesbian Index	1.03

Comparative Statistics

	All	GL couples	GL rank
Presence of children, among households	51%	30%	20
Seniors (55+), among adults	29%	25%	9
Nonwhite, among adults	77%	59%	1
Females, among adults	50%	48%	43
Rural, among households	9%	12%	39

Top Hawaii Metro Areas

(among 331 metro areas nationwide)

	GL rank	Gay male rank	Lesbian rank
Honolulu MSA	117	86	132

Top Hawaii Communities

(among 1,360 communities nationwide with 50 or more GL couples)

	GL rank	Gay male rank	Lesbian rank
Kihei	74	54	150
Kaneohe	572	722	390
Kailua	610	955	290
Honolulu	701	382	1,033
Hilo	1,127	1,124	1,064

Gay Male Index Rank: 11   Lesbian Index Rank: 19   Gay/Lesbian-Supportive Laws Rank: 16

Ages of Same-Sex Unmarried Partners

Age	Percent
18–24	5%
25–34	17%
35–44	29%
45–54	24%
55+	25%

Race/Ethnicity of Householder in Same-Sex Unmarried Partner Households

White 41%
Other 51%
Black 2%
Hispanic 6%

Presence of Children under Age 18 in Same-Sex Unmarried Partner Households

No children 70%   Children 30%

IDAHO

Concentration of Gay/Lesbian Couples (by tract)

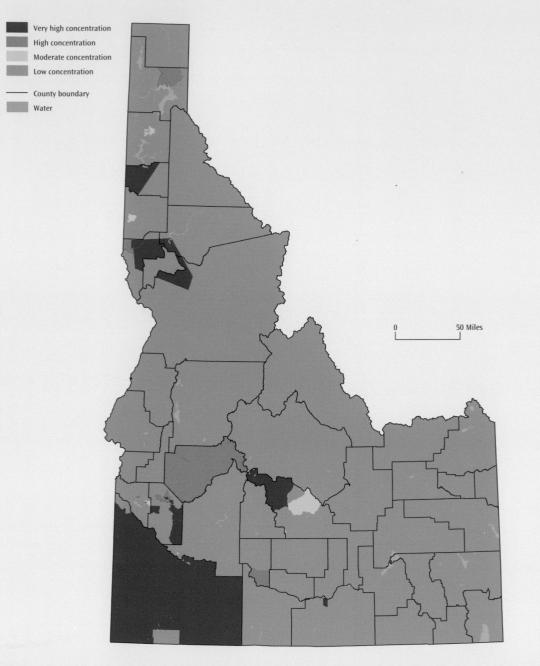

- Very high concentration
- High concentration
- Moderate concentration
- Low concentration
- County boundary
- Water

Concentration of Gay Male Couples (by county)

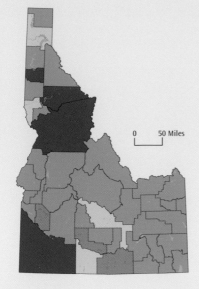

0   50 Miles

Concentration of Lesbian Couples (by county)

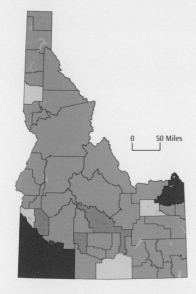

0   50 Miles

Indices

Gay/Lesbian Index	0.71
Gay Male Index	0.67
Lesbian Index	0.74

Comparative Statistics

	All	GL couples	GL rank
Presence of children, among households	50%	31%	16
Seniors (55+), among adults	27%	24%	11
Nonwhite, among adults	12%	11%	41
Females, among adults	50%	52%	23
Rural, among households	34%	34%	15

Top Idaho Metro Areas

(among 331 metro areas nationwide)

	GL rank	Gay male rank	Lesbian rank
Boise City MSA	177	219	135
Pocatello MSA	287	275	289

Top Idaho Communities

(among 1,360 communities nationwide with 50 or more GL couples)

	GL rank	Gay male rank	Lesbian rank
Boise City	756	827	627
Pocatello	1,228	1,184	1,171
Nampa	1,245	1,347	912
Coeur d'Alene	1,260	1,150	1,268

Gay Male Index Rank: 43   Lesbian Index Rank: 42   Gay/Lesbian-Supportive Laws Rank: 43

Ages of Same-Sex Unmarried Partners

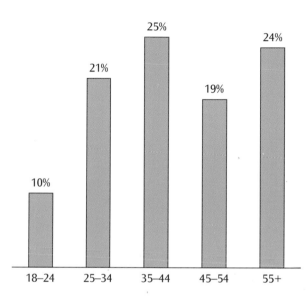

Race/Ethnicity of Householder in Same-Sex Unmarried Partner Households

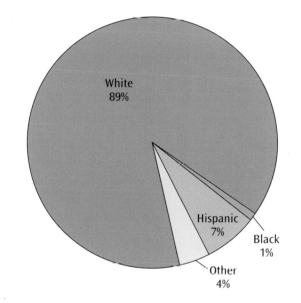

Presence of Children under Age 18 in Same-Sex Unmarried Partner Households

ILLINOIS

Concentration of Gay/Lesbian Couples (by tract)

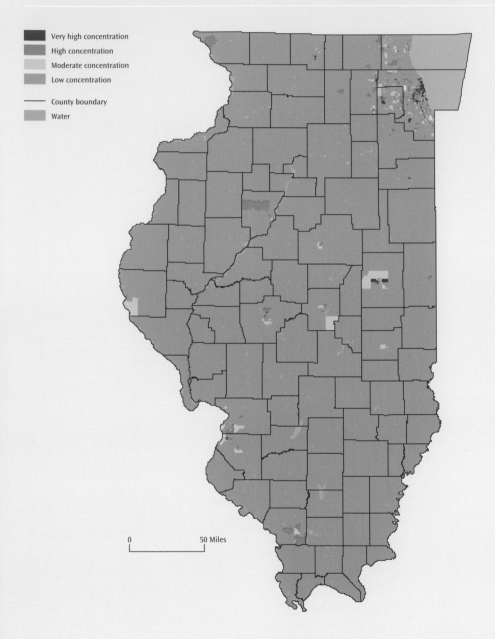

Very high concentration
High concentration
Moderate concentration
Low concentration
County boundary
Water

0   50 Miles

Concentration of Gay Male Couples (by county)

0   50 Miles

Concentration of Lesbian Couples (by county)

0   50 Miles

Indices

Gay/Lesbian Index	0.88
Gay Male Index	0.93
Lesbian Index	0.84

Comparative Statistics

	All	GL couples	GL rank
Presence of children, among households	50%	29%	22
Seniors (55+), among adults	28%	18%	36
Nonwhite, among adults	32%	32%	11
Females, among adults	52%	47%	46
Rural, among households	12%	8%	47

Top Illinois Metro Areas

(among 331 metro areas nationwide)

	GL rank	Gay male rank	Lesbian rank
Chicago PMSA	76	45	133
Champaign-Urbana MSA	132	218	76
Springfield MSA	208	150	251
St. Louis MSA*	213	190	230
Bloomington-Normal MSA	231	286	154

Top Illinois Communities

(among 1,360 communities nationwide with 50 or more GL couples)

	GL rank	Gay male rank	Lesbian rank
Oak Park	77	74	95
Evanston	139	161	156
Chicago	146	96	356
Forest Park	174	188	191
Cicero	288	210	469

Gay Male Index Rank: 20   Lesbian Index Rank: 32   Gay/Lesbian-Supportive Laws Rank: 12

Ages of Same-Sex Unmarried Partners

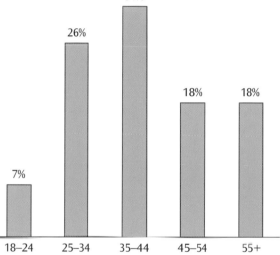

- 18–24: 7%
- 25–34: 26%
- 35–44: 31%
- 45–54: 18%
- 55+: 18%

Race/Ethnicity of Householder in Same-Sex Unmarried Partner Households

- White 68%
- Black 14%
- Hispanic 14%
- Other 4%

Presence of Children under Age 18 in Same-Sex Unmarried Partner Households

- No children 71%
- Children 29%

* Metropolitan area spans more than one state.

INDIANA

Concentration of Gay/Lesbian Couples (by tract)

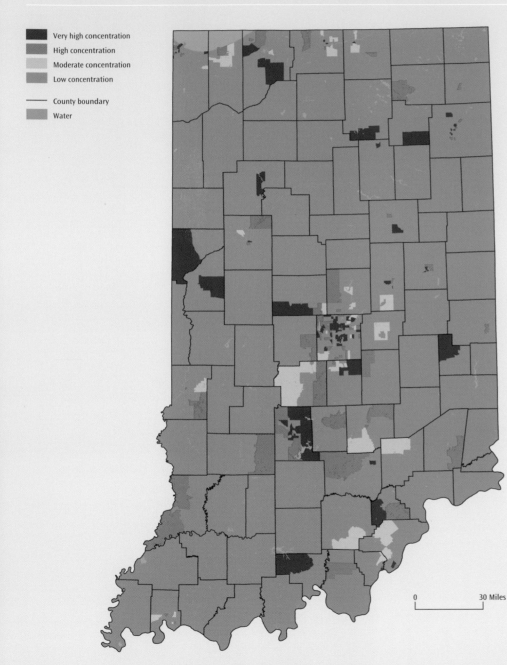

Very high concentration
High concentration
Moderate concentration
Low concentration

County boundary
Water

0   30 Miles

Concentration of Gay Male Couples (by county)

0   30 Miles

Concentration of Lesbian Couples (by county)

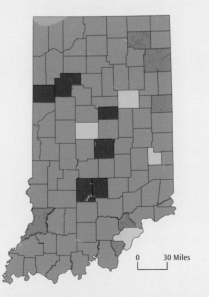

0   30 Miles

Indices

Gay/Lesbian Index	0.77
Gay Male Index	0.76
Lesbian Index	0.79

Comparative Statistics

	All	GL couples	GL rank
Presence of children, among households	47%	28%	27
Seniors (55+), among adults	28%	20%	29
Nonwhite, among adults	14%	14%	36
Females, among adults	52%	51%	32
Rural, among households	29%	24%	22

Top Indiana Metro Areas

(among 331 metro areas nationwide)

	GL rank	Gay male rank	Lesbian rank
Bloomington MSA	25	39	21
Indianapolis MSA	97	67	125
Louisville MSA*	139	110	147
Muncie MSA	193	122	264
Cincinnati PMSA*	195	170	217

Top Indiana Communities

(among 1,360 communities nationwide with 50 or more GL couples)

	GL rank	Gay male rank	Lesbian rank
Indianapolis	318	259	440
Bloomington	340	304	406
New Albany	719	540	848
South Bend	775	662	818
Jeffersonville	781	660	832

Gay Male Index Rank: 33   Lesbian Index Rank: 35   Gay/Lesbian-Supportive Laws Rank: 27

Ages of Same-Sex Unmarried Partners

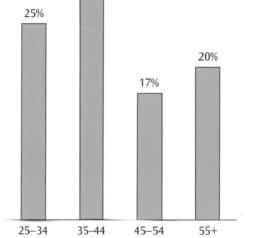

Race/Ethnicity of Householder in Same-Sex Unmarried Partner Households

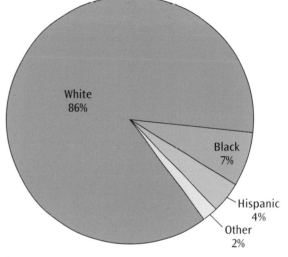

Presence of Children under Age 18 in Same-Sex Unmarried Partner Households

No children 72% | Children 28%

* Metropolitan area spans more than one state.

93

IOWA

Concentration of Gay/Lesbian Couples (by tract)

Very high concentration
High concentration
Moderate concentration
Low concentration

County boundary
Water

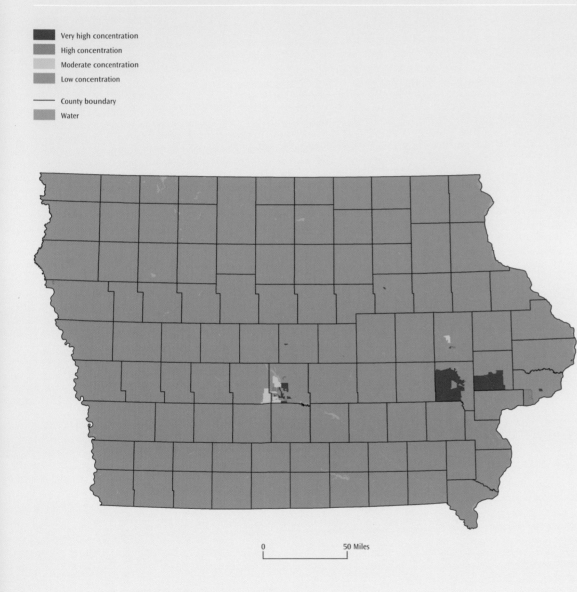

0   50 Miles

Concentration of Gay Male Couples (by county)

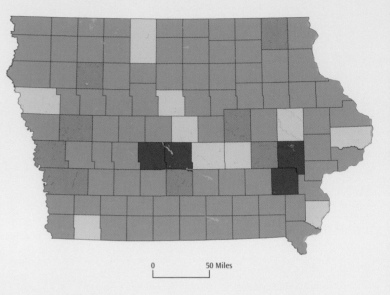

0   50 Miles

Concentration of Lesbian Couples (by county)

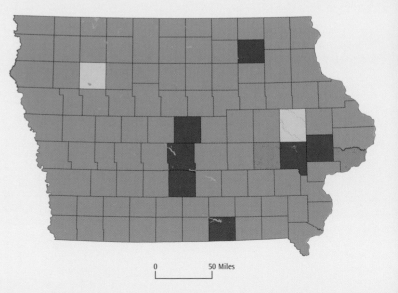

0   50 Miles

Indices

Gay/Lesbian Index	0.57
Gay Male Index	0.54
Lesbian Index	0.59

Comparative Statistics

	All	GL couples	GL rank
Presence of children, among households	45%	27%	31
Seniors (55+), among adults	32%	23%	16
Nonwhite, among adults	7%	8%	46
Females, among adults	52%	52%	25
Rural, among households	39%	32%	16

Top Iowa Metro Areas

(among 331 metro areas nationwide)

	GL rank	Gay male rank	Lesbian rank
Iowa City MSA	32	107	16
Des Moines MSA	162	118	204
Omaha MSA*	249	223	268
Davenport-Moline-Rock Island MSA*	297	271	308
Cedar Rapids MSA	303	295	304

Top Iowa Communities

(among 1,360 communities nationwide with 50 or more GL couples)

	GL rank	Gay male rank	Lesbian rank
Iowa City	210	706	85
Des Moines	540	399	713
Ames	1,122	1,265	877
West Des Moines	1,132	936	1,218
Davenport	1,214	1,160	1,180

Gay Male Index Rank: 47   Lesbian Index Rank: 48   Gay/Lesbian-Supportive Laws Rank: 20

Ages of Same-Sex Unmarried Partners

18–24	25–34	35–44	45–54	55+
10%	23%	26%	18%	23%

Race/Ethnicity of Householder in Same-Sex Unmarried Partner Households

White 92%
Black 2%
Hispanic 3%
Other 3%

Presence of Children under Age 18 in Same-Sex Unmarried Partner Households

No children 73%
Children 27%

* Metropolitan area spans more than one state.

KANSAS

Concentration of Gay/Lesbian Couples (by tract)

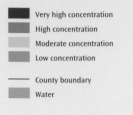

Very high concentration
High concentration
Moderate concentration
Low concentration

County boundary
Water

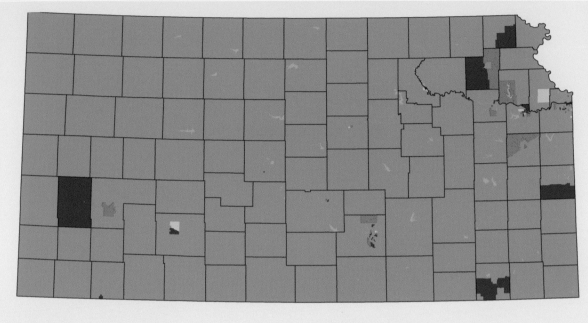

0   50 Miles

Concentration of Gay Male Couples (by county)

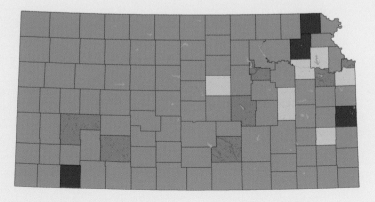

0   50 Miles

Concentration of Lesbian Couples (by county)

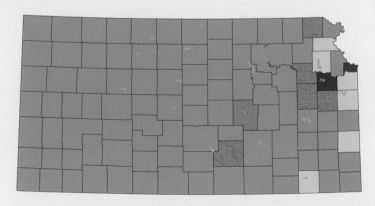

0   50 Miles

Indices

Gay/Lesbian Index	0.68
Gay Male Index	0.64
Lesbian Index	0.72

Comparative Statistics

	All	GL couples	GL rank
Presence of children, among households	48%	34%	8
Seniors (55+), among adults	29%	22%	19
Nonwhite, among adults	17%	18%	27
Females, among adults	51%	52%	20
Rural, among households	29%	24%	21

Top Kansas Metro Areas

(among 331 metro areas nationwide)

	GL rank	Gay male rank	Lesbian rank
Lawrence MSA	59	91	33
Kansas City MSA*	143	104	169
Wichita MSA	201	195	200
Topeka MSA	224	246	184

Top Kansas Communities

(among 1,360 communities nationwide with 50 or more GL couples)

	GL rank	Gay male rank	Lesbian rank
Lawrence	396	529	291
Kansas City	871	788	913
Wichita	892	845	892
Topeka	956	1,012	842
Shawnee	1,067	1,256	773

Gay Male Index Rank: 45   Lesbian Index Rank: 44   Gay/Lesbian-Supportive Laws Rank: 32

Ages of Same-Sex Unmarried Partners

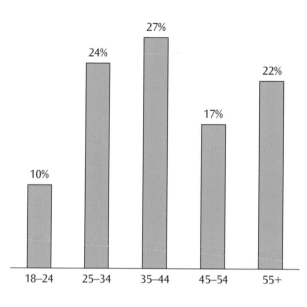

Race/Ethnicity of Householder in Same-Sex Unmarried Partner Households

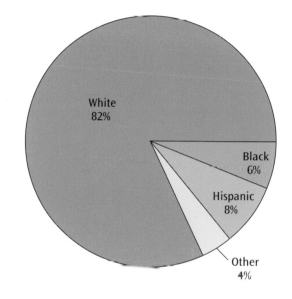

Presence of Children under Age 18 in Same-Sex Unmarried Partner Households

No children 66%   Children 34%

* Metropolitan area spans more than one state.

KENTUCKY

Concentration of Gay/Lesbian Couples (by tract)

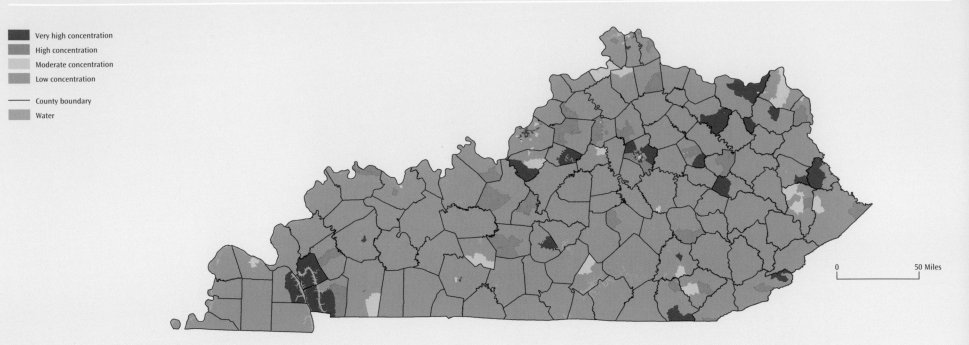

Very high concentration
High concentration
Moderate concentration
Low concentration
County boundary
Water

0   50 Miles

Concentration of Gay Male Couples (by county)

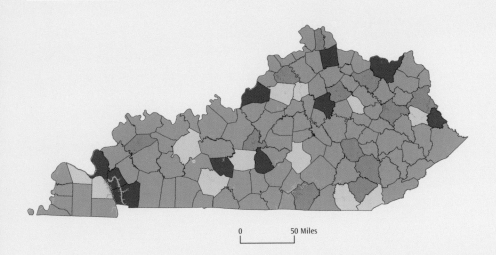

0   50 Miles

Concentration of Lesbian Couples (by county)

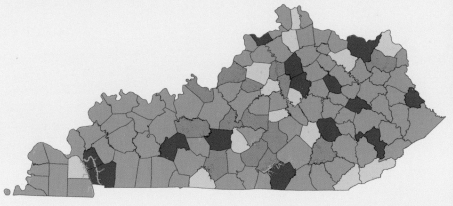

0   50 Miles

Indices

Gay/Lesbian Index	0.79
Gay Male Index	0.73
Lesbian Index	0.86

Comparative Statistics

	All	GL couples	GL rank
Presence of children, among households	46%	29%	25
Seniors (55+), among adults	29%	24%	12
Nonwhite, among adults	11%	11%	42
Females, among adults	52%	53%	11
Rural, among households	44%	39%	13

Top Kentucky Metro Areas
(among 331 metro areas nationwide)

	GL rank	Gay male rank	Lesbian rank
Lexington MSA	89	101	83
Louisville MSA*	139	110	147
Cincinnati PMSA*	195	170	217
Huntington-Ashland MSA*	219	215	213
Evansville-Henderson MSA*	250	237	256

Top Kentucky Communities
(among 1,360 communities nationwide with 50 or more GL couples)

	GL rank	Gay male rank	Lesbian rank
Covington	292	244	399
Louisville	320	272	422
Lexington-Fayette	338	351	332
Frankfort	672	647	632
Bowling Green	814	884	694

Gay Male Index Rank: 40   Lesbian Index Rank: 30   Gay/Lesbian-Supportive Laws Rank: 27

Ages of Same-Sex Unmarried Partners

Race/Ethnicity of Householder in Same-Sex Unmarried Partner Households

Presence of Children under Age 18 in Same-Sex Unmarried Partner Households

* Metropolitan area spans more than one state.

LOUISIANA

Concentration of Gay/Lesbian Couples (by tract)

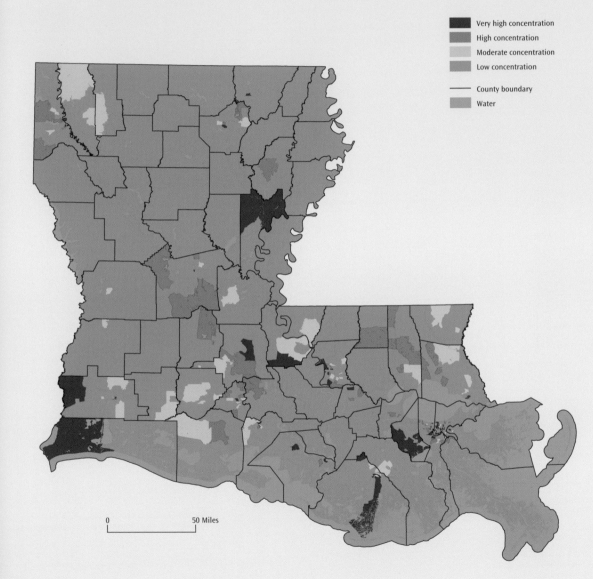

■ Very high concentration
■ High concentration
□ Moderate concentration
■ Low concentration
— County boundary
■ Water

0   50 Miles

Concentration of Gay Male Couples (by county)

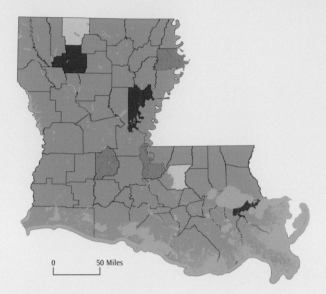

0   50 Miles

Concentration of Lesbian Couples (by county)

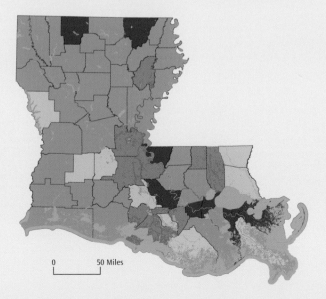

0   50 Miles

Indices

Gay/Lesbian Index	0.94
Gay Male Index	0.89
Lesbian Index	1.00

Comparative Statistics

	All	GL couples	GL rank
Presence of children, among households	50%	35%	5
Seniors (55+), among adults	28%	22%	18
Nonwhite, among adults	37%	34%	9
Females, among adults	53%	53%	19
Rural, among households	27%	23%	26

Top Louisiana Metro Areas

(among 331 metro areas nationwide)

	GL rank	Gay male rank	Lesbian rank
New Orleans MSA	38	28	44
Lafayette MSA	146	174	116
Baton Rouge MSA	148	130	160
Alexandria MSA	152	168	131
Houma MSA	153	183	123

Top Louisiana Communities

(among 1,360 communities nationwide with 50 or more GL couples)

	GL rank	Gay male rank	Lesbian rank
New Orleans	121	77	304
Marrero	392	664	215
Terrytown	401	535	294
Harvey	410	1,156	122
New Iberia	487	877	221

Gay Male Index Rank: 23   Lesbian Index Rank: 22   Gay/Lesbian-Supportive Laws Rank: 32

Ages of Same-Sex Unmarried Partners

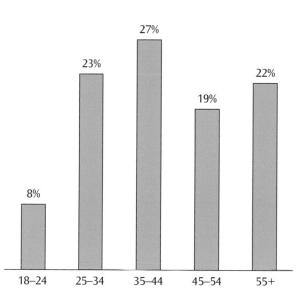

18–24	25–34	35–44	45–54	55+
8%	23%	27%	19%	22%

Race/Ethnicity of Householder in Same-Sex Unmarried Partner Households

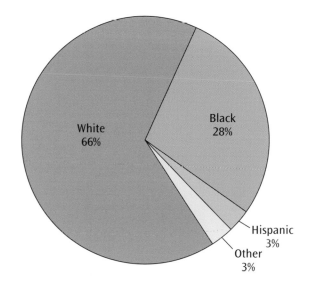

White 66%
Black 28%
Hispanic 3%
Other 3%

Presence of Children under Age 18 in Same-Sex Unmarried Partner Households

No children 65%   Children 35%

MAINE

Concentration of Gay/Lesbian Couples (by tract)

Very high concentration
High concentration
Moderate concentration
Low concentration
County boundary
Water

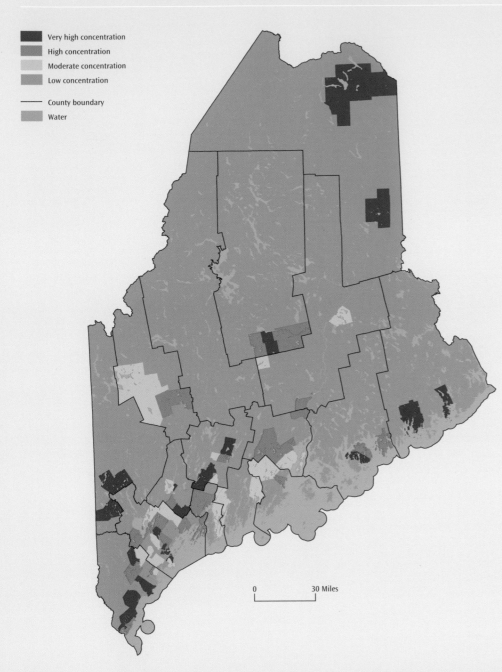

0   30 Miles

Concentration of Gay Male Couples (by county)

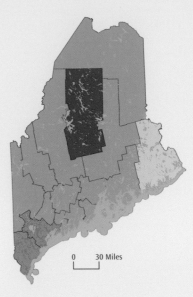

0   30 Miles

Concentration of Lesbian Couples (by county)

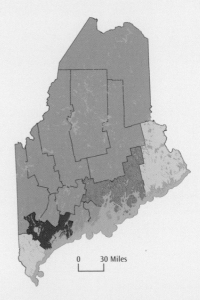

0   30 Miles

Indices

Gay/Lesbian Index	1.16
Gay Male Index	1.01
Lesbian Index	1.32

Comparative Statistics

	All	GL couples	GL rank
Presence of children, among households	43%	22%	47
Seniors (55+), among adults	31%	20%	28
Nonwhite, among adults	4%	3%	50
Females, among adults	52%	56%	6
Rural, among households	60%	56%	2

Top Maine Metro Areas

(among 331 metro areas nationwide)

	GL rank	Gay male rank	Lesbian rank
Portland MSA	8	18	7
Portsmouth-Rochester PMSA*	53	97	24
Bangor MSA	82	200	28
Lewiston-Auburn MSA	103	84	109

Top Maine Communities

(among 1,360 communities nationwide with 50 or more GL couples)

	GL rank	Gay male rank	Lesbian rank
Portland	55	64	47
South Portland	156	375	88
Auburn	346	273	473
Augusta	453	787	231
Biddeford	495	531	441

Ages of Same-Sex Unmarried Partners

Race/Ethnicity of Householder in Same-Sex Unmarried Partner Households

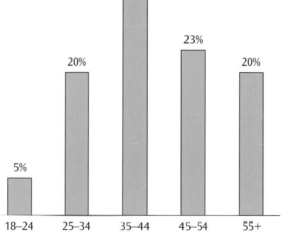

Presence of Children under Age 18 in Same-Sex Unmarried Partner Households

No children 78%   Children 22%

* Metropolitan area spans more than one state.

103

MARYLAND

Concentration of Gay/Lesbian Couples (by tract)

Very high concentration
High concentration
Moderate concentration
Low concentration
County boundary
Water

0   30 Miles

Concentration of Gay Male Couples (by county)

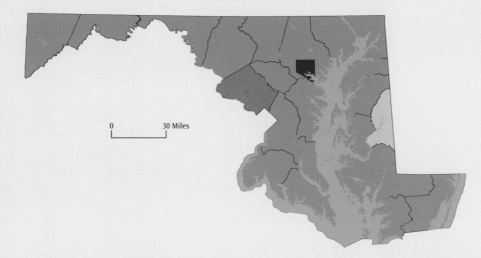

0   30 Miles

Concentration of Lesbian Couples (by county)

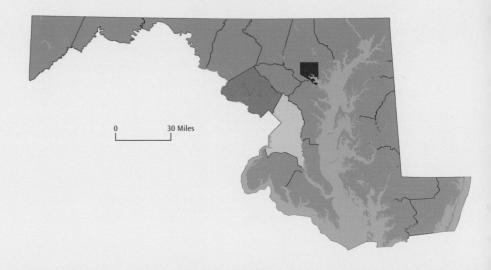

0   30 Miles

Gay Male Index Rank: 21   **Lesbian Index Rank: 14**   **Gay/Lesbian-Supportive Laws Rank: 15**

Indices

Gay/Lesbian Index	1.01
Gay Male Index	0.93
Lesbian Index	1.09

Comparative Statistics

	All	GL couples	GL rank
Presence of children, among households	49%	29%	24
Seniors (55+), among adults	27%	17%	42
Nonwhite, among adults	38%	33%	10
Females, among adults	53%	53%	10
Rural, among households	14%	10%	41

Top Maryland Metro Areas

(among 331 metro areas nationwide)

	GL rank	Gay male rank	Lesbian rank
Washington PMSA*	24	13	66
Baltimore PMSA	75	81	78
Wilmington-Newark PMSA*	84	65	104
Hagerstown PMSA	165	98	232
Cumberland MSA*	301	296	300

Top Maryland Communities

(among 1,360 communities nationwide with 50 or more GL couples)

	GL rank	Gay male rank	Lesbian rank
Takoma Park	16	25	7
Hyattsville	47	153	20
Silver Spring	89	111	81
Baltimore	187	198	202
Wheaton-Glenmont	217	279	182

Ages of Same-Sex Unmarried Partners

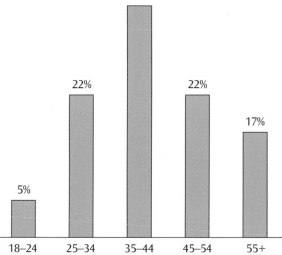

Race/Ethnicity of Householder in Same-Sex Unmarried Partner Households

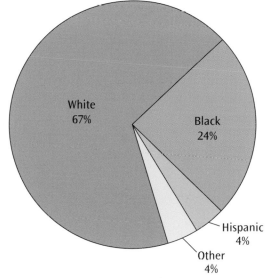

Presence of Children under Age 18 in Same-Sex Unmarried Partner Households

No children 71%   Children 29%

* Metropolitan area spans more than one state.

MASSACHUSETTS

Concentration of Gay/Lesbian Couples (by tract)

Very high concentration
High concentration
Moderate concentration
Low concentration
County boundary
Water

0   20 Miles

Concentration of Gay Male Couples (by county)

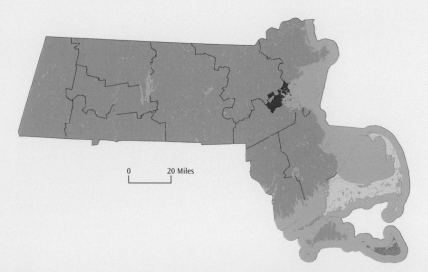

0   20 Miles

Concentration of Lesbian Couples (by county)

0   20 Miles

Indices

Gay/Lesbian Index	1.24
Gay Male Index	1.14
Lesbian Index	1.34

Comparative Statistics

	All	GL couples	GL rank
Presence of children, among households	48%	22%	46
Seniors (55+), among adults	29%	17%	43
Nonwhite, among adults	18%	15%	34
Females, among adults	53%	54%	9
Rural, among households	9%	8%	46

Top Massachusetts Metro Areas

(among 331 metro areas nationwide)

	GL rank	Gay male rank	Lesbian rank
Boston PMSA*	19	20	23
Springfield MSA	22	146	8
Barnstable-Yarmouth MSA	35	33	34
Providence-Fall River-Warwick MSA*	65	73	63
Lawrence PMSA*	88	136	50

Top Massachusetts Communities

(among 1,360 communities nationwide with 50 or more GL couples)

	GL rank	Gay male rank	Lesbian rank
Provincetown	1	1	1
Northampton	9	354	3
Easthampton	34	771	8
Cambridge	46	94	28
Boston	48	35	112

Gay Male Index Rank: 9   **Lesbian Index Rank: 4**   **Gay/Lesbian-Supportive Laws Rank: 6**

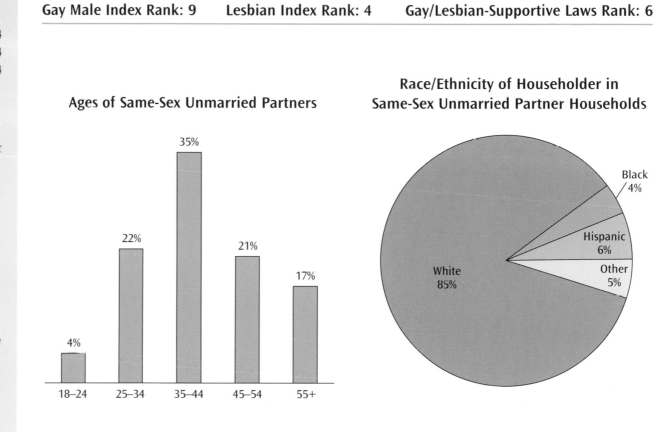

Ages of Same-Sex Unmarried Partners

- 18–24: 4%
- 25–34: 22%
- 35–44: 35%
- 45–54: 21%
- 55+: 17%

Race/Ethnicity of Householder in Same-Sex Unmarried Partner Households

- White 85%
- Black 4%
- Hispanic 6%
- Other 5%

Presence of Children under Age 18 in Same-Sex Unmarried Partner Households

- No children 78%
- Children 22%

* Metropolitan area spans more than one state.

MICHIGAN

Concentration of Gay/Lesbian Couples (by tract)

Concentration of Gay Male Couples (by county)

Concentration of Lesbian Couples (by county)

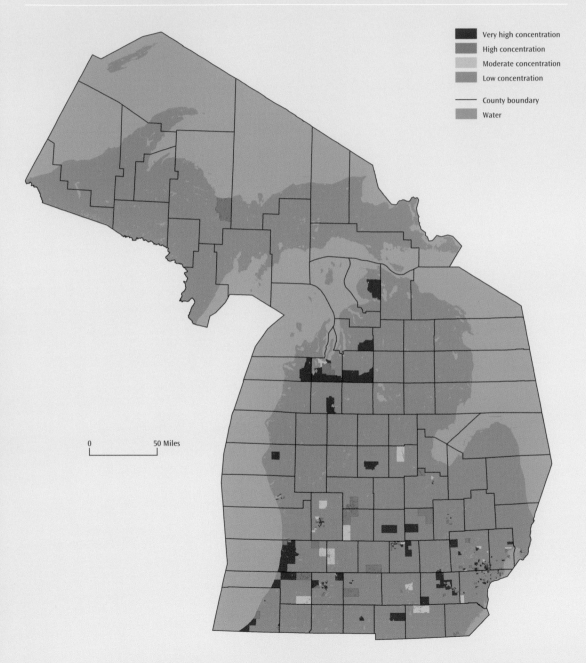

Very high concentration
High concentration
Moderate concentration
Low concentration
County boundary
Water

0   50 Miles

Indices

Gay/Lesbian Index	0.72
Gay Male Index	0.67
Lesbian Index	0.76

Comparative Statistics

	All	GL couples	GL rank
Presence of children, among households	47%	28%	29
Seniors (55+), among adults	28%	21%	20
Nonwhite, among adults	21%	22%	23
Females, among adults	52%	53%	18
Rural, among households	25%	22%	28

Top Michigan Metro Areas

(among 331 metro areas nationwide)

	GL rank	Gay male rank	Lesbian rank
Ann Arbor PMSA	91	143	53
Lansing-East Lansing MSA	111	144	82
Benton Harbor MSA	182	155	210
Kalamazoo-Battle Creek MSA	199	216	171
Grand Rapids-Muskegon-Holland MSA	211	169	246

Top Michigan Communities

(among 1,360 communities nationwide with 50 or more GL couples)

	GL rank	Gay male rank	Lesbian rank
Ferndale	45	36	93
Ypsilanti	116	162	104
Ann Arbor	151	405	74
Lansing	196	278	164
Royal Oak	262	171	524

Gay Male Index Rank: 42   Lesbian Index Rank: 40   Gay/Lesbian-Supportive Laws Rank: 32

Ages of Same-Sex Unmarried Partners

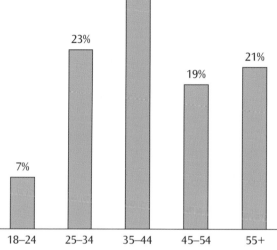

18–24: 7%
25–34: 23%
35–44: 29%
45–54: 19%
55+: 21%

Race/Ethnicity of Householder in Same-Sex Unmarried Partner Households

White 78%
Black 14%
Hispanic 4%
Other 4%

Presence of Children under Age 18 in Same-Sex Unmarried Partner Households

No children 72%

Children 28%

MINNESOTA

Concentration of Gay/Lesbian Couples (by tract)

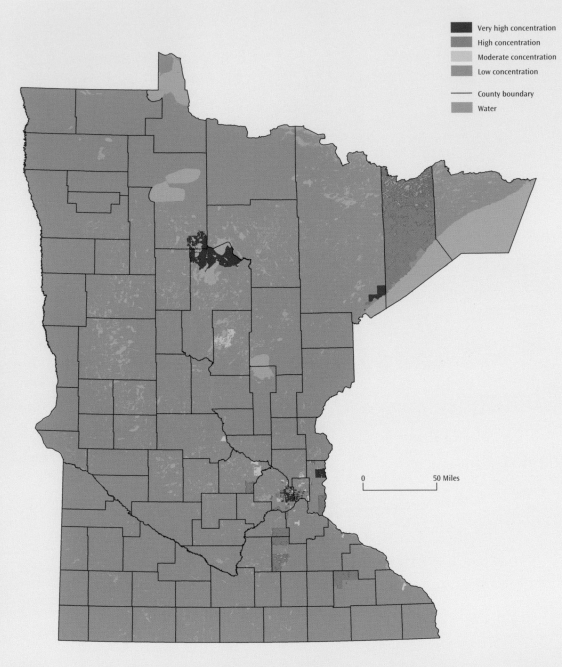

Very high concentration
High concentration
Moderate concentration
Low concentration

County boundary
Water

0   50 Miles

Concentration of Gay Male Couples (by county)

0   50 Miles

Concentration of Lesbian Couples (by county)

0   50 Miles

Indices

Gay/Lesbian Index	0.85
Gay Male Index	0.79
Lesbian Index	0.92

Comparative Statistics

	All	GL couples	GL rank
Presence of children, among households	48%	19%	50
Seniors (55+), among adults	28%	16%	45
Nonwhite, among adults	12%	11%	44
Females, among adults	51%	53%	13
Rural, among households	29%	18%	32

Top Minnesota Metro Areas

(among 331 metro areas nationwide)

	GL rank	Gay male rank	Lesbian rank
Minneapolis- St. Paul MSA*	63	69	58
La Crosse MSA*	289	328	202
Rochester MSA	294	304	283
Duluth-Superior MSA*	296	318	269
St. Cloud MSA	316	320	299

Top Minnesota Communities

(among 1,360 communities nationwide with 50 or more GL couples)

	GL rank	Gay male rank	Lesbian rank
Minneapolis	33	32	37
Golden Valley	63	37	245
St. Paul	192	423	107
St. Louis Park	209	189	275
Richfield	472	518	401

Gay Male Index Rank: 30   Lesbian Index Rank: 26   Gay/Lesbian-Supportive Laws Rank: 9

Ages of Same-Sex Unmarried Partners

18–24	25–34	35–44	45–54	55+
7%	24%	33%	20%	16%

Race/Ethnicity of Householder in Same-Sex Unmarried Partner Households

White 89%
Black 3%
Hispanic 3%
Other 4%

Presence of Children under Age 18 in Same-Sex Unmarried Partner Households

No children 81%

Children 19%

* Metropolitan area spans more than one state.

MISSISSIPPI

Concentration of Gay/Lesbian Couples (by tract)

Very high concentration
High concentration
Moderate concentration
Low concentration
County boundary
Water

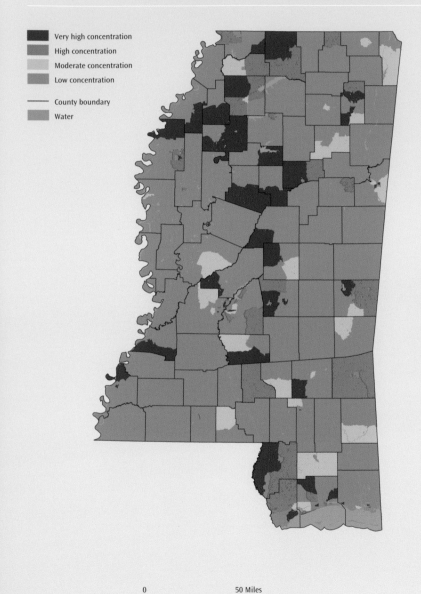

0   50 Miles

Concentration of Gay Male Couples (by county)

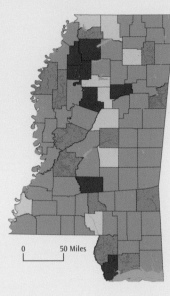

0   50 Miles

Concentration of Lesbian Couples (by county)

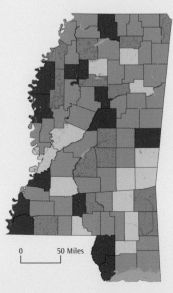

0   50 Miles

Indices

Gay/Lesbian Index	0.81
Gay Male Index	0.75
Lesbian Index	0.86

Comparative Statistics

	All	GL couples	GL rank
Presence of children, among households	49%	41%	1
Seniors (55+), among adults	28%	26%	5
Nonwhite, among adults	39%	41%	4
Females, among adults	53%	53%	16
Rural, among households	51%	52%	4

Top Mississippi Metro Areas

(among 331 metro areas nationwide)

	GL rank	Gay male rank	Lesbian rank
Memphis MSA*	125	90	144
Biloxi-Gulfport-Pascagoula MSA	157	116	198
Jackson MSA	172	152	187
Hattiesburg MSA	299	272	309

Top Mississippi Communities

(among 1,360 communities nationwide with 50 or more GL couples)

	GL rank	Gay male rank	Lesbian rank
Natchez	414	476	357
Pearl	463	863	210
Greenville	732	975	425
Jackson	838	583	1,048
Gulfport	858	640	1,022

Gay Male Index Rank: 34   Lesbian Index Rank: 29   Gay/Lesbian-Supportive Laws Rank: 47

Ages of Same-Sex Unmarried Partners

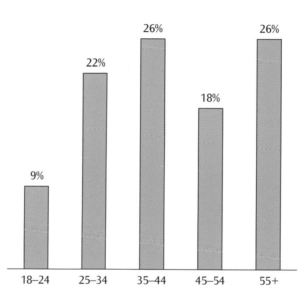

9%	22%	26%	18%	26%
18–24	25–34	35–44	45–54	55+

Race/Ethnicity of Householder in Same-Sex Unmarried Partner Households

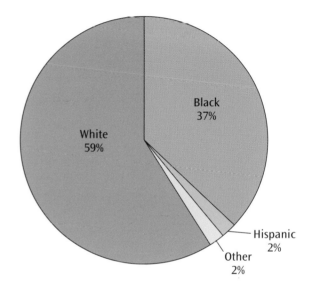

White 59%
Black 37%
Hispanic 2%
Other 2%

Presence of Children under Age 18 in Same-Sex Unmarried Partner Households

No children 59%	Children 41%

* Metropolitan area spans more than one state.

MISSOURI

Concentration of Gay/Lesbian Couples (by tract)

Very high concentration
High concentration
Moderate concentration
Low concentration
County boundary
Water

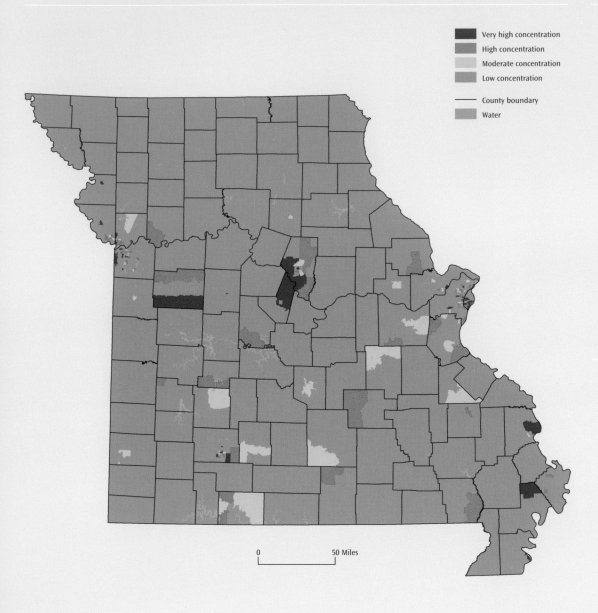

0   50 Miles

Concentration of Gay Male Couples (by county)

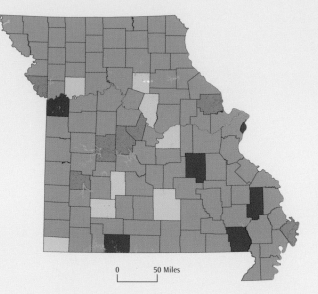

0   50 Miles

Concentration of Lesbian Couples (by county)

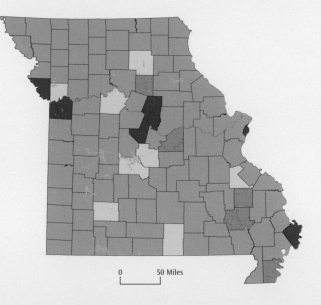

0   50 Miles

Indices

Gay/Lesbian Index	0.76
Gay Male Index	0.75
Lesbian Index	0.77

Comparative Statistics

	All	GL couples	GL rank
Presence of children, among households	46%	26%	35
Seniors (55+), among adults	30%	21%	22
Nonwhite, among adults	16%	16%	29
Females, among adults	52%	50%	34
Rural, among households	31%	24%	23

Top Missouri Metro Areas

(among 331 metro areas nationwide)

	GL rank	Gay male rank	Lesbian rank
Columbia MSA	98	161	48
Kansas City MSA*	143	104	169
St. Louis MSA*	213	190	230
Springfield MSA	226	193	248
St. Joseph MSA	262	228	279

Top Missouri Communities

(among 1,360 communities nationwide with 50 or more GL couples)

	GL rank	Gay male rank	Lesbian rank
St. Louis	149	108	300
Kansas City	193	139	360
University City	404	267	684
Columbia	717	912	463
Springfield	926	761	1,017

Gay Male Index Rank: 35   Lesbian Index Rank: 38   Gay/Lesbian-Supportive Laws Rank: 32

Ages of Same-Sex Unmarried Partners

- 18–24: 9%
- 25–34: 24%
- 35–44: 29%
- 45–54: 17%
- 55+: 21%

Race/Ethnicity of Householder in Same-Sex Unmarried Partner Households

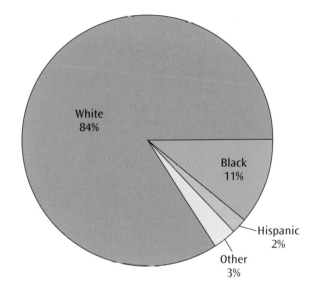

- White 84%
- Black 11%
- Hispanic 2%
- Other 3%

Presence of Children under Age 18 in Same-Sex Unmarried Partner Households

- No children 74%
- Children 26%

* Metropolitan area spans more than one state.

MONTANA

Concentration of Gay/Lesbian Couples (by tract)

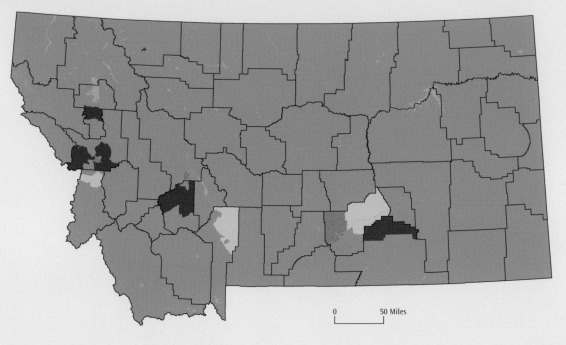

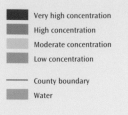

- Very high concentration
- High concentration
- Moderate concentration
- Low concentration
- County boundary
- Water

0   50 Miles

Concentration of Gay Male Couples (by county)

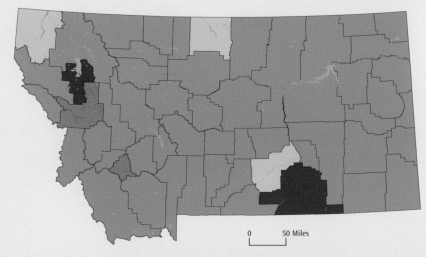

0   50 Miles

Concentration of Lesbian Couples (by county)

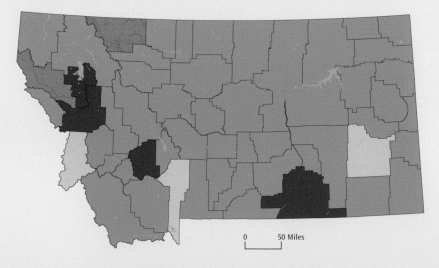

0   50 Miles

Indices

Gay/Lesbian Index	0.60
Gay Male Index	0.54
Lesbian Index	0.66

Comparative Statistics

	All	GL couples	GL rank
Presence of children, among households	45%	32%	13
Seniors (55+), among adults	31%	25%	8
Nonwhite, among adults	10%	13%	39
Females, among adults	51%	55%	7
Rural, among households	46%	49%	5

Top Montana Metro Areas

(among 331 metro areas nationwide)

	GL rank	Gay male rank	Lesbian rank
Missoula MSA	123	230	52
Billings MSA	309	290	321
Great Falls MSA	323	315	322

Top Montana Communities

(among 1,360 communities nationwide with 50 or more GL couples)

	GL rank	Gay male rank	Lesbian rank
Missoula	904	923	812
Billings	1,328	1,237	1,335
Great Falls	1,348	1,320	1,346

Gay Male Index Rank: 48 **Lesbian Index Rank: 46** **Gay/Lesbian-Supportive Laws Rank: 32**

Ages of Same-Sex Unmarried Partners

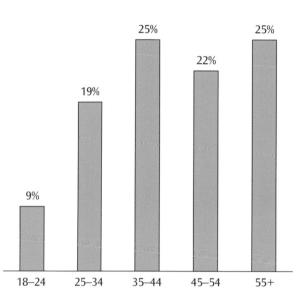

Race/Ethnicity of Householder in Same-Sex Unmarried Partner Households

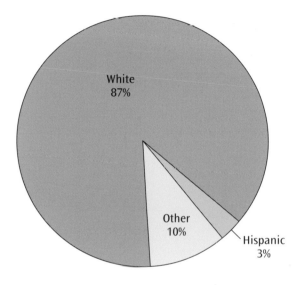

Presence of Children under Age 18 in Same-Sex Unmarried Partner Households

No children 68% | Children 32%

NEBRASKA

Concentration of Gay/Lesbian Couples (by tract)

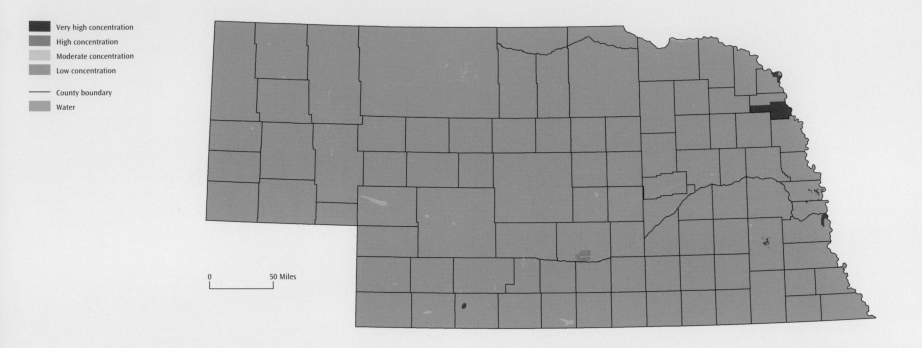

Very high concentration
High concentration
Moderate concentration
Low concentration
County boundary
Water

0   50 Miles

Concentration of Gay Male Couples (by county)

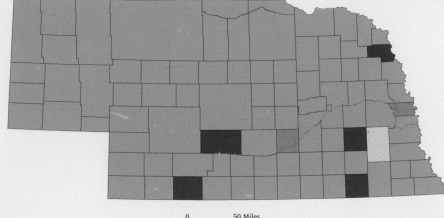

0   50 Miles

Concentration of Lesbian Couples (by county)

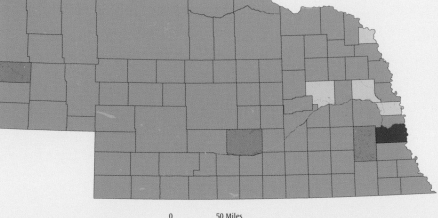

0   50 Miles

Indices

Gay/Lesbian Index	0.62
Gay Male Index	0.58
Lesbian Index	0.65

Comparative Statistics

	All	GL couples	GL rank
Presence of children, among households	47%	29%	26
Seniors (55+), among adults	30%	24%	10
Nonwhite, among adults	13%	13%	38
Females, among adults	51%	52%	21
Rural, among households	30%	23%	24

Top Nebraska Metro Areas

(among 331 metro areas nationwide)

	GL rank	Gay male rank	Lesbian rank
Lincoln MSA	220	270	148
Omaha MSA*	249	223	268
Sioux City MSA*	310	294	316

Top Nebraska Communities

(among 1,360 communities nationwide with 50 or more GL couples)

	GL rank	Gay male rank	Lesbian rank
Omaha	1,016	886	1,069
Lincoln	1,076	1,170	899
Grand Island	1,255	993	1,323

Gay Male Index Rank: 46   Lesbian Index Rank: 47   Gay/Lesbian-Supportive Laws Rank: 27

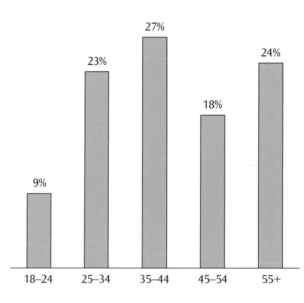

Ages of Same-Sex Unmarried Partners

18–24: 9%
25–34: 23%
35–44: 27%
45–54: 18%
55+: 24%

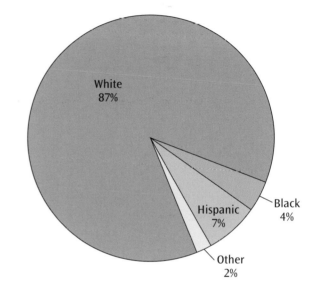

Race/Ethnicity of Householder in Same-Sex Unmarried Partner Households

White 87%
Hispanic 7%
Black 4%
Other 2%

Presence of Children under Age 18 in Same-Sex Unmarried Partner Households

No children 71%
Children 29%

* Metropolitan area spans more than one state.

NEVADA

Concentration of Gay/Lesbian Couples (by tract)

Very high concentration
High concentration
Moderate concentration
Low concentration

— County boundary
Water

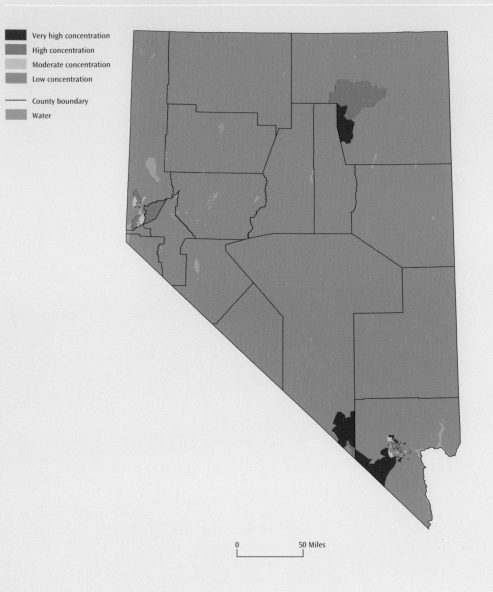

0   50 Miles

Concentration of Gay Male Couples (by county)

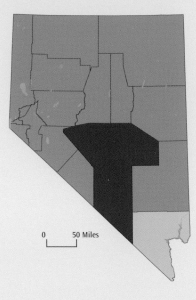

0   50 Miles

Concentration of Lesbian Couples (by county)

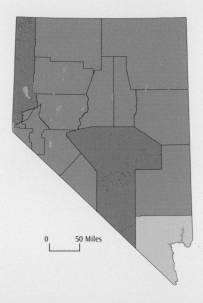

0   50 Miles

Indices

Gay/Lesbian Index	1.17
Gay Male Index	1.28
Lesbian Index	1.07

Comparative Statistics

	All	GL couples	GL rank
Presence of children, among households	47%	31%	17
Seniors (55+), among adults	28%	18%	39
Nonwhite, among adults	35%	30%	15
Females, among adults	49%	45%	49
Rural, among households	8%	7%	48

Top Nevada Metro Areas

(among 331 metro areas nationwide)

	GL rank	Gay male rank	Lesbian rank
Reno MSA	37	29	41
Las Vegas MSA*	40	19	91

Top Nevada Communities

(among 1,360 communities nationwide with 50 or more GL couples)

	GL rank	Gay male rank	Lesbian rank
North Las Vegas	144	158	166
Sun Valley	150	291	96
Pahrump	175	114	443
Winchester	265	92	1,104
Spring Valley	272	136	760

Gay Male Index Rank: 2   Lesbian Index Rank: 17   Gay/Lesbian-Supportive Laws Rank: 12

Ages of Same-Sex Unmarried Partners

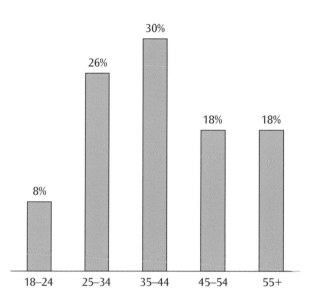

- 18–24: 8%
- 25–34: 26%
- 35–44: 30%
- 45–54: 18%
- 55+: 18%

Race/Ethnicity of Householder in Same-Sex Unmarried Partner Households

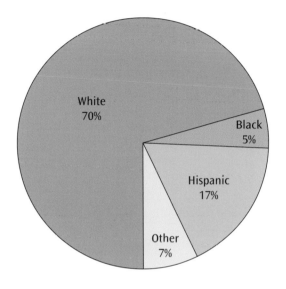

- White 70%
- Black 5%
- Hispanic 17%
- Other 7%

Presence of Children under Age 18 in Same-Sex Unmarried Partner Households

No children 69%	Children 31%

* Metropolitan area spans more than one state.

NEW HAMPSHIRE

Concentration of Gay/Lesbian Couples (by tract)

Very high concentration
High concentration
Moderate concentration
Low concentration

County boundary
Water

0   20 Miles

Concentration of Gay Male Couples (by county)

0   20 Miles

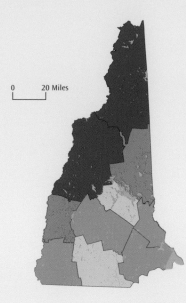

Concentration of Lesbian Couples (by county)

0   20 Miles

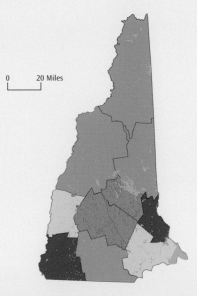

Indices

Gay/Lesbian Index	1.01
Gay Male Index	0.85
Lesbian Index	1.17

Comparative Statistics

	All	GL couples	GL rank
Presence of children, among households	47%	24%	42
Seniors (55+), among adults	28%	18%	37
Nonwhite, among adults	5%	4%	48
Females, among adults	52%	57%	4
Rural, among households	41%	44%	9

Top New Hampshire Metro Areas

(among 331 metro areas nationwide)

	GL rank	Gay male rank	Lesbian rank
Boston PMSA*	19	20	23
Portsmouth-Rochester PMSA*	53	97	24
Lawrence PMSA*	88	136	50
Nashua PMSA	94	120	69
Manchester PMSA	101	89	102

Top New Hampshire Communities

(among 1,360 communities nationwide with 50 or more GL couples)

	GL rank	Gay male rank	Lesbian rank
Portsmouth	189	207	196
Dover	354	411	302
Manchester	642	533	685
Concord	646	980	309
Nashua	741	691	709

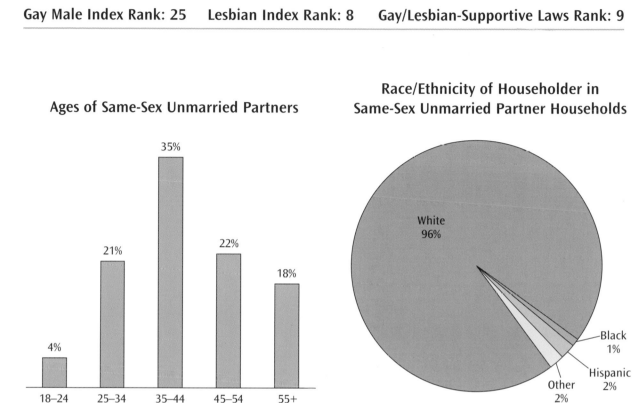

Ages of Same-Sex Unmarried Partners

- 18–24: 4%
- 25–34: 21%
- 35–44: 35%
- 45–54: 22%
- 55+: 18%

Race/Ethnicity of Householder in Same-Sex Unmarried Partner Households

- White 96%
- Black 1%
- Hispanic 2%
- Other 2%

Presence of Children under Age 18 in Same-Sex Unmarried Partner Households

- No children 76%
- Children 24%

* Metropolitan area spans more than one state.

NEW JERSEY

Concentration of Gay/Lesbian Couples (by tract)

Very high concentration
High concentration
Moderate concentration
Low concentration
County boundary
Water

0   20 Miles

Concentration of Gay Male Couples (by county)

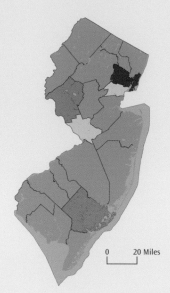

0   20 Miles

Concentration of Lesbian Couples (by county)

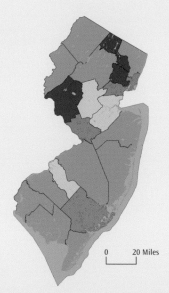

0   20 Miles

Indices

Gay/Lesbian Index	0.96
Gay Male Index	0.95
Lesbian Index	0.98

Comparative Statistics

	All	GL couples	GL rank
Presence of children, among households	50%	30%	21
Seniors (55+), among adults	30%	20%	26
Nonwhite, among adults	34%	34%	7
Females, among adults	52%	50%	35
Rural, among households	6%	5%	49

Top New Jersey Metro Areas

(among 331 metro areas nationwide)

	GL rank	Gay male rank	Lesbian rank
Jersey City PMSA	16	6	70
Newark PMSA	72	60	94
Trenton PMSA	78	71	93
Philadelphia PMSA*	96	72	119
Atlantic-Cape May PMSA	107	76	128

Top New Jersey Communities

(among 1,360 communities nationwide with 50 or more GL couples)

	GL rank	Gay male rank	Lesbian rank
Maplewood	44	44	58
Plainfield	51	49	61
Highland Park	80	541	24
Montclair	93	117	86
Jersey City	111	72	301

Gay Male Index Rank: 19   Lesbian Index Rank: 23   Gay/Lesbian-Supportive Laws Rank: 2

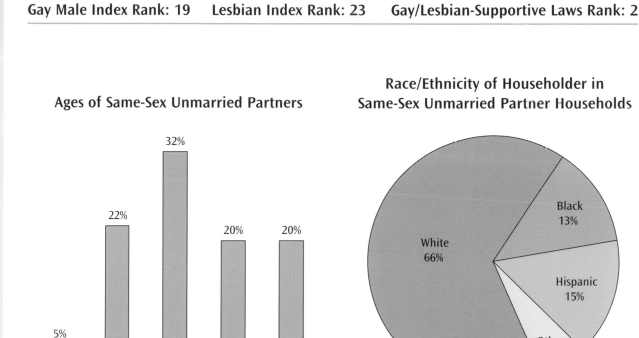

Ages of Same-Sex Unmarried Partners

- 18–24: 5%
- 25–34: 22%
- 35–44: 32%
- 45–54: 20%
- 55+: 20%

Race/Ethnicity of Householder in Same-Sex Unmarried Partner Households

- White 66%
- Black 13%
- Hispanic 15%
- Other 6%

Presence of Children under Age 18 in Same-Sex Unmarried Partner Households

- No children 70%
- Children 30%

* Metropolitan area spans more than one state.

NEW MEXICO

Concentration of Gay/Lesbian Couples (by tract)

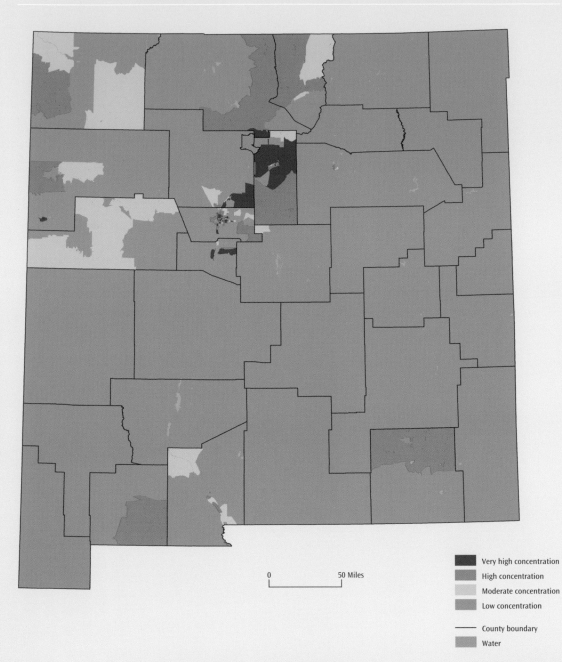

Concentration of Gay Male Couples (by county)

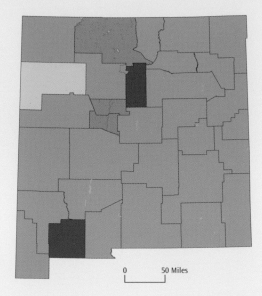

Concentration of Lesbian Couples (by county)

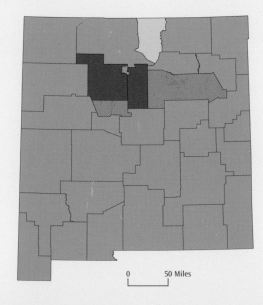

Very high concentration
High concentration
Moderate concentration
Low concentration

County boundary
Water

0   50 Miles

Indices

Gay/Lesbian Index	1.18
Gay Male Index	0.98
Lesbian Index	1.37

Comparative Statistics

	All	GL couples	GL rank
Presence of children, among households	50%	31%	15
Seniors (55+), among adults	28%	20%	25
Nonwhite, among adults	55%	46%	2
Females, among adults	52%	58%	3
Rural, among households	25%	23%	25

Top New Mexico Metro Areas

(among 331 metro areas nationwide)

	GL rank	Gay male rank	Lesbian rank
Santa Fe MSA	4	8	3
Albuquerque MSA	14	47	12
Las Cruces MSA	79	142	39

Top New Mexico Communities

(among 1,360 communities nationwide with 50 or more GL couples)

	GL rank	Gay male rank	Lesbian rank
Eldorado at Santa Fe	14	26	6
Santa Fe	71	110	52
South Valley	94	192	51
Albuquerque	220	391	136
Rio Rancho	471	1,006	174

Gay Male Index Rank: 16   **Lesbian Index Rank: 2**   **Gay/Lesbian-Supportive Laws Rank: 17**

Ages of Same-Sex Unmarried Partners

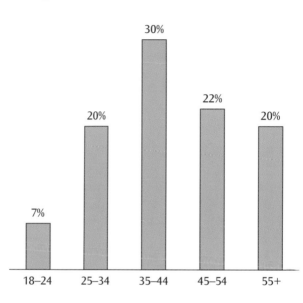

Race/Ethnicity of Householder in Same-Sex Unmarried Partner Households

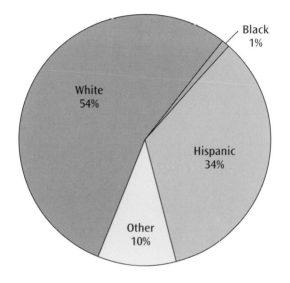

Presence of Children under Age 18 in Same-Sex Unmarried Partner Households

No children 69%   Children 31%

NEW YORK

Concentration of Gay/Lesbian Couples (by tract)

Very high concentration
High concentration
Moderate concentration
Low concentration

—— County boundary
Water

0   50 Miles

Concentration of Gay Male Couples (by county)

0   50 Miles

Concentration of Lesbian Couples (by county)

0   50 Miles

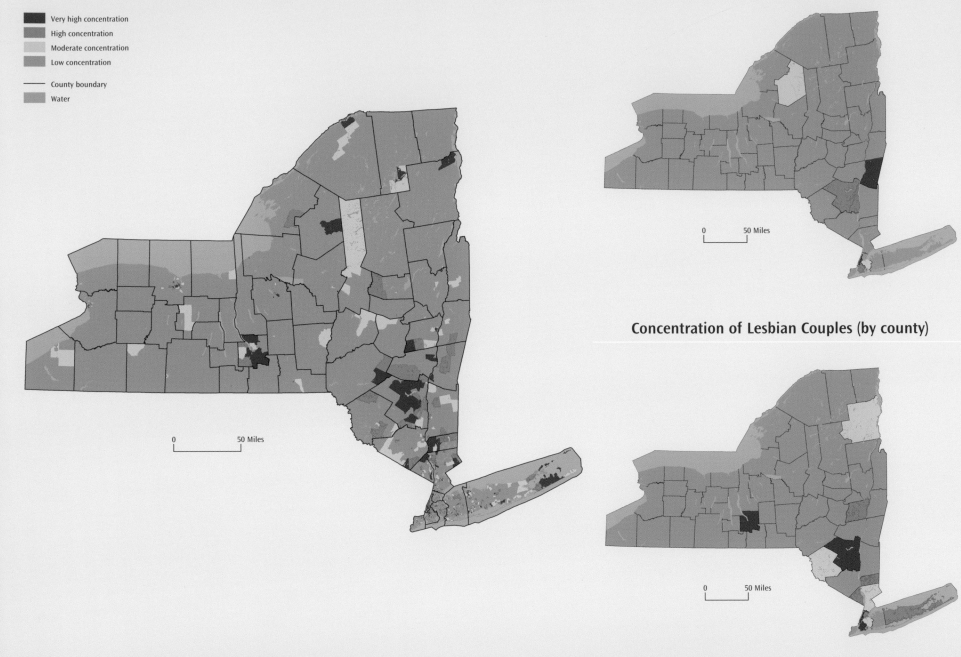

Indices

Gay/Lesbian Index	1.17
Gay Male Index	1.22
Lesbian Index	1.12

Comparative Statistics

	All	GL couples	GL rank
Presence of children, among households	49%	27%	30
Seniors (55+), among adults	29%	20%	32
Nonwhite, among adults	38%	34%	8
Females, among adults	53%	47%	45
Rural, among households	13%	9%	43

Top New York Metro Areas

(among 331 metro areas nationwide)

	GL rank	Gay male rank	Lesbian rank
New York PMSA	11	5	35
Newburgh PMSA*	60	58	60
Nassau-Suffolk PMSA	81	87	87
Dutchess County PMSA	105	103	95
Albany-Schenectady-Troy MSA	128	163	98

Top New York Communities

(among 1,360 communities nationwide with 50 or more GL couples)

	GL rank	Gay male rank	Lesbian rank
Ithaca	50	202	19
Ossining	96	85	120
Albany	123	174	101
Freeport	130	164	126
Rochester	136	129	177

Gay Male Index Rank: 4   **Lesbian Index Rank: 13**   **Gay/Lesbian-Supportive Laws Rank: 6**

Ages of Same-Sex Unmarried Partners

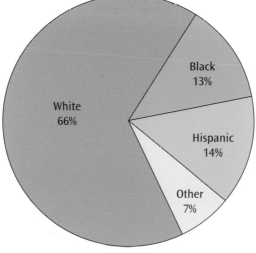

- 18–24: 5%
- 25–34: 23%
- 35–44: 32%
- 45–54: 21%
- 55+: 20%

Race/Ethnicity of Householder in Same-Sex Unmarried Partner Households

- White 66%
- Black 13%
- Hispanic 14%
- Other 7%

Presence of Children under Age 18 in Same-Sex Unmarried Partner Households

- No children 73%
- Children 27%

* Metropolitan area spans more than one state.

NORTH CAROLINA

Concentration of Gay/Lesbian Couples (by tract)

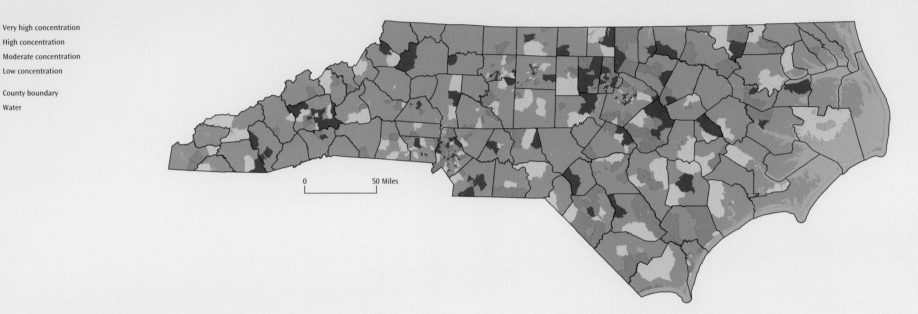

Very high concentration
High concentration
Moderate concentration
Low concentration
County boundary
Water

0 ___ 50 Miles

Concentration of Gay Male Couples (by county)

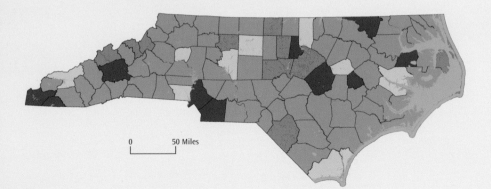

0 ___ 50 Miles

Concentration of Lesbian Couples (by county)

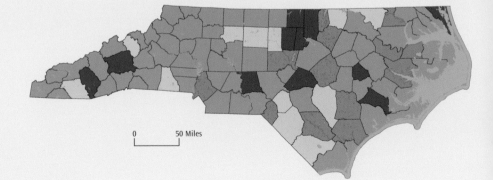

0 ___ 50 Miles

Indices

Gay/Lesbian Index	0.92
Gay Male Index	0.88
Lesbian Index	0.95

Gay Male Index Rank: 24   Lesbian Index Rank: 24   Gay/Lesbian-Supportive Laws Rank: 47

Comparative Statistics

	All	GL couples	GL rank
Presence of children, among households	46%	31%	18
Seniors (55+), among adults	28%	20%	27
Nonwhite, among adults	30%	29%	16
Females, among adults	52%	52%	26
Rural, among households	40%	38%	14

Top North Carolina Metro Areas

(among 331 metro areas nationwide)

	GL rank	Gay male rank	Lesbian rank
Asheville MSA	20	44	17
Raleigh-Durham-Chapel Hill MSA	56	55	54
Charlotte-Gastonia-Rock Hill MSA*	92	56	134
Greensboro-Winston Salem-High Point MSA	131	114	137
Wilmington MSA	166	102	228

Top North Carolina Communities

(among 1,360 communities nationwide with 50 or more GL couples)

	GL rank	Gay male rank	Lesbian rank
Asheville	97	133	70
Monroe	126	88	253
Durham	163	275	116
Charlotte	388	258	675
Carrboro	408	606	262

Ages of Same-Sex Unmarried Partners

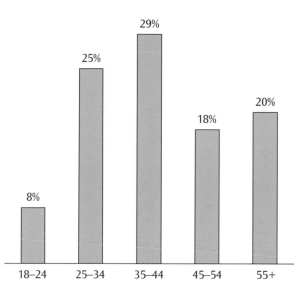

Race/Ethnicity of Householder in Same-Sex Unmarried Partner Households

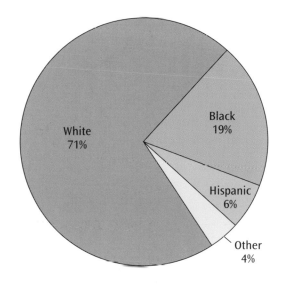

Presence of Children under Age 18 in Same-Sex Unmarried Partner Households

No children 69%   Children 31%

* Metropolitan area spans more than one state.

NORTH DAKOTA

Concentration of Gay/Lesbian Couples (by tract)

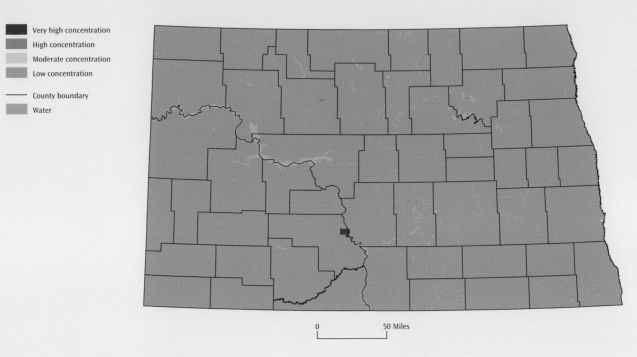

Very high concentration
High concentration
Moderate concentration
Low concentration

— County boundary
Water

0   50 Miles

Concentration of Gay Male Couples (by county)

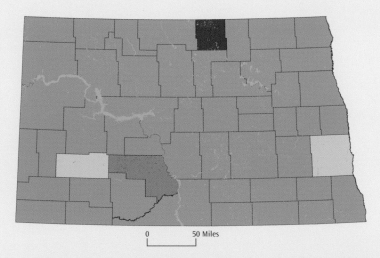

0   50 Miles

Concentration of Lesbian Couples (by county)

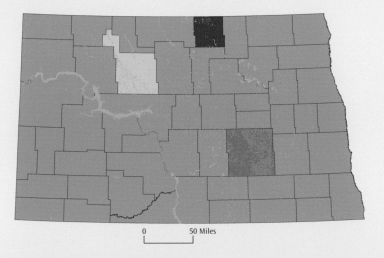

0   50 Miles

Indices

Gay/Lesbian Index	0.48
Gay Male Index	0.49
Lesbian Index	0.48

Comparative Statistics

	All	GL couples	GL rank
Presence of children, among households	46%	23%	43
Seniors (55+), among adults	31%	35%	1
Nonwhite, among adults	8%	10%	45
Females, among adults	51%	49%	41
Rural, among households	44%	45%	8

Top North Dakota Metro Areas

(among 331 metro areas nationwide)

	GL rank	Gay male rank	Lesbian rank
Fargo-Moorhead MSA*	318	273	327
Bismarck MSA	328	312	329
Grand Forks MSA*	329	330	325

Top North Dakota Communities

(among 1,360 communities nationwide with 50 or more GL couples)

	GL rank	Gay male rank	Lesbian rank
Fargo	1,337	1,224	1,351
Bismarck	1,357	1,331	1,355

Gay Male Index Rank: 49   **Lesbian Index Rank: 50**   **Gay/Lesbian-Supportive Laws Rank: 40**

Ages of Same-Sex Unmarried Partners

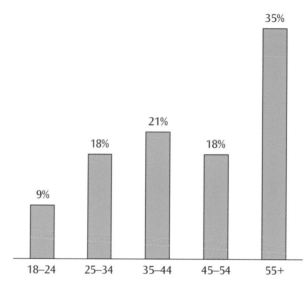

Race/Ethnicity of Householder in Same-Sex Unmarried Partner Households

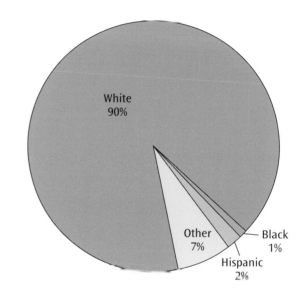

Presence of Children under Age 18 in Same-Sex Unmarried Partner Households

No children 77%   Children 23%

* Metropolitan area spans more than one state.

133

OHIO

Concentration of Gay/Lesbian Couples (by tract)

Very high concentration
High concentration
Moderate concentration
Low concentration
County boundary
Water

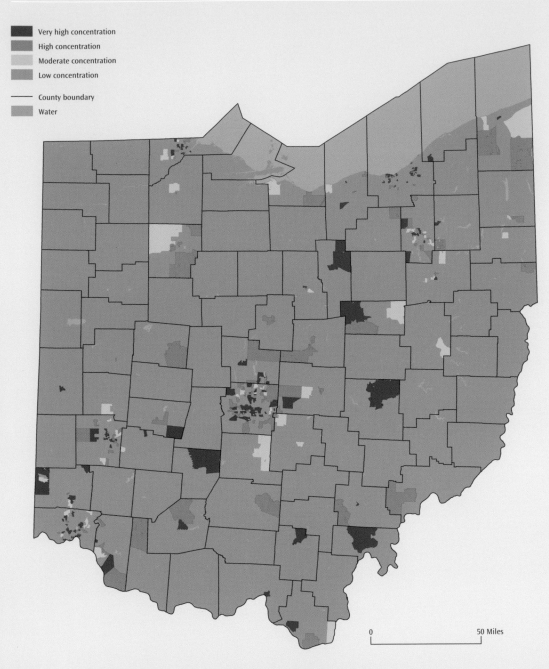

Concentration of Gay Male Couples (by county)

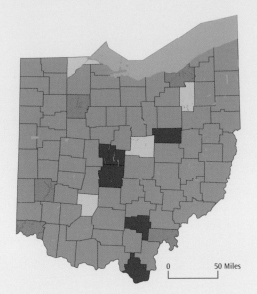

Concentration of Lesbian Couples (by county)

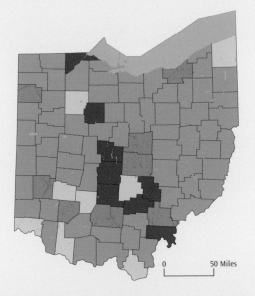

Indices

Indices	
Gay/Lesbian Index	0.75
Gay Male Index	0.73
Lesbian Index	0.78

Comparative Statistics

	All	GL couples	GL rank
Presence of children, among households	46%	26%	33
Seniors (55+), among adults	30%	21%	23
Nonwhite, among adults	16%	16%	31
Females, among adults	52%	51%	28
Rural, among households	23%	17%	33

Top Ohio Metro Areas

(among 331 metro areas nationwide)

	GL rank	Gay male rank	Lesbian rank
Columbus MSA	48	34	62
Toledo MSA	188	203	163
Cincinnati PMSA*	195	170	217
Dayton-Springfield MSA	216	198	221
Huntington-Ashland MSA*	219	215	213

Top Ohio Communities

(among 1,360 communities nationwide with 50 or more GL couples)

	GL rank	Gay male rank	Lesbian rank
Cleveland Heights	118	130	137
Lakewood	129	80	339
Columbus	159	137	242
Dayton	451	332	646
East Cleveland	479	756	260

Ages of Same-Sex Unmarried Partners

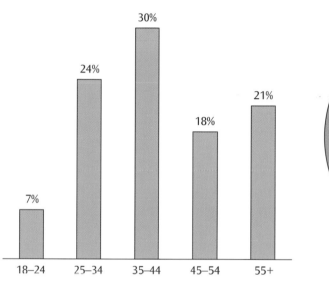

Race/Ethnicity of Householder in Same-Sex Unmarried Partner Households

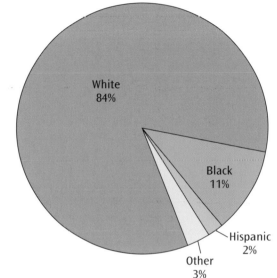

Presence of Children under Age 18 in Same-Sex Unmarried Partner Households

No children 74%   Children 26%

* Metropolitan area spans more than one state.

OKLAHOMA

Concentration of Gay/Lesbian Couples (by tract)

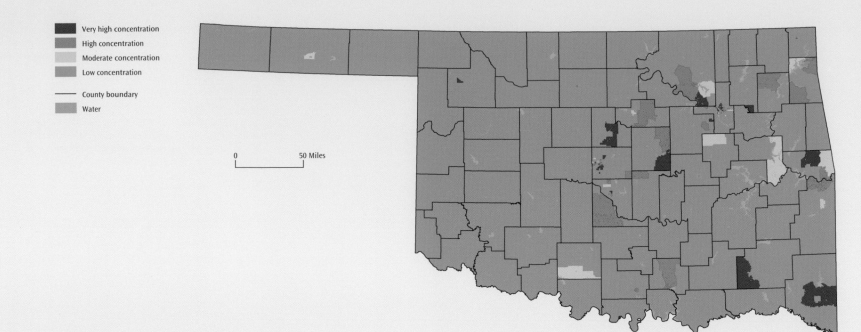

Very high concentration
High concentration
Moderate concentration
Low concentration

County boundary
Water

0   50 Miles

Concentration of Gay Male Couples (by county)

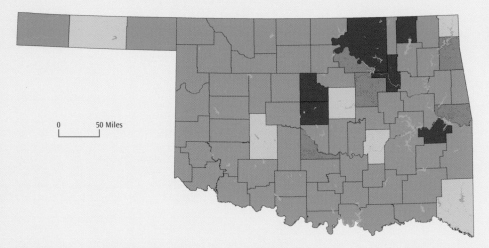

0   50 Miles

Concentration of Lesbian Couples (by county)

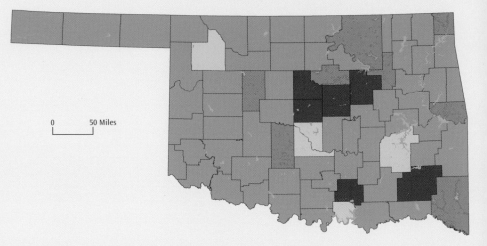

0   50 Miles

Indices

Gay/Lesbian Index	0.76
Gay Male Index	0.73
Lesbian Index	0.79

Comparative Statistics

	All	GL couples	GL rank
Presence of children, among households	46%	32%	12
Seniors (55+), among adults	30%	23%	17
Nonwhite, among adults	26%	24%	20
Females, among adults	52%	51%	27
Rural, among households	35%	31%	19

Top Oklahoma Metro Areas

(among 331 metro areas nationwide)

	GL rank	Gay male rank	Lesbian rank
Oklahoma City MSA	147	131	156
Tulsa MSA	163	115	209
Fort Smith MSA*	246	235	252
Enid MSA	295	316	270
Lawton MSA	305	307	297

Top Oklahoma Communities

(among 1,360 communities nationwide with 50 or more GL couples)

	GL rank	Gay male rank	Lesbian rank
Oklahoma City	637	491	739
Tulsa	710	502	880
Norman	1,013	1,000	954
Stillwater	1,078	1,091	1,004
Moore	1,195	1,328	906

Ages of Same-Sex Unmarried Partners

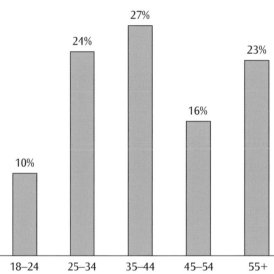

- 18–24: 10%
- 25–34: 24%
- 35–44: 27%
- 45–54: 16%
- 55+: 23%

Race/Ethnicity of Householder in Same-Sex Unmarried Partner Households

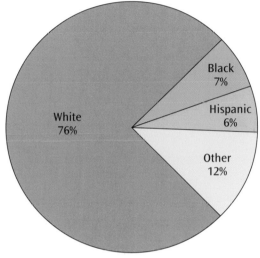

- White 76%
- Black 7%
- Hispanic 6%
- Other 12%

Presence of Children under Age 18 in Same-Sex Unmarried Partner Households

No children 68%	Children 32%

* Metropolitan area spans more than one state.

OREGON

Concentration of Gay/Lesbian Couples (by tract)

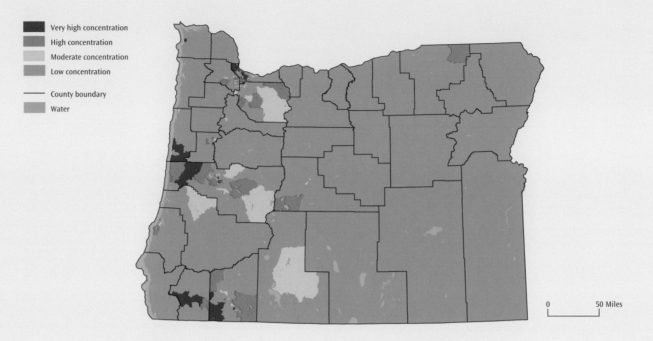

Very high concentration
High concentration
Moderate concentration
Low concentration
County boundary
Water

0   50 Miles

Concentration of Gay Male Couples (by county)

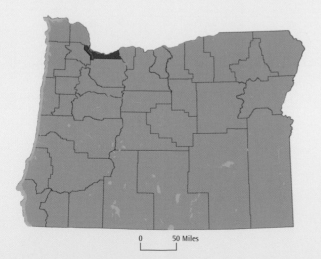

0   50 Miles

Concentration of Lesbian Couples (by county)

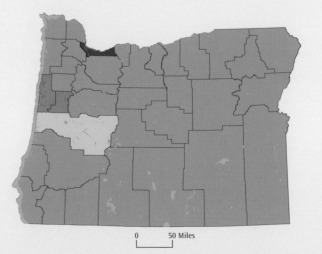

0   50 Miles

Indices

Gay/Lesbian Index	1.19
Gay Male Index	1.01
Lesbian Index	1.37

Comparative Statistics

	All	GL couples	GL rank
Presence of children, among households	45%	23%	44
Seniors (55+), among adults	29%	17%	40
Nonwhite, among adults	16%	13%	40
Females, among adults	51%	57%	5
Rural, among households	21%	17%	34

Top Oregon Metro Areas

(among 331 metro areas nationwide)

	GL rank	Gay male rank	Lesbian rank
Portland-Vancouver PMSA*	17	32	19
Eugene-Springfield MSA	26	92	13
Medford-Ashland MSA	46	70	27
Corvallis MSA	58	322	9
Salem PMSA	120	154	92

Top Oregon Communities

(among 1,360 communities nationwide with 50 or more GL couples)

	GL rank	Gay male rank	Lesbian rank
Portland	43	69	31
Ashland	103	513	39
Eugene	165	610	64
Milwaukie	485	970	188
Corvallis	491	1,334	103

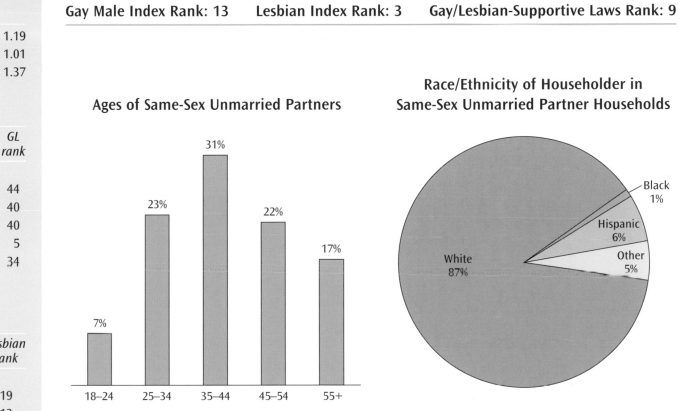

Ages of Same-Sex Unmarried Partners

18–24: 7%
25–34: 23%
35–44: 31%
45–54: 22%
55+: 17%

Race/Ethnicity of Householder in Same-Sex Unmarried Partner Households

White 87%
Black 1%
Hispanic 6%
Other 5%

Presence of Children under Age 18 in Same-Sex Unmarried Partner Households

No children 77%
Children 23%

* Metropolitan area spans more than one state.

PENNSYLVANIA

Concentration of Gay/Lesbian Couples (by tract)

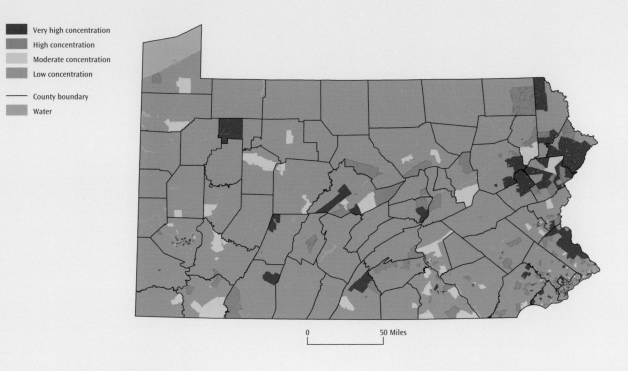

Very high concentration
High concentration
Moderate concentration
Low concentration

County boundary
Water

0   50 Miles

Concentration of Gay Male Couples (by county)

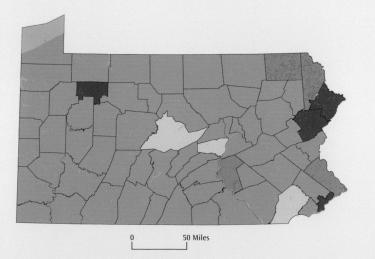

0   50 Miles

Concentration of Lesbian Couples (by county)

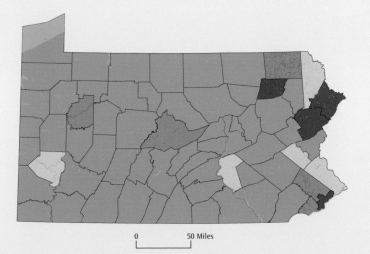

0   50 Miles

Gay Male Index Rank: 31 Lesbian Index Rank: 34 Gay/Lesbian-Supportive Laws Rank: 20

Indices

Gay/Lesbian Index	0.78
Gay Male Index	0.77
Lesbian Index	0.80

Comparative Statistics

	All	GL couples	GL rank
Presence of children, among households	44%	26%	34
Seniors (55+), among adults	33%	24%	13
Nonwhite, among adults	16%	17%	28
Females, among adults	53%	50%	33
Rural, among households	23%	20%	31

Top Pennsylvania Metro Areas

(among 331 metro areas nationwide)

	GL rank	Gay male rank	Lesbian rank
Newburgh PMSA*	60	58	60
Philadelphia PMSA*	96	72	119
State College MSA	151	129	175
Allentown-Bethlehem-Easton MSA	222	205	225
Harrisburg-Lebanon-Carlisle MSA	232	184	267

Top Pennsylvania Communities

(among 1,360 communities nationwide with 50 or more GL couples)

	GL rank	Gay male rank	Lesbian rank
Wilkinsburg	109	135	114
Harrisburg	113	70	337
Lancaster	278	497	159
Philadelphia	290	233	412
Easton	316	216	546

Ages of Same-Sex Unmarried Partners

18–24	25–34	35–44	45–54	55+
5%	21%	30%	20%	24%

Race/Ethnicity of Householder in Same-Sex Unmarried Partner Households

White 83%
Black 11%
Hispanic 4%
Other 3%

Presence of Children under Age 18 in Same-Sex Unmarried Partner Households

No children 74%
Children 26%

* Metropolitan area spans more than one state.

RHODE ISLAND

Concentration of Gay/Lesbian Couples (by tract)

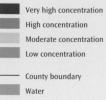

- Very high concentration
- High concentration
- Moderate concentration
- Low concentration

—— County boundary

Water

0   10 Miles

Concentration of Gay Male Couples (by county)

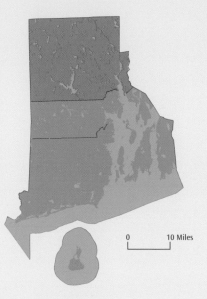

0   10 Miles

Concentration of Lesbian Couples (by county)

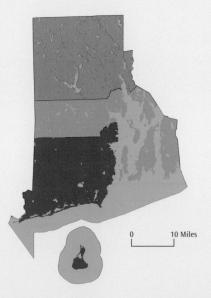

0   10 Miles

Indices

Gay/Lesbian Index	1.07
Gay Male Index	1.01
Lesbian Index	1.14

Comparative Statistics

	All	GL couples	GL rank
Presence of children, among households	46%	23%	45
Seniors (55+), among adults	30%	20%	30
Nonwhite, among adults	18%	15%	33
Females, among adults	53%	53%	17
Rural, among households	9%	9%	44

Top Rhode Island Metro Areas

(among 331 metro areas nationwide)

	GL rank	Gay male rank	Lesbian rank
Providence-Fall River-Warwick MSA*	65	73	63
New London-Norwich MSA*	133	177	97

Top Rhode Island Communities

(among 1,360 communities nationwide with 50 or more GL couples)

	GL rank	Gay male rank	Lesbian rank
Providence	106	90	163
Pawtucket	493	618	373
Newport	689	437	936
North Providence	724	459	966
Cranston	730	602	804

Gay Male Index Rank: 15   **Lesbian Index Rank: 11**   **Gay/Lesbian-Supportive Laws Rank: 5**

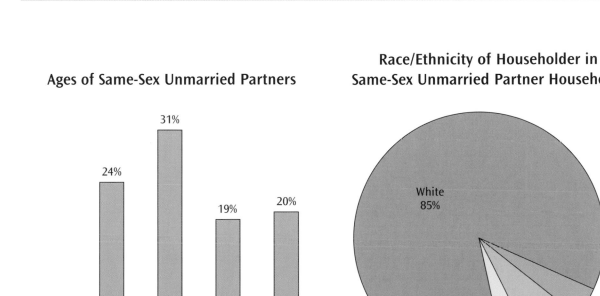

Ages of Same-Sex Unmarried Partners

- 18–24: 6%
- 25–34: 24%
- 35–44: 31%
- 45–54: 19%
- 55+: 20%

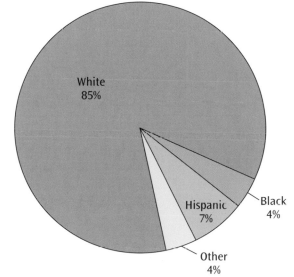

Race/Ethnicity of Householder in Same-Sex Unmarried Partner Households

- White 85%
- Hispanic 7%
- Black 4%
- Other 4%

Presence of Children under Age 18 in Same-Sex Unmarried Partner Households

- No children 77%
- Children 23%

* Metropolitan area spans more than one state.

SOUTH CAROLINA

Concentration of Gay/Lesbian Couples (by tract)

Very high concentration
High concentration
Moderate concentration
Low concentration

County boundary
Water

0   50 Miles

Concentration of Gay Male Couples (by county)

0   50 Miles

Concentration of Lesbian Couples (by county)

0   50 Miles

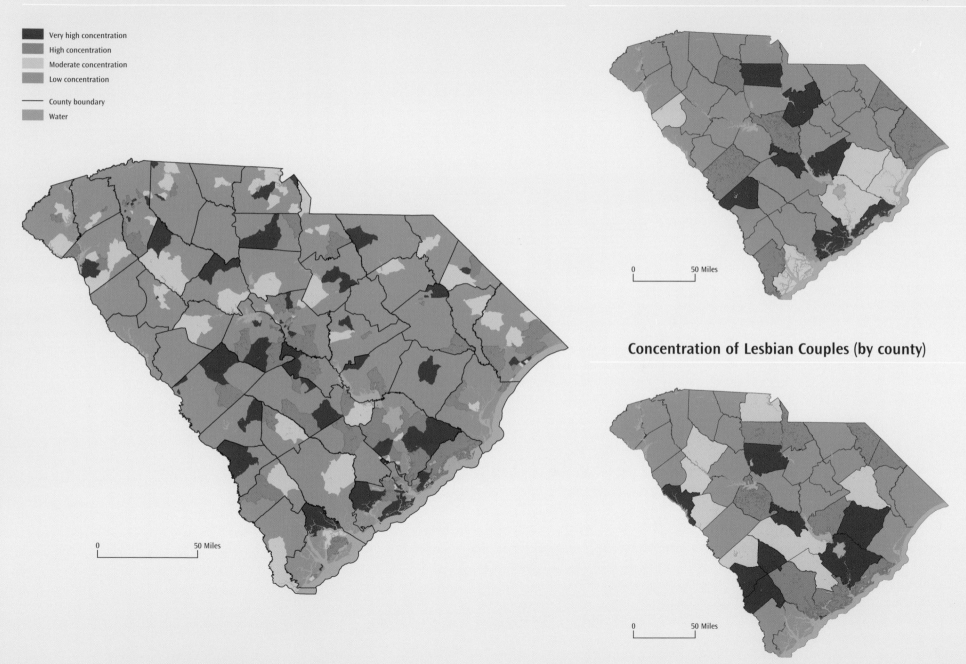

Indices

Gay/Lesbian Index	0.88
Gay Male Index	0.81
Lesbian Index	0.94

Comparative Statistics

	All	GL couples	GL rank
Presence of children, among households	46%	36%	4
Seniors (55+), among adults	29%	24%	15
Nonwhite, among adults	34%	35%	6
Females, among adults	52%	53%	12
Rural, among households	40%	40%	12

Top South Carolina Metro Areas

(among 331 metro areas nationwide)

	GL rank	Gay male rank	Lesbian rank
Charleston-North Charleston MSA	66	63	81
Charlotte-Gastonia-Rock Hill MSA*	92	56	134
Columbia MSA	122	133	105
Myrtle Beach MSA	124	77	181
Augusta-Aiken MSA*	149	128	170

Top South Carolina Communities

(among 1,360 communities nationwide with 50 or more GL couples)

	GL rank	Gay male rank	Lesbian rank
Myrtle Beach	335	102	1,253
Charleston	406	320	549
Columbia	557	404	720
Greenwood	574	702	414
Mount Pleasant	687	467	891

Ages of Same-Sex Unmarried Partners

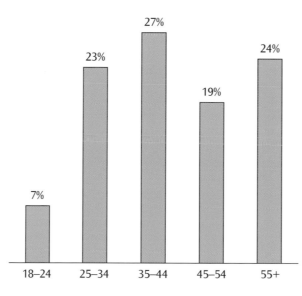

Race/Ethnicity of Householder in Same-Sex Unmarried Partner Households

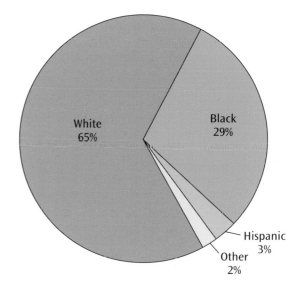

Presence of Children under Age 18 in Same-Sex Unmarried Partner Households

No children 64%

Children 36%

* Metropolitan area spans more than one state.

SOUTH DAKOTA

Concentration of Gay/Lesbian Couples (by tract)

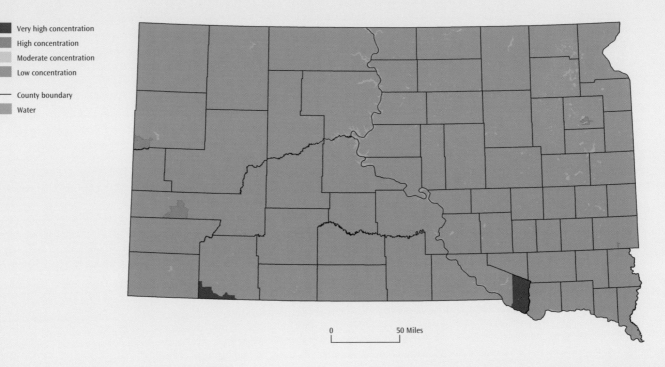

Very high concentration
High concentration
Moderate concentration
Low concentration

County boundary
Water

0   50 Miles

Concentration of Gay Male Couples (by county)

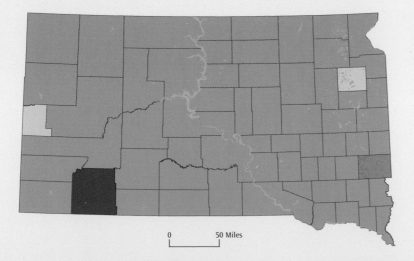

0   50 Miles

Concentration of Lesbian Couples (by county)

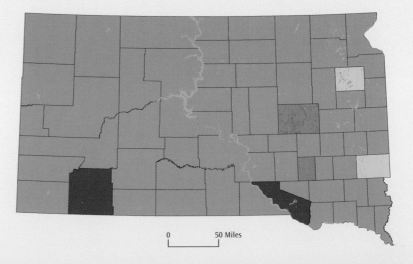

0   50 Miles

Indices

Gay/Lesbian Index	0.50
Gay Male Index	0.47
Lesbian Index	0.54

Comparative Statistics

	All	GL couples	GL rank
Presence of children, among households	47%	40%	2
Seniors (55+), among adults	31%	29%	2
Nonwhite, among adults	12%	14%	37
Females, among adults	51%	53%	15
Rural, among households	48%	47%	6

Top South Dakota Metro Areas

(among 331 metro areas nationwide)

	GL rank	Gay male rank	Lesbian rank
Sioux Falls MSA	320	310	320
Rapid City MSA	330	326	330

Top South Dakota Communities

(among 1,360 communities nationwide with 50 or more GL couples)

	GL rank	Gay male rank	Lesbian rank
Sioux Falls	1,317	1,304	1,278
Rapid City	1,355	1,343	1,347

Ages of Same-Sex Unmarried Partners

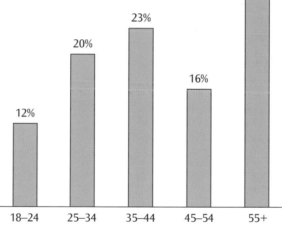

18–24	25–34	35–44	45–54	55+
12%	20%	23%	16%	29%

Race/Ethnicity of Householder in Same-Sex Unmarried Partner Households

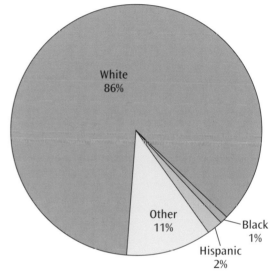

White 86%
Other 11%
Black 1%
Hispanic 2%

Presence of Children under Age 18 in Same-Sex Unmarried Partner Households

No children 60%   Children 40%

147

TENNESSEE

Concentration of Gay/Lesbian Couples (by tract)

Very high concentration
High concentration
Moderate concentration
Low concentration
County boundary
Water

0   50 Miles

Concentration of Gay Male Couples (by county)

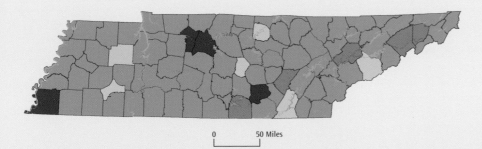

0   50 Miles

Concentration of Lesbian Couples (by county)

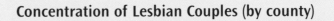

0   50 Miles

Indices

Gay/Lesbian Index	0.81
Gay Male Index	0.80
Lesbian Index	0.82

Comparative Statistics

	All	GL couples	GL rank
Presence of children, among households	45%	30%	19
Seniors (55+), among adults	29%	21%	21
Nonwhite, among adults	21%	20%	26
Females, among adults	52%	50%	36
Rural, among households	36%	31%	18

Top Tennessee Metro Areas

(among 331 metro areas nationwide)

	GL rank	Gay male rank	Lesbian rank
Nashville MSA	93	57	130
Memphis MSA*	125	90	144
Knoxville MSA	155	166	139
Chattanooga MSA*	171	132	211
Jackson MSA	230	208	234

Top Tennessee Communities

(among 1,360 communities nationwide with 50 or more GL couples)

	GL rank	Gay male rank	Lesbian rank
Nashville-Davidson	323	214	582
Knoxville	558	685	404
Memphis	602	466	710
Chattanooga	790	616	921
Cleveland	916	781	989

Ages of Same-Sex Unmarried Partners

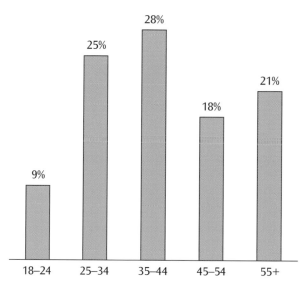

Race/Ethnicity of Householder in Same-Sex Unmarried Partner Households

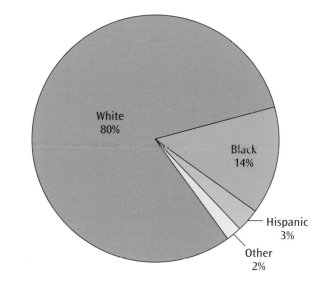

Presence of Children under Age 18 in Same-Sex Unmarried Partner Households

No children 70%	Children 30%

* Metropolitan area spans more than one state.

TEXAS

Concentration of Gay/Lesbian Couples (by tract)

Very high concentration
High concentration
Moderate concentration
Low concentration
County boundary
Water

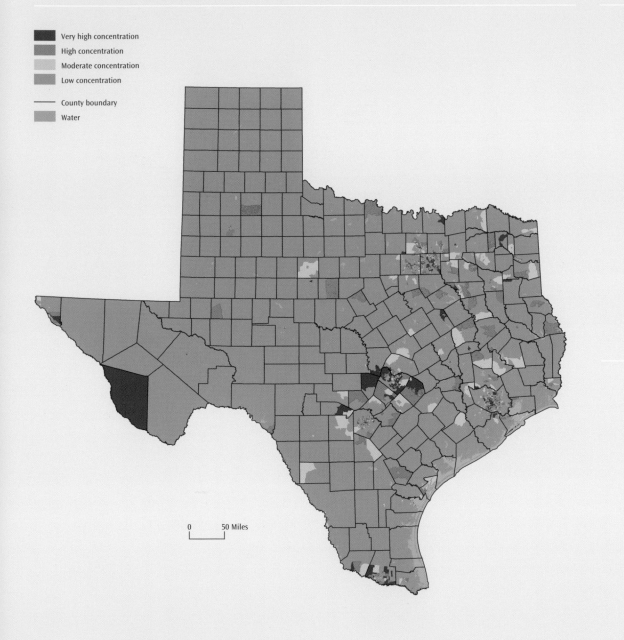

Concentration of Gay Male Couples (by county)

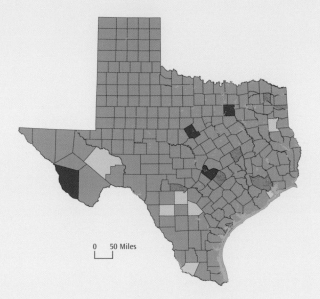

0   50 Miles

Concentration of Lesbian Couples (by county)

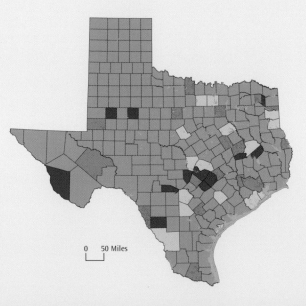

0   50 Miles

0   50 Miles

Indices

Gay/Lesbian Index	1.03
Gay Male Index	1.03
Lesbian Index	1.03

Comparative Statistics

	All	GL couples	GL rank
Presence of children, among households	54%	35%	7
Seniors (55+), among adults	25%	17%	41
Nonwhite, among adults	48%	42%	3
Females, among adults	51%	49%	37
Rural, among households	17%	14%	35

Top Texas Metro Areas

(among 331 metro areas nationwide)

	GL rank	Gay male rank	Lesbian rank
Austin-San Marcos MSA	10	16	20
Dallas PMSA	27	14	84
Houston PMSA	44	30	61
McAllen-Edinburg-Mission MSA	62	79	45
Galveston-Texas City PMSA	67	54	99

Top Texas Communities

(among 1,360 communities nationwide with 50 or more GL couples)

	GL rank	Gay male rank	Lesbian rank
Dallas	78	45	279
Austin	114	123	138
Galveston	115	97	190
Bellaire	131	104	223
Socorro	154	442	69

Gay Male Index Rank: 12   Lesbian Index Rank: 20   Gay/Lesbian-Supportive Laws Rank: 27

Ages of Same-Sex Unmarried Partners

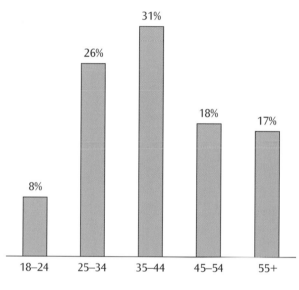

Race/Ethnicity of Householder in Same-Sex Unmarried Partner Households

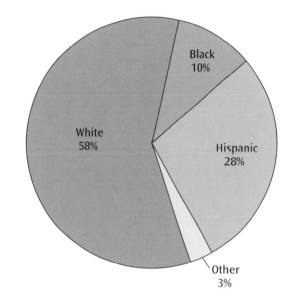

Presence of Children under Age 18 in Same-Sex Unmarried Partner Households

No children 65%   Children 35%

UTAH

Concentration of Gay/Lesbian Couples (by tract)

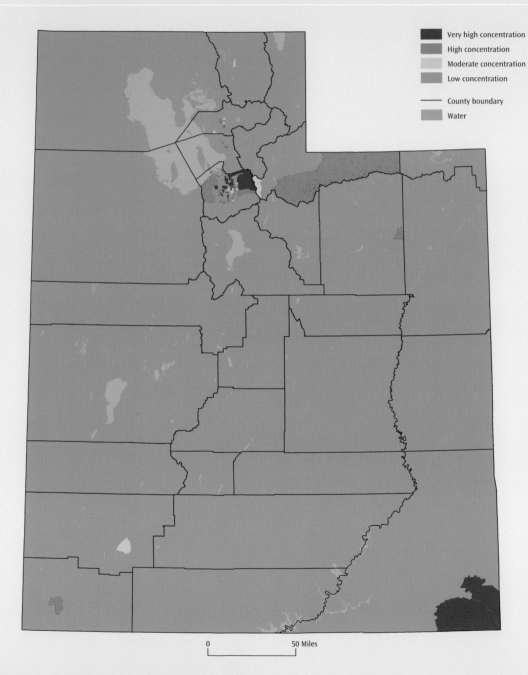

Very high concentration
High concentration
Moderate concentration
Low concentration
—— County boundary
Water

0   50 Miles

Concentration of Gay Male Couples (by county)

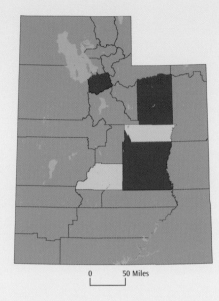

0   50 Miles

Concentration of Lesbian Couples (by county)

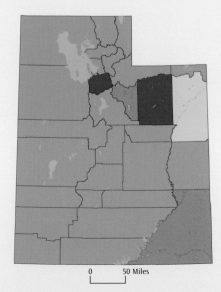

0   50 Miles

Indices

Gay/Lesbian Index	0.85
Gay Male Index	0.83
Lesbian Index	0.87

Comparative Statistics

	All	GL couples	GL rank
Presence of children, among households	58%	33%	9
Seniors (55+), among adults	22%	16%	46
Nonwhite, among adults	15%	16%	30
Females, among adults	51%	51%	31
Rural, among households	12%	10%	42

Top Utah Metro Areas

(among 331 metro areas nationwide)

	GL rank	Gay male rank	Lesbian rank
Flagstaff MSA*	61	113	30
Salt Lake City-Ogden MSA	86	66	107
Provo-Orem MSA	327	327	324

Top Utah Communities

(among 1,360 communities nationwide with 50 or more GL couples)

	GL rank	Gay male rank	Lesbian rank
Salt Lake City	84	63	130
South Salt Lake	319	400	255
Kearns	486	686	306
West Valley City	561	519	555
Midvale	627	772	431

Gay Male Index Rank: 26   Lesbian Index Rank: 28   Gay/Lesbian-Supportive Laws Rank: 47

Ages of Same-Sex Unmarried Partners

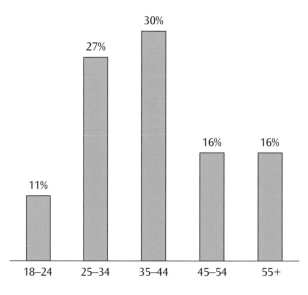

Race/Ethnicity of Householder in Same-Sex Unmarried Partner Households

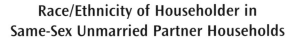
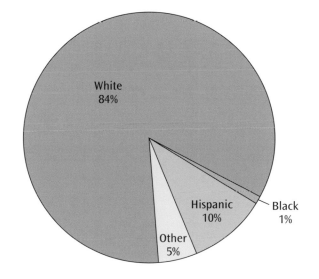

White 84%
Hispanic 10%
Black 1%
Other 5%

Presence of Children under Age 18 in Same-Sex Unmarried Partner Households

No children 67%   Children 33%

* Metropolitan area spans more than one state.

VERMONT

Concentration of Gay/Lesbian Couples (by tract)

Concentration of Gay Male Couples (by county)

Concentration of Lesbian Couples (by county)

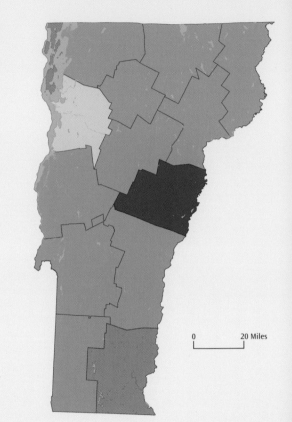

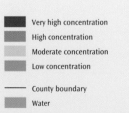

Very high concentration

High concentration

Moderate concentration

Low concentration

County boundary

Water

0   20 Miles

Indices

Gay/Lesbian Index	1.43
Gay Male Index	1.11
Lesbian Index	1.75

Comparative Statistics

	All	GL couples	GL rank
Presence of children, among households	46%	25%	37
Seniors (55+), among adults	29%	19%	33
Nonwhite, among adults	4%	4%	49
Females, among adults	52%	61%	1
Rural, among households	62%	65%	1

Top Vermont Metro Areas

(among 331 metro areas nationwide)

	GL rank	Gay male rank	Lesbian rank
Burlington MSA	9	51	6

Top Vermont Communities

(among 1,360 communities nationwide with 50 or more GL couples)

	GL rank	Gay male rank	Lesbian rank
Burlington	92	183	54

Gay Male Index Rank: 10   **Lesbian Index Rank: 1**   **Gay/Lesbian-Supportive Laws Rank: 1**

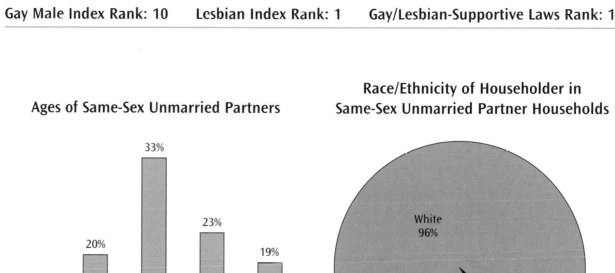

Ages of Same-Sex Unmarried Partners

18–24: 5%
25–34: 20%
35–44: 33%
45–54: 23%
55+: 19%

Race/Ethnicity of Householder in Same-Sex Unmarried Partner Households

White 96%
Other 2%
Hispanic 1%
Black 1%

Presence of Children under Age 18 in Same-Sex Unmarried Partner Households

No children 75%
Children 25%

VIRGINIA

Concentration of Gay/Lesbian Couples (by tract)

Very high concentration
High concentration
Moderate concentration
Low concentration
County boundary
Water

0   50 Miles

Concentration of Gay Male Couples (by county)

0   50 Miles

Concentration of Lesbian Couples (by county)

0   50 Miles

Indices

Gay/Lesbian Index	0.91
Gay Male Index	0.92
Lesbian Index	0.89

Comparative Statistics

	All	GL couples	GL rank
Presence of children, among households	48%	25%	39
Seniors (55+), among adults	27%	19%	34
Nonwhite, among adults	30%	25%	19
Females, among adults	52%	49%	40
Rural, among households	27%	22%	27

Top Virginia Metro Areas

(among 331 metro areas nationwide)

	GL rank	Gay male rank	Lesbian rank
Washington PMSA*	24	13	66
Charlottesville MSA	115	181	59
Richmond-Petersburg MSA	142	112	161
Roanoke MSA	185	175	188
Norfolk-Virginia Beach-Newport News MSA*	203	199	191

Top Virginia Communities

(among 1,360 communities nationwide with 50 or more GL couples)

	GL rank	Gay male rank	Lesbian rank
Arlington	54	29	455
Rose Hill	57	43	98
Alexandria	75	42	322
Jefferson	87	53	207
Groveton	128	66	504

Ages of Same-Sex Unmarried Partners

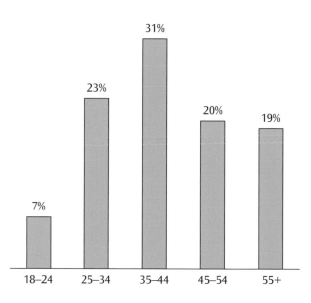

Race/Ethnicity of Householder in Same-Sex Unmarried Partner Households

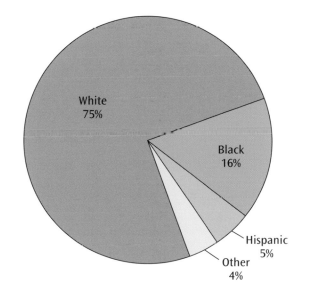

Presence of Children under Age 18 in Same-Sex Unmarried Partner Households

No children 75%	Children 25%

* Metropolitan area spans more than one state.

WASHINGTON

Concentration of Gay/Lesbian Couples (by tract)

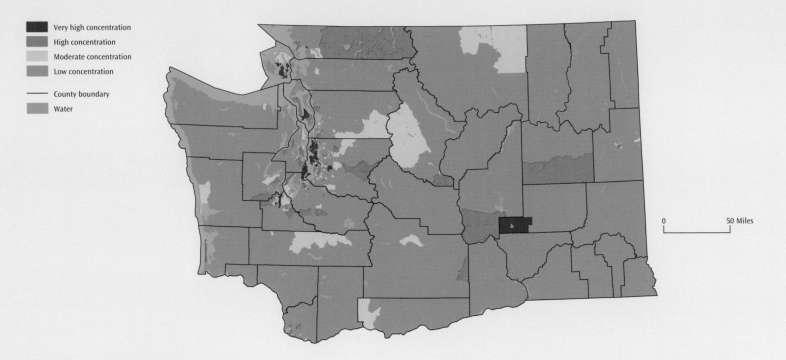

Very high concentration
High concentration
Moderate concentration
Low concentration
County boundary
Water

0   50 Miles

Concentration of Gay Male Couples (by county)

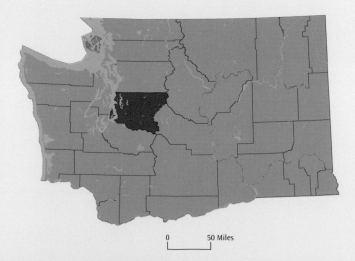

0   50 Miles

Concentration of Lesbian Couples (by county)

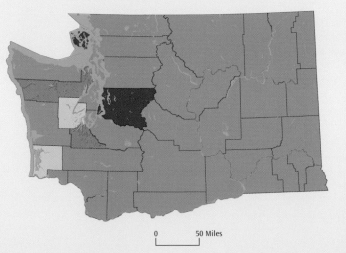

0   50 Miles

Indices

Gay/Lesbian Index	1.24
Gay Male Index	1.18
Lesbian Index	1.30

Comparative Statistics

	All	GL couples	GL rank
Presence of children, among households	48%	22%	49
Seniors (55+), among adults	26%	15%	49
Nonwhite, among adults	21%	16%	32
Females, among adults	51%	52%	22
Rural, among households	18%	14%	36

Top Washington Metro Areas

(among 331 metro areas nationwide)

	GL rank	Gay male rank	Lesbian rank
Seattle-Bellevue-Everett PMSA	6	4	15
Portland-Vancouver PMSA*	17	32	19
Olympia PMSA	34	172	11
Bremerton PMSA	69	78	68
Bellingham MSA	100	162	49

Top Washington Communities

(among 1,360 communities nationwide with 50 or more GL couples)

	GL rank	Gay male rank	Lesbian rank
Vashon	20	60	5
Seattle	25	22	21
Bryn Mawr-Skyway	62	58	87
Tukwila	91	87	108
Olympia	95	632	30

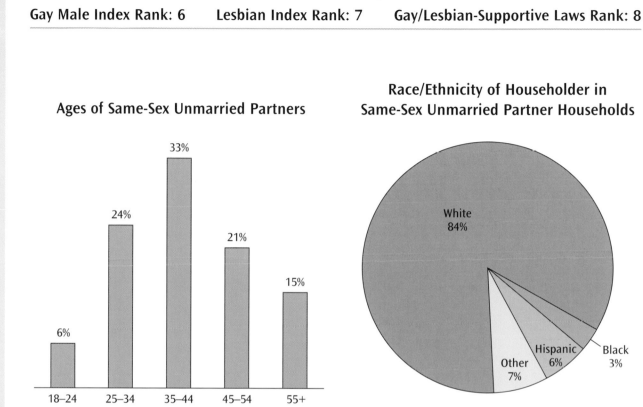

Ages of Same-Sex Unmarried Partners

- 18–24: 6%
- 25–34: 24%
- 35–44: 33%
- 45–54: 21%
- 55+: 15%

Race/Ethnicity of Householder in Same-Sex Unmarried Partner Households

- White 84%
- Other 7%
- Hispanic 6%
- Black 3%

Presence of Children under Age 18 in Same-Sex Unmarried Partner Households

- No children 78%
- Children 22%

* Metropolitan area spans more than one state.

WEST VIRGINIA

Concentration of Gay/Lesbian Couples (by tract)

Concentration of Gay Male Couples (by county)

Very high concentration
High concentration
Moderate concentration
Low concentration
County boundary
Water

Concentration of Lesbian Couples (by county)

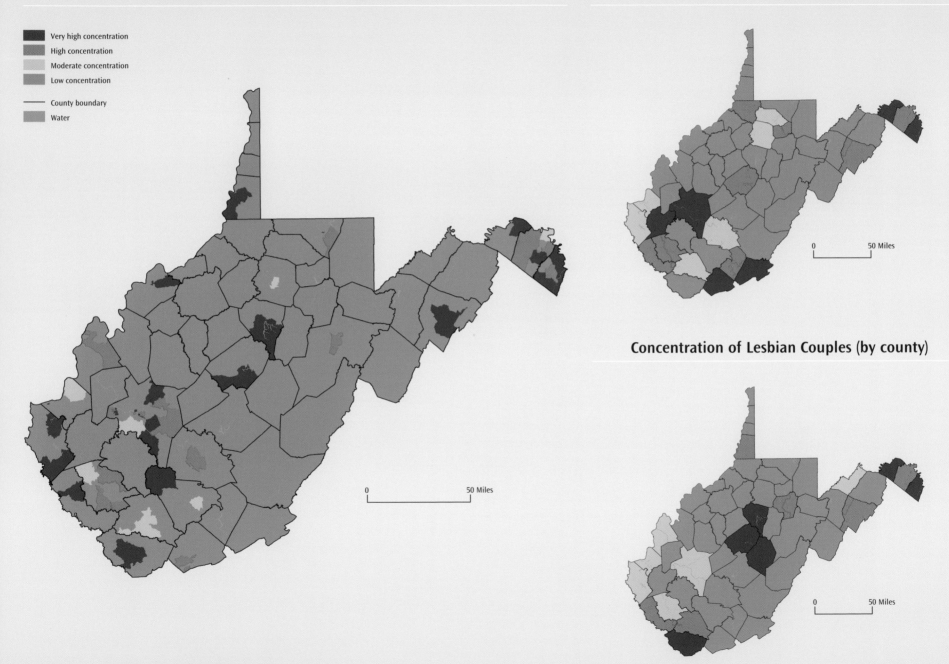

0   50 Miles

0   50 Miles

0   50 Miles

Indices

Gay/Lesbian Index	0.70
Gay Male Index	0.71
Lesbian Index	0.69

Comparative Statistics

	All	GL couples	GL rank
Presence of children, among households	42%	32%	14
Seniors (55+), among adults	33%	28%	4
Nonwhite, among adults	5%	5%	47
Females, among adults	52%	49%	42
Rural, among households	54%	52%	3

Top West Virginia Metro Areas

(among 331 metro areas nationwide)

	GL rank	Gay male rank	Lesbian rank
Charleston MSA	183	109	257
Huntington-Ashland MSA*	219	215	213
Parkersburg-Marietta MSA*	282	266	291
Cumberland MSA*	301	296	300
Wheeling MSA*	304	301	302

Top West Virginia Communities

(among 1,360 communities nationwide with 50 or more GL couples)

	GL rank	Gay male rank	Lesbian rank
Charleston	563	323	893
Huntington	745	682	729
Parkersburg	1,241	1,172	1,211

Ages of Same-Sex Unmarried Partners

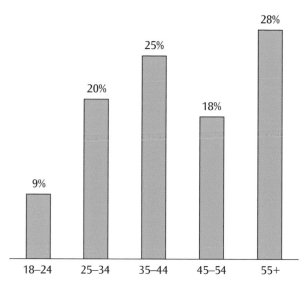

18–24: 9%
25–34: 20%
35–44: 25%
45–54: 18%
55+: 28%

Race/Ethnicity of Householder in Same-Sex Unmarried Partner Households

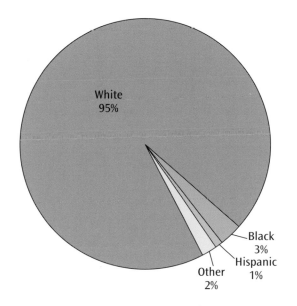

White 95%
Black 3%
Hispanic 1%
Other 2%

Presence of Children under Age 18 in Same-Sex Unmarried Partner Households

No children 68%   Children 32%

* Metropolitan area spans more than one state.

WISCONSIN

Concentration of Gay/Lesbian Couples (by tract)

Concentration of Gay Male Couples (by county)

Concentration of Lesbian Couples (by county)

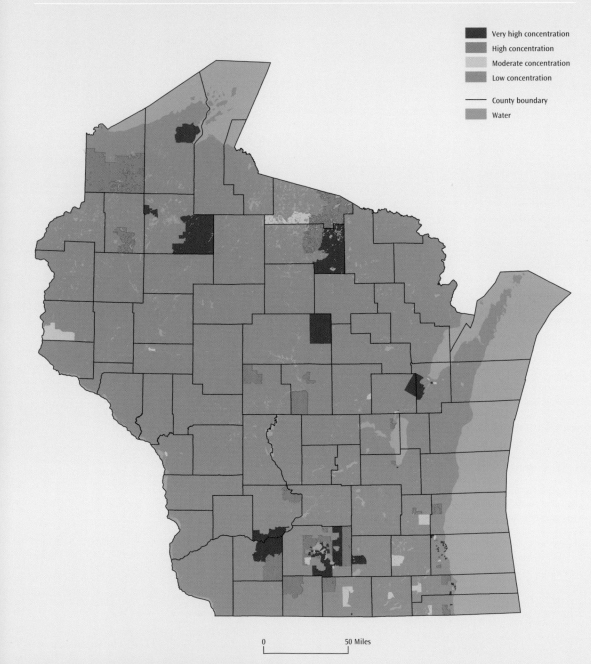

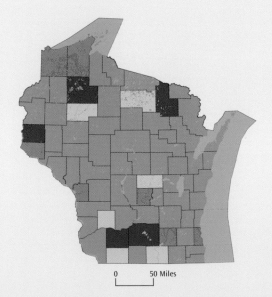

Very high concentration
High concentration
Moderate concentration
Low concentration
County boundary
Water

0   50 Miles

0   50 Miles

0   50 Miles

Indices

Gay/Lesbian Index	0.70
Gay Male Index	0.65
Lesbian Index	0.75

Comparative Statistics

	All	GL couples	GL rank
Presence of children, among households	46%	24%	40
Seniors (55+), among adults	29%	19%	35
Nonwhite, among adults	13%	14%	35
Females, among adults	51%	53%	14
Rural, among households	32%	27%	20

Top Wisconsin Metro Areas

(among 331 metro areas nationwide)

	GL rank	Gay male rank	Lesbian rank
Madison MSA	13	52	10
Minneapolis-St. Paul MSA*	63	69	58
Milwaukee-Waukesha PMSA	212	165	254
Kenosha PMSA	239	214	255
Racine PMSA	263	225	281

Top Wisconsin Communities

(among 1,360 communities nationwide with 50 or more GL couples)

	GL rank	Gay male rank	Lesbian rank
Madison	100	251	49
Milwaukee	552	386	752
Wauwatosa	898	968	751
Racine	928	689	1,081
Superior	1,025	1,141	825

Gay Male Index Rank: 44   Lesbian Index Rank: 41   Gay/Lesbian-Supportive Laws Rank: 12

Ages of Same-Sex Unmarried Partners

- 18–24: 8%
- 25–34: 23%
- 35–44: 31%
- 45–54: 19%
- 55+: 19%

Race/Ethnicity of Householder in Same-Sex Unmarried Partner Households

- White 86%
- Black 6%
- Hispanic 5%
- Other 3%

Presence of Children under Age 18 in Same-Sex Unmarried Partner Households

- No children 76%
- Children 24%

* Metropolitan area spans more than one state.

163

WYOMING

Concentration of Gay/Lesbian Couples (by tract)

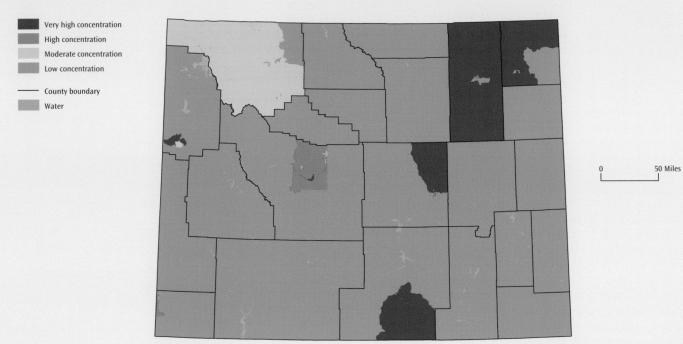

Very high concentration
High concentration
Moderate concentration
Low concentration

County boundary
Water

0   50 Miles

Concentration of Gay Male Couples (by county)

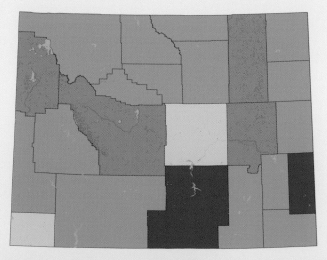

0   50 Miles

Concentration of Lesbian Couples (by county)

0   50 Miles

Indices

Gay/Lesbian Index	0.74
Gay Male Index	0.75
Lesbian Index	0.73

Comparative Statistics

	All	GL couples	GL rank
Presence of children, among households	46%	33%	11
Seniors (55+), among adults	28%	28%	3
Nonwhite, among adults	11%	11%	43
Females, among adults	50%	49%	39
Rural, among households	35%	40%	11

Top Wyoming Metro Areas

(among 331 metro areas nationwide)

	GL rank	Gay male rank	Lesbian rank
Casper MSA	145	135	152
Cheyenne MSA	321	317	319

Top Wyoming Communities

(among 1,360 communities nationwide with 50 or more GL couples)

	GL rank	Gay male rank	Lesbian rank
Casper	939	1,028	774
Cheyenne	1,349	1,314	1,348

Gay Male Index Rank: 36   Lesbian Index Rank: 43   Gay/Lesbian-Supportive Laws Rank: 27

Ages of Same-Sex Unmarried Partners

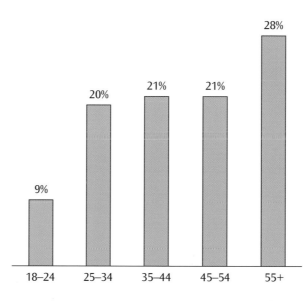

Race/Ethnicity of Householder in Same-Sex Unmarried Partner Households

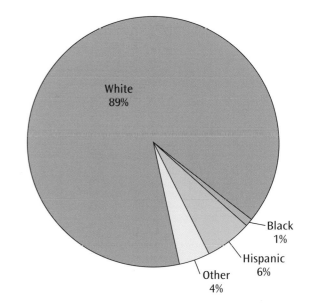

Presence of Children under Age 18 in Same-Sex Unmarried Partner Households

No children 67%   Children 33%

165

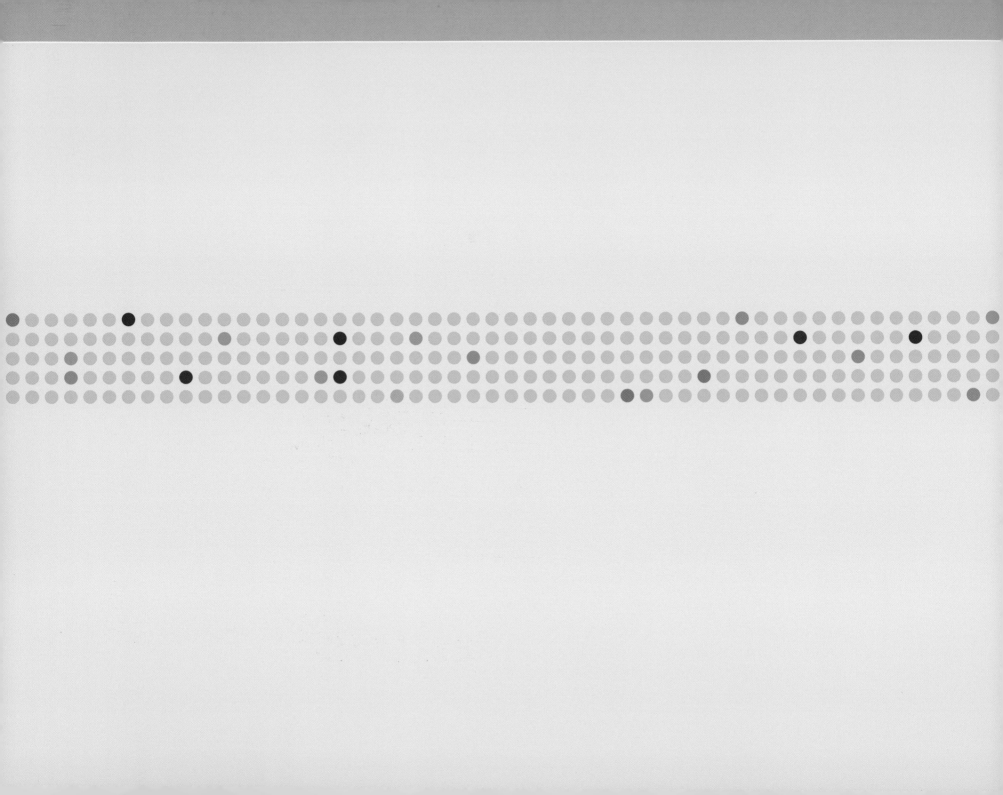

Seattle
WASHINGTON
Portland
OREGON
MONTANA
NORTH DAKOTA
MINNESOTA
Minneapolis
St. Paul
WISCONSIN
MICHIGAN
VERMONT
MAINE
NEW HAMPSHIRE
Boston MASSACHUSETTS
NEW YORK
RHODE ISLAND
CONNECTICUT
IDAHO
SOUTH DAKOTA
WYOMING
IOWA
NEBRASKA
Chicago
ILLINOIS
INDIANA
Columbus
OHIO
PENNSYLVANIA
Philadelphia
New York
NEW JERSEY
DELAWARE
MARYLAND
Oakland
San Francisco
CALIFORNIA
NEVADA
UTAH
Denver
COLORADO
KANSAS
Kansas City
MISSOURI
VIRGINIA
Washington DISTRICT OF COLUMBIA
KENTUCKY
NORTH CAROLINA
Los Angeles
ARIZONA
Albuquerque
Nashville
TENNESSEE
SOUTH CAROLINA
Phoenix
San Diego
NEW MEXICO
OKLAHOMA
ARKANSAS
Atlanta
Dallas
TEXAS
MISSISSIPPI
LOUISIANA
ALABAMA
GEORGIA
Austin
Houston
New Orleans
Orlando
FLORIDA
Fort Lauderdale
Miami

0   200   Miles

How to Read the City Maps

1   The large city map presents same-sex unmarried partner concentration at the census tract level. Tracts are designed to contain a similar number of housing units, so some tracts are geographically larger than others, even within the same city. The boundaries overlaid on the city map are ZIP Code Tabulation Areas, which roughly resemble postal service ZIP Codes. These are provided for reference only and are not intended to represent true ZIP Code boundaries. The different colors indicate the relative concentration of same-sex couples only within the area shown.

2   This legend defines the corresponding concentration level for each color on the map. Note that these concentrations are relative only to the area shown on the map. Any areal unit with an Index value of 1.0 or less is colored green. In addition, any tract on the main Gay/Lesbian city map with 10 or fewer gay or lesbian couples is colored green out of concern for the validity of these data. Similarly, tracts on the separate Gay Male and Lesbian city maps with five or fewer gay male or lesbian couples, respectively, are colored green. Areas with Index values greater than 1.0—i.e., areas with an overrepresentation of same-sex couples—were divided into three roughly equal groups, varying in color from yellow (moderate concentration) to red (very high concentration).

3   The two smaller city maps present separate tract-level concentrations for same-sex male and female couples. The different colors indicate the relative concentration of male or female couples in counties only within the area shown.

4   These indices indicate the associated MSA/PMSA's concentration of all same-sex couples, male couples, and female couples, relative to the United States.

5   These indices and rankings are presented at the city level rather than at the broader MSA/PMSA level. The city's Gay/Lesbian Index, Gay Male Index, and Lesbian Index, all of which are relative to the U.S., are shown along with two rankings. The first shows rankings for each Index among the 50 largest U.S. cities, if applicable. The second shows each ranking among the 1,360 communities with 50 or more same-sex unmarried partner couples.

6   This chart shows the distribution of all people counted as same-sex couples among five age categories: 18 to 24; 25 to 34; 35 to 44; 45 to 54; and 55 and older, based on U.S. Census tabulations. As only county-level data were available from Census, this chart shows statistics for the metropolitan statistical area (MSA) or primary metropolitan statistical area (PMSA) associated with the city.

7   This chart shows the share of all same-sex couple households in the associated MSA/PMSA that are headed by a white householder, a black householder, a Hispanic householder, or a householder of some other race/ethnicity.

8   These numbers indicate where the city's metropolitan area ranks among the 331 MSAs and PMSAs in the United States, based on its Gay/Lesbian Index, Gay Male Index, and Lesbian Index values.

9   These statistics compare demographic characteristics of the same-sex couple population in the associated MSA/PMSA with the MSA/PMSA's general population. The Gay/Lesbian Rank column gives that MSA/PMSA's rank among the 331 MSAs and PMSAs for each same-sex couple population measure. Ranks are high to low, meaning an MSA/PMSA ranked number one has the highest percentage in that characteristic.

10 This table lists the top five ZIP Codes in the area shown on the maps, based on their Gay/Lesbian Index, Gay Male Index, and Lesbian Index values.

11 This chart shows the share of all same-sex couple households with at least one child under the age of 18 present, based on U.S. Census tabulations. As only county-level data were available from Census, this chart shows statistics for the MSA or PMSA associated with the city.

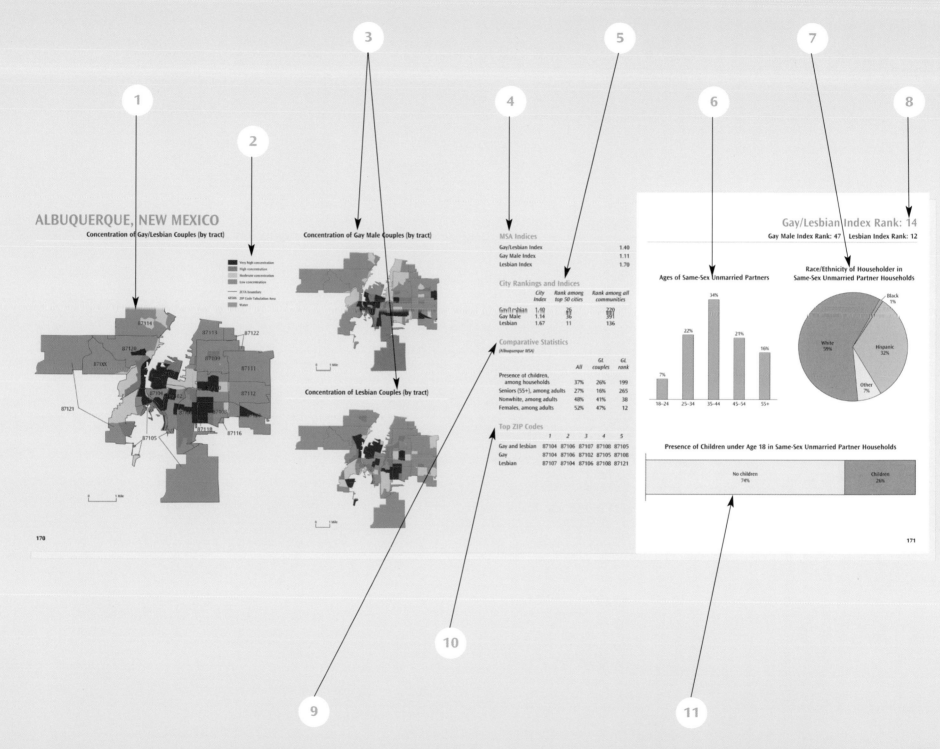

ALBUQUERQUE, NEW MEXICO

Concentration of Gay/Lesbian Couples (by tract)

Very high concentration
High concentration
Moderate concentration
Low concentration

ZCTA Boundary
68506 ZIP Code Tabulation Area
Water

87114
87113
87122
87120
87111
871XX
87109
87111
87112
87104
87121
87108
87118
87116
87105

0   1 Mile

Concentration of Gay Male Couples (by tract)

0   1 Mile

Concentration of Lesbian Couples (by tract)

0   1 Mile

MSA Indices

Gay/Lesbian Index	1.40
Gay Male Index	1.11
Lesbian Index	1.70

City Rankings and Indices

	City Index	Rank among top 50 cities	Rank among all communities
Gay/Lesbian	1.40	26	220
Gay Male	1.14	36	391
Lesbian	1.67	11	136

Comparative Statistics
(Albuquerque MSA)

	All	GL couples	GL rank
Presence of children, among households	37%	26%	199
Seniors (55+), among adults	27%	16%	265
Nonwhite, among adults	48%	41%	38
Females, among adults	52%	47%	12

Top ZIP Codes

	1	2	3	4	5
Gay and lesbian	87104	87106	87107	87108	87105
Gay	87104	87106	87102	87105	87108
Lesbian	87107	87104	87106	87108	87121

Gay/Lesbian Index Rank: 14

Gay Male Index Rank: 47   Lesbian Index Rank: 12

Ages of Same-Sex Unmarried Partners

Age	%
18–24	7%
25–34	22%
35–44	34%
45–54	21%
55+	16%

Race/Ethnicity of Householder in Same-Sex Unmarried Partner Households

White 59%
Hispanic 32%
Other 7%
Black 1%

Presence of Children under Age 18 in Same-Sex Unmarried Partner Households

No children 74%   Children 26%

ALBUQUERQUE, NEW MEXICO

Concentration of Gay/Lesbian Couples (by tract)

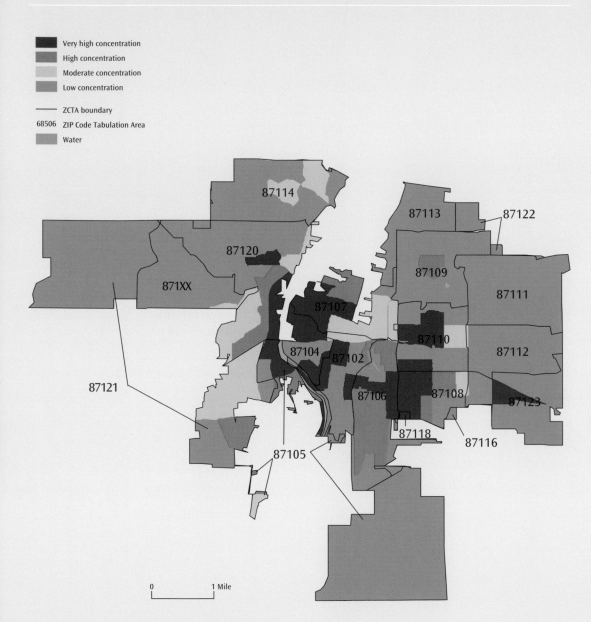

Very high concentration
High concentration
Moderate concentration
Low concentration

ZCTA boundary
68506 ZIP Code Tabulation Area
Water

87114

87113   87122

87120

871XX

87109

87111

87107

87110

87104 87102

87112

87121

87106   87108   87123

87118   87116

87105

0   1 Mile

Concentration of Gay Male Couples (by tract)

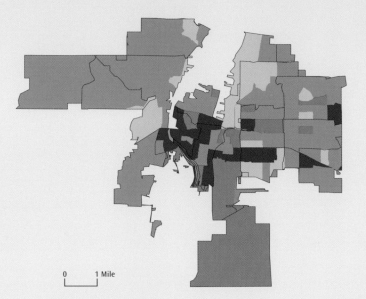

0   1 Mile

Concentration of Lesbian Couples (by tract)

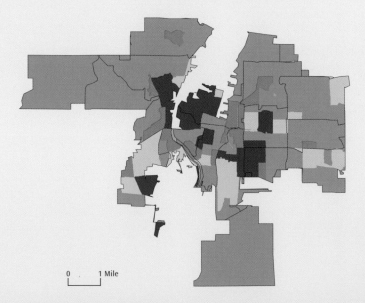

0   1 Mile

MSA Indices

Gay/Lesbian Index	1.40
Gay Male Index	1.11
Lesbian Index	1.70

City Rankings and Indices

	City Index	Rank among top 50 cities	Rank among all communities
Gay/Lesbian	1.40	26	220
Gay Male	1.14	36	391
Lesbian	1.67	11	136

Comparative Statistics

(Albuquerque MSA)

	All	GL couples	GL rank
Presence of children, among households	37%	26%	199
Seniors (55+), among adults	27%	16%	265
Nonwhite, among adults	48%	41%	38
Females, among adults	52%	47%	12

Top ZIP Codes

	1	2	3	4	5
Gay and lesbian	87104	87106	87107	87108	87105
Gay	87104	87106	87102	87105	87108
Lesbian	87107	87104	87106	87108	87121

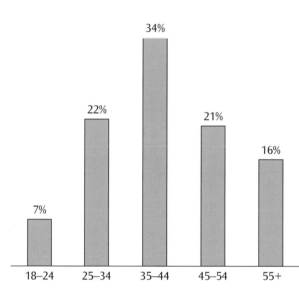

Ages of Same-Sex Unmarried Partners

- 18–24: 7%
- 25–34: 22%
- 35–44: 34%
- 45–54: 21%
- 55+: 16%

Race/Ethnicity of Householder in Same-Sex Unmarried Partner Households

- White 59%
- Hispanic 32%
- Other 7%
- Black 1%

Presence of Children under Age 18 in Same-Sex Unmarried Partner Households

- No children 74%
- Children 26%

ATLANTA, GEORGIA

Concentration of Gay/Lesbian Couples (by tract)

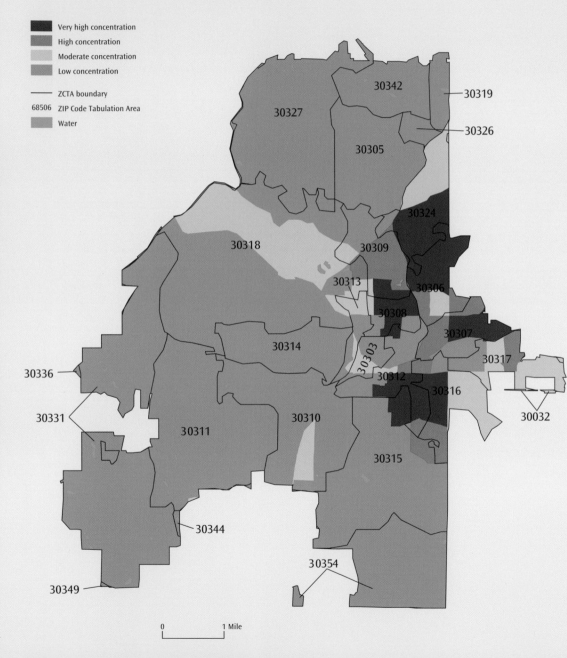

Very high concentration
High concentration
Moderate concentration
Low concentration

— ZCTA boundary
68506 ZIP Code Tabulation Area
Water

30342
30319
30327
30326
30305
30324
30318
30309
30313
30306
30308
30307
30303
30314
30317
30336
30312
30316
30032
30331
30310
30311
30315
30344
30354
30349

0   1 Mile

Concentration of Gay Male Couples (by tract)

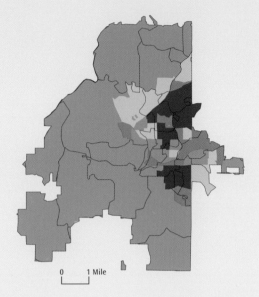

0   1 Mile

Concentration of Lesbian Couples (by tract)

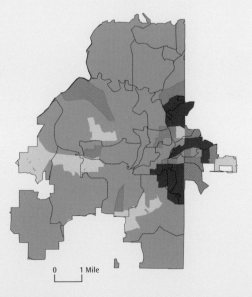

0   1 Mile

MSA Indices

Gay/Lesbian Index	1.40
Gay Male Index	1.56
Lesbian Index	1.24

City Rankings and Indices

	City Index	Rank among top 50 cities	Rank among all communities
Gay/Lesbian	2.99	4	31
Gay Male	4.19	2	20
Lesbian	1.75	10	118

Comparative Statistics

(Atlanta MSA)

	All	GL couples	GL rank
Presence of children, among households	40%	22%	278
Seniors (55+), among adults	20%	10%	325
Nonwhite, among adults	38%	28%	100
Females, among adults	51%	34%	37

Top ZIP Codes

	1	2	3	4	5
Gay and lesbian	30324	30306	30308	30307	30309
Gay	30308	30324	30306	30309	30312
Lesbian	30307	30306	30324	30316	30317

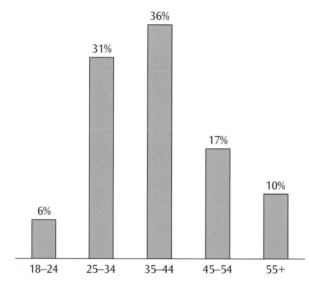

Ages of Same-Sex Unmarried Partners

- 18–24: 6%
- 25–34: 31%
- 35–44: 36%
- 45–54: 17%
- 55+: 10%

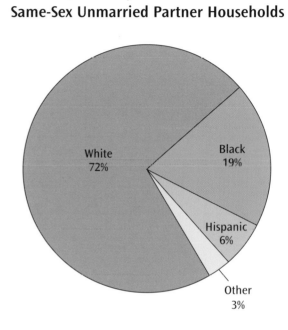

Race/Ethnicity of Householder in Same-Sex Unmarried Partner Households

- White 72%
- Black 19%
- Hispanic 6%
- Other 3%

Presence of Children under Age 18 in Same-Sex Unmarried Partner Households

- No children 78%
- Children 22%

173

AUSTIN, TEXAS

Concentration of Gay/Lesbian Couples (by tract)

Concentration of Gay Male Couples (by tract)

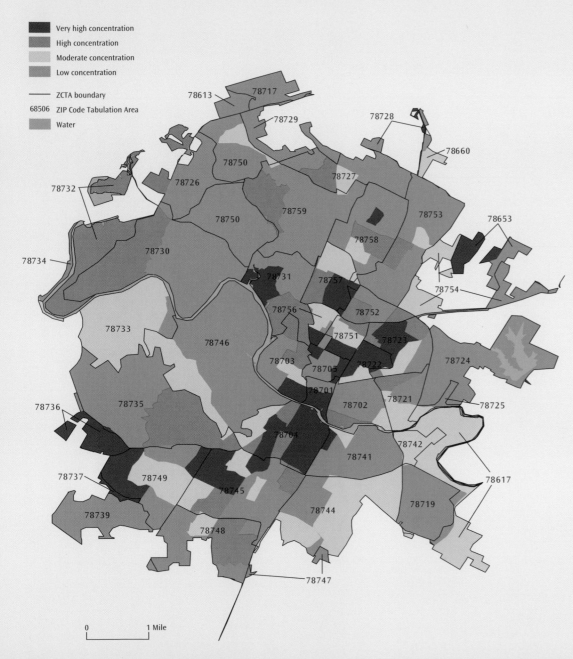

Legend:
- Very high concentration
- High concentration
- Moderate concentration
- Low concentration
- ——— ZCTA boundary
- 68506 ZIP Code Tabulation Area
- Water

78613 78717 78729 78728 78660
78750 78727 78753 78653
78732 78726 78759 78758 78754
78734 78750 78730 78731 78757 78752
78733 78756 78751 78723 78724
78746 78703 78705 78722
78701 78702 78721 78725
78736 78735 78742
78737 78749 78741 78617
78745 78719
78739 78744
78748 78747

0   1 Mile

0   1 Mile

Concentration of Lesbian Couples (by tract)

0   1 Mile

MSA Indices

Gay/Lesbian Index	1.47
Gay Male Index	1.41
Lesbian Index	1.52

City Rankings and Indices

	City Index	Rank among top 50 cities	Rank among all communities
Gay/Lesbian	1.69	14	114
Gay Male	1.72	21	123
Lesbian	1.66	12	138

Comparative Statistics

(Austin-San Marcos MSA)

	All	GL couples	GL rank
Presence of children, among households	36%	21%	279
Seniors (55+), among adults	18%	9%	327
Nonwhite, among adults	36%	29%	97
Females, among adults	49%	42%	20

Top ZIP Codes

	1	2	3	4	5
Gay and lesbian	78722	78723	78704	78757	78751
Gay	78722	78723	78703	78757	78752
Lesbian	78722	78704	78757	78748	78723

Ages of Same-Sex Unmarried Partners

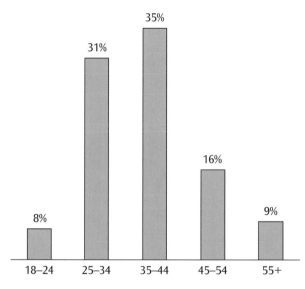

Race/Ethnicity of Householder in Same-Sex Unmarried Partner Households

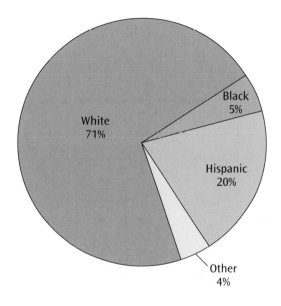

Presence of Children under Age 18 in Same-Sex Unmarried Partner Households

No children 79%

Children 21%

175

BOSTON, MASSACHUSETTS

Concentration of Gay/Lesbian Couples (by tract)

Concentration of Gay Male Couples (by tract)

Concentration of Lesbian Couples (by tract)

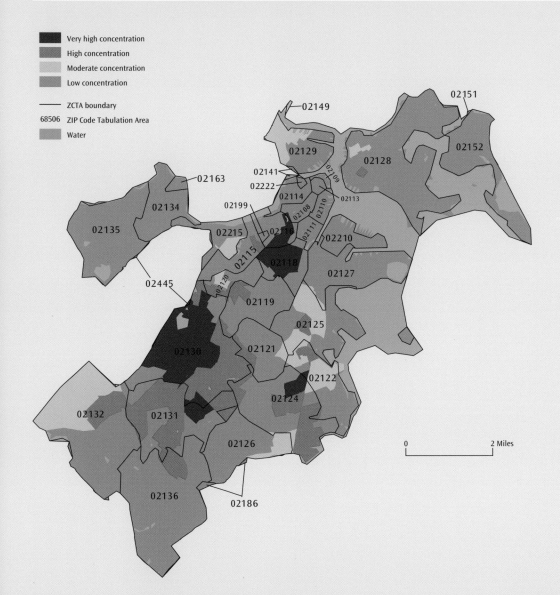

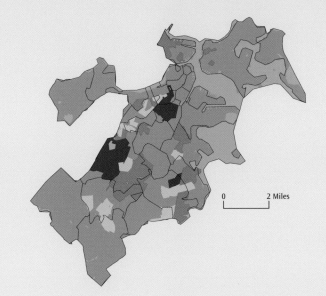

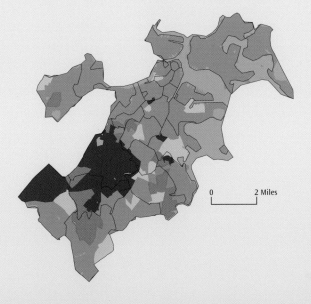

Very high concentration

High concentration

Moderate concentration

Low concentration

ZCTA boundary

68506 ZIP Code Tabulation Area

Water

02149
02151
02129
02128
02152
02141
02109
02163
02222
02114
02113
02134
02199
02108
02110
02135
02215
02116
02111
02210
02115
02127
02118
02445
02120
02119
02130
02125
02121
02132
02131
02122
02124
02126
02136
02186

0   2 Miles

0   2 Miles

0   2 Miles

MSA Indices

Gay/Lesbian Index	1.36
Gay Male Index	1.34
Lesbian Index	1.38

City Rankings and Indices

	City Index	Rank among top 50 cities	Rank among all communities
Gay/Lesbian	2.33	9	48
Gay Male	2.85	6	35
Lesbian	1.78	9	112

Comparative Statistics

(Boston PMSA)

	All	GL couples	GL rank
Presence of children, among households	31%	21%	292
Seniors (55+), among adults	28%	14%	291
Nonwhite, among adults	18%	15%	210
Females, among adults	53%	38%	23

Top ZIP Codes

	1	2	3	4	5
Gay and lesbian	02118	02130	02116	02131	02120
Gay	02118	02116	02130	02120	02122
Lesbian	02130	02131	02120	02132	02124

Ages of Same-Sex Unmarried Partners

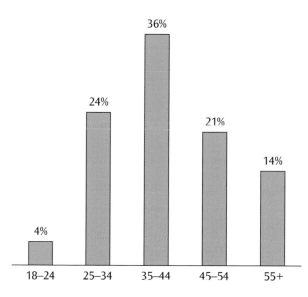

Race/Ethnicity of Householder in Same-Sex Unmarried Partner Households

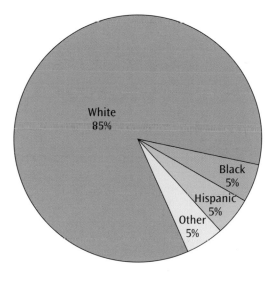

Presence of Children under Age 18 in Same-Sex Unmarried Partner Households

No children 79%   Children 21%

CHICAGO, ILLINOIS

Concentration of Gay/Lesbian Couples (by tract)

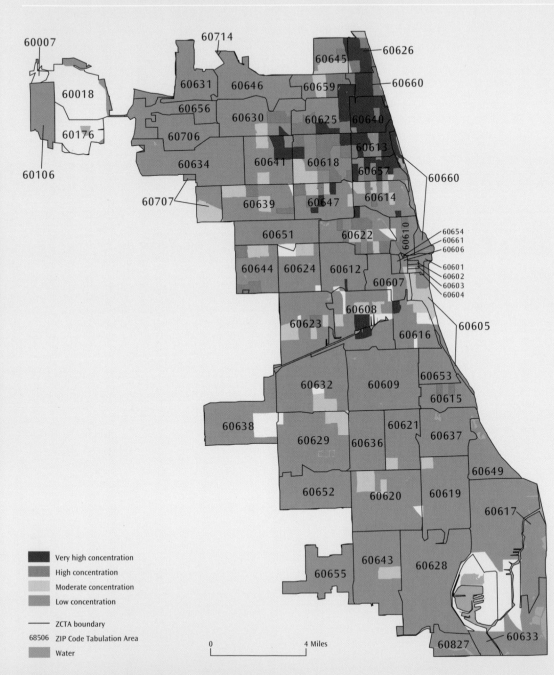

60007
60018
60176
60106
60714
60645
60626
60631
60646
60659
60660
60656
60630
60625
60640
60706
60613
60634
60641
60618
60657
60660
60707
60639
60647
60614
60651
60622
60610
60654
60661
60606
60601
60602
60603
60604
60644
60624
60612
60607
60605
60623
60608
60616
60632
60609
60653
60615
60638
60621
60637
60629
60636
60652
60620
60619
60649
60617
60643
60628
60655
60827
60633

Legend

- **Very high concentration**
- High concentration
- Moderate concentration
- Low concentration

— ZCTA boundary
68506 ZIP Code Tabulation Area
Water

0   4 Miles

Concentration of Gay Male Couples (by tract)

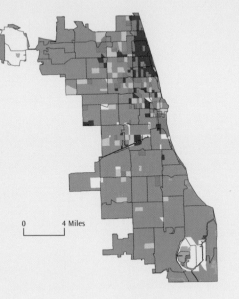

0   4 Miles

Concentration of Lesbian Couples (by tract)

0   4 Miles

MSA Indices

Gay/Lesbian Index	1.03
Gay Male Index	1.12
Lesbian Index	0.94

City Rankings and Indices

	City Index	Rank among top 50 cities	Rank among all communities
Gay/Lesbian	1.57	18	146
Gay Male	1.86	17	96
Lesbian	1.28	26	356

Comparative Statistics

(Chicago PMSA)

	All	GL couples	GL rank
Presence of children, among households	38%	29%	149
Seniors (55+), among adults	26%	17%	248
Nonwhite, among adults	38%	38%	50
Females, among adults	52%	26%	133

Top ZIP Codes

	1	2	3	4	5
Gay and lesbian	60640	60660	60613	60657	60626
Gay	60640	60613	60660	60657	60626
Lesbian	60640	60660	60659	60618	60626

Gay/Lesbian Index Rank: 76

Gay Male Index Rank: 45   Lesbian Index Rank: 133

Ages of Same-Sex Unmarried Partners

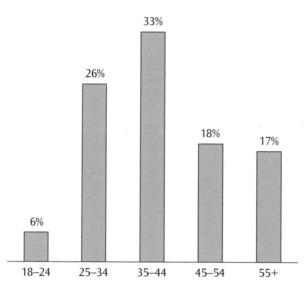

Race/Ethnicity of Householder in Same-Sex Unmarried Partner Households

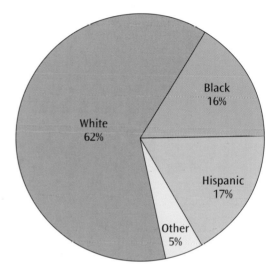

Presence of Children under Age 18 in Same-Sex Unmarried Partner Households

179

COLUMBUS, OHIO

Concentration of Gay/Lesbian Couples (by tract)

43035
43065
43035
43240
43082
43016
43081
43235
43085
43229
43054
43017
43231
43220
43214
43221
43224
43202
43026
43230
43221
43211
43210
43004
43212
43219
43228
43201
43215
43203
43209
43213
43204
43222
43205
43119
43206
43227
43068
43223
43232
43147
43109
43110
43123
43207
43125
43137
43137
43217

Very high concentration
High concentration
Moderate concentration
Low concentration
ZCTA boundary
68506 ZIP Code Tabulation Area
Water

0   4 Miles

Concentration of Gay Male Couples (by tract)

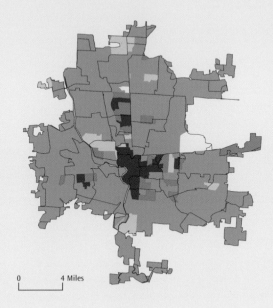

0   4 Miles

Concentration of Lesbian Couples (by tract)

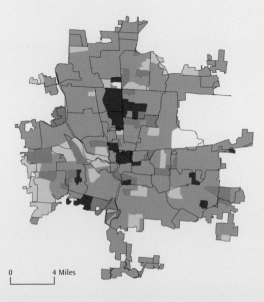

0   4 Miles

MSA Indices

Gay/Lesbian Index	1.16
Gay Male Index	1.18
Lesbian Index	1.14

City Rankings and Indices

	City Index	Rank among top 50 cities	Rank among all communities
Gay/Lesbian	1.52	21	159
Gay Male	1.64	23	137
Lesbian	1.41	17	242

Comparative Statistics

(Columbus MSA)

	All	GL couples	GL rank
Presence of children, among households	35%	20%	304
Seniors (55+), among adults	24%	12%	316
Nonwhite, among adults	18%	15%	218
Females, among adults	52%	32%	62

Top ZIP Codes

	1	2	3	4	5
Gay and lesbian	43215	43205	43202	43206	43201
Gay	43215	43205	43206	43201	43203
Lesbian	43202	43214	43215	43201	43211

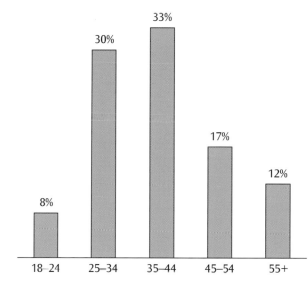

Ages of Same-Sex Unmarried Partners

- 18–24: 8%
- 25–34: 30%
- 35–44: 33%
- 45–54: 17%
- 55+: 12%

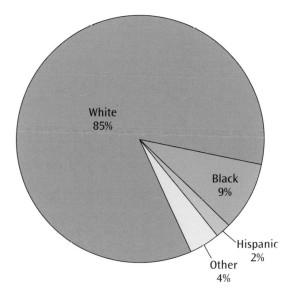

Race/Ethnicity of Householder in Same-Sex Unmarried Partner Households

- White 85%
- Black 9%
- Hispanic 2%
- Other 4%

Presence of Children under Age 18 in Same-Sex Unmarried Partner Households

- No children 80%
- Children 20%

DALLAS, TEXAS

Concentration of Gay/Lesbian Couples (by tract)

Very high concentration
High concentration
Moderate concentration
Low concentration

ZCTA boundary
68506 ZIP Code Tabulation Area
Water

Concentration of Gay Male Couples (by tract)

Concentration of Lesbian Couples (by tract)

75287
75252
75080
75248
75240
75081
75019
75006
75063
75234
75244
75251
75243
75229
75230
75041
75220
75231
75238
75039
75225
75209
75218
75205
75235
75214
75228
75061
75206
75219
75247
75204
75224
75060
75207
75223
75149
75212
75226
75227
75202
75210
75208
75203
75215
75211
75217
75051
75224
75052
75233
75236
75237
75216
75241
75253
75249
75232
75159
75141
75115
75134
75173
75098
75087
75088
75043
75182
75126

0   6 Miles

182

MSA Indices

Gay/Lesbian Index	1.29
Gay Male Index	1.48
Lesbian Index	1.10

City Rankings and Indices

	City Index	Rank among top 50 cities	Rank among all communities
Gay/Lesbian	1.96	12	78
Gay Male	2.54	9	45
Lesbian	1.36	19	279

Comparative Statistics

(Dallas PMSA)

	All	GL couples	GL rank
Presence of children, among households	40%	25%	224
Seniors (55+), among adults	21%	11%	320
Nonwhite, among adults	40%	34%	68
Females, among adults	51%	31%	84

Top ZIP Codes

	1	2	3	4	5
Gay and lesbian	75219	75208	75235	75209	75229
Gay	75219	75208	75235	75209	75204
Lesbian	75208	75218	75229	75233	75220

Ages of Same-Sex Unmarried Partners

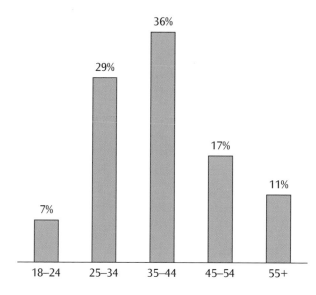

Race/Ethnicity of Householder in Same-Sex Unmarried Partner Households

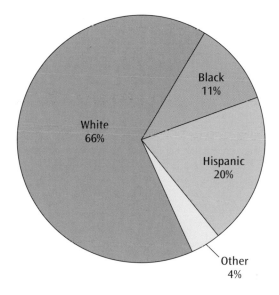

Presence of Children under Age 18 in Same-Sex Unmarried Partner Households

No children 75%   Children 25%

DENVER, COLORADO

Concentration of Gay/Lesbian Couples (by tract)

Very high concentration
High concentration
Moderate concentration
Low concentration

ZCTA boundary
68506 ZIP Code Tabulation Area
Water

80249

80221
80212
80211
80216
80205
80207
80202
80204
80203
80218
80220
80206
80230
80209
80246
80224
80012
80219
80223
80210
80231
80232
80222
80014
80227
80236
80237
80235
80110
80123

0   5 Miles

Concentration of Gay Male Couples (by tract)

0   5 Miles

Concentration of Lesbian Couples (by tract)

0   5 Miles

MSA Indices

Gay/Lesbian Index	1.29
Gay Male Index	1.28
Lesbian Index	1.30

City Rankings and Indices

	City Index	Rank among top 50 cities	Rank among all communities
Gay/Lesbian	2.16	10	59
Gay Male	2.49	10	50
Lesbian	1.83	8	99

Comparative Statistics

(Denver PMSA)

	All	GL couples	GL rank
Presence of children, among households	35%	19%	307
Seniors (55+), among adults	23%	11%	323
Nonwhite, among adults	26%	23%	141
Females, among adults	50%	36%	31

Top ZIP Codes

	1	2	3	4	5
Gay and lesbian	80218	80206	80220	80223	80211
Gay	80218	80206	80203	80220	80223
Lesbian	80212	80206	80211	80220	80210

Ages of Same-Sex Unmarried Partners

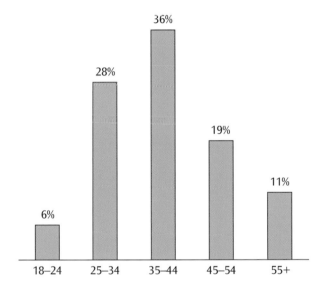

Race/Ethnicity of Householder in Same-Sex Unmarried Partner Households

White 77%
Black 4%
Hispanic 15%
Other 4%

Presence of Children under Age 18 in Same-Sex Unmarried Partner Households

No children 81%   Children 19%

HOUSTON, TEXAS

Concentration of Gay/Lesbian Couples (by tract)

Concentration of Gay Male Couples (by tract)

Concentration of Lesbian Couples (by tract)

Very high concentration
High concentration
Moderate concentration
Low concentration

ZCTA boundary
68506 ZIP Code Tabulation Area
Water

0   10 Miles

MSA Indices

Gay/Lesbian Index	1.19
Gay Male Index	1.22
Lesbian Index	1.15

City Rankings and Indices

	City Index	Rank among top 50 cities	Rank among all communities
Gay/Lesbian	1.50	23	166
Gay Male	1.69	22	126
Lesbian	1.31	22	323

Comparative Statistics

(Houston PMSA)

	All	GL couples	GL rank
Presence of children, among households	43%	33%	90
Seniors (55+), among adults	21%	13%	309
Nonwhite, among adults	51%	45%	29
Females, among adults	51%	32%	61

Top ZIP Codes

	1	2	3	4	5
Gay and lesbian	77006	77019	77008	77098	77018
Gay	77006	77019	77098	77008	77007
Lesbian	77006	77018	77008	77013	77019

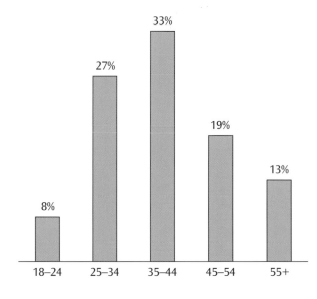

Ages of Same-Sex Unmarried Partners

18–24: 8%
25–34: 27%
35–44: 33%
45–54: 19%
55+: 13%

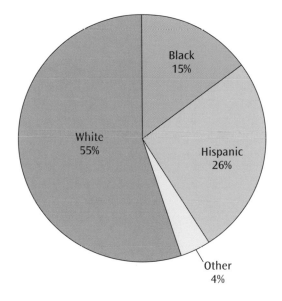

Race/Ethnicity of Householder in Same-Sex Unmarried Partner Households

White 55%
Black 15%
Hispanic 26%
Other 4%

Presence of Children under Age 18 in Same-Sex Unmarried Partner Households

No children 67%
Children 33%

KANSAS CITY, KANSAS/MISSOURI

Concentration of Gay/Lesbian Couples (by tract)

64163
64165
64164
64166
64167
64079
64153
64154
64156
64157
64155
64152
64151
64118
64119
64158
66109
64105
64116
64117
64161
66104
66115
64120
66101
66112
66102
64123
64053
66106
64124
64125
64106
66012
66111
66105
64127
64126
64108
64103
64109
64128
64111
64129
64112
64130
64113
64131
64110
64136
64114
64132
64133
64137
64138
64139
64134
64145
64146
64147
64149
64012

Legend:
- Very high concentration
- High concentration
- Moderate concentration
- Low concentration
- ZCTA boundary
- 68506 ZIP Code Tabulation Area
- Water

0 — 1 Mile

Concentration of Gay Male Couples (by tract)

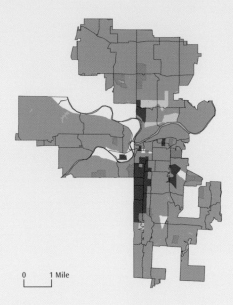

0 — 1 Mile

Concentration of Lesbian Couples (by tract)

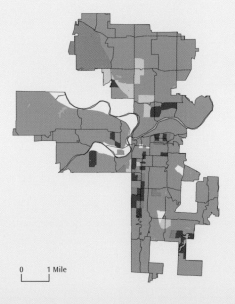

0 — 1 Mile

188

MSA Indices

Gay/Lesbian Index	0.88
Gay Male Index	0.89
Lesbian Index	0.88

City Rankings and Indices

	City Index	Rank among top 50 cities	Rank among all communities
(Kansas City, Missouri)			
Gay/Lesbian	1.45	25	193
Gay Male	1.62	24	139
Lesbian	1.27	27	360
(Kansas City, Kansas)			
Gay/Lesbian	0.89	NA	871
Gay Male	0.86	NA	788
Lesbian	0.91	NA	913

Comparative Statistics

(Kansas City MSA)

	All	GL couples	GL rank
Presence of children, among households	36%	23%	256
Seniors (55+), among adults	27%	15%	270
Nonwhite, among adults	20%	19%	170
Females, among adults	52%	24%	169

Top ZIP Codes

	1	2	3	4	5
Gay and lesbian	64110	64113	64109	64111	64112
Gay	64113	64110	64111	64109	64112
Lesbian	64110	64109	64113	64111	64114

NA = not applicable

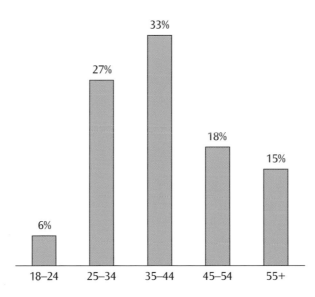

Ages of Same-Sex Unmarried Partners

18–24: 6%
25–34: 27%
35–44: 33%
45–54: 18%
55+: 15%

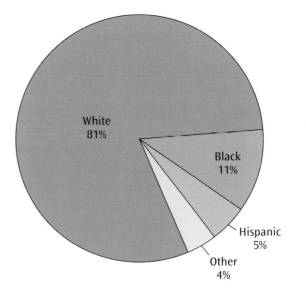

Race/Ethnicity of Householder in Same-Sex Unmarried Partner Households

White 81%
Black 11%
Hispanic 5%
Other 4%

Presence of Children under Age 18 in Same-Sex Unmarried Partner Households

No children 77%
Children 23%

LOS ANGELES, CALIFORNIA

Concentration of Gay/Lesbian Couples (by tract)

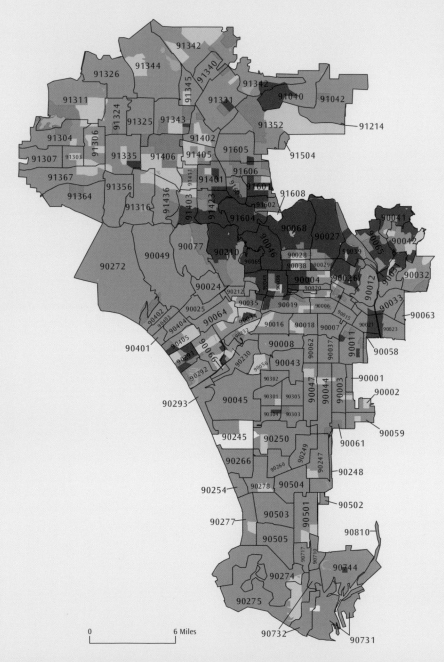

Legend:
- Very high concentration
- High concentration
- Moderate concentration
- Low concentration
- —— ZCTA boundary
- 68506 ZIP Code Tabulation Area
- Water

0 _____ 6 Miles

Concentration of Gay Male Couples (by tract)

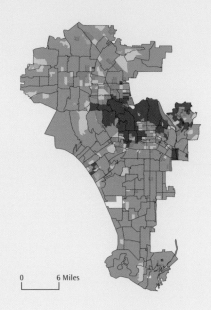

0 ___ 6 Miles

Concentration of Lesbian Couples (by tract)

0 ___ 6 Miles

MSA Indices

Gay/Lesbian Index	1.43
Gay Male Index	1.62
Lesbian Index	1.23

City Rankings and Indices

	City Index	Rank among top 50 cities	Rank among all communities
(Los Angeles)			
Gay/Lesbian	1.68	15	117
Gay Male	2.04	13	73
Lesbian	1.30	23	328
(West Hollywood)			
Gay/Lesbian	7.38	NA	4
Gay Male	12.82	NA	4
Lesbian	1.79	NA	111

Comparative Statistics

(Los Angeles-Long Beach PMSA)

	All	GL couples	GL rank
Presence of children, among households	41%	28%	152
Seniors (55+), among adults	24%	15%	283
Nonwhite, among adults	65%	48%	20
Females, among adults	51%	34%	38

Top ZIP Codes

	1	2	3	4	5
Gay and lesbian	90069	90068	90046	90039	90026
Gay	90069	90068	90046	90039	90027
Lesbian	90065	90039	90069	90291	91401

NA = not applicable

Ages of Same-Sex Unmarried Partners

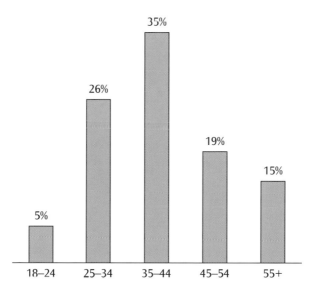

Race/Ethnicity of Householder in Same-Sex Unmarried Partner Households

Presence of Children under Age 18 in Same-Sex Unmarried Partner Households

No children 72%   Children 28%

MIAMI-FT. LAUDERDALE, FLORIDA

Concentration of Gay/Lesbian Couples
(by tract)

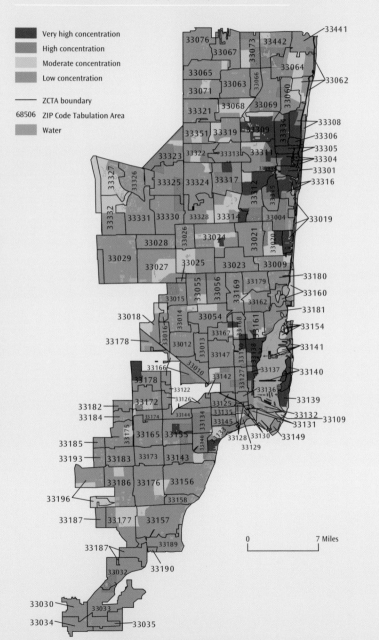

Very high concentration
High concentration
Moderate concentration
Low concentration

—— ZCTA boundary

68506 ZIP Code Tabulation Area

Water

Concentration of Gay Male Couples
(by tract)

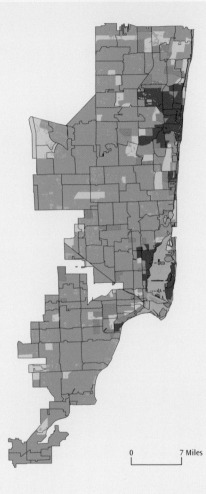

0   7 Miles

Concentration of Lesbian Couples
(by tract)

0   7 Miles

0   7 Miles

MSA Indices

Gay/Lesbian Index	1.47
Gay Male Index	1.77
Lesbian Index	1.16

City Rankings and Indices

	City Index	Rank among top 50 cities	Rank among all communities
(Miami)			
Gay/Lesbian	1.54	20	155
Gay Male	1.90	16	89
Lesbian	1.18	31	477
(Ft. Lauderdale)			
Gay/Lesbian	3.68	NA	23
Gay Male	5.89	NA	14
Lesbian	1.40	NA	247

Comparative Statistics

(Miami-Ft. Lauderdale CMSA)

	All	GL couples	GL rank
Presence of children, among households	36%	23%	263
Seniors (55+), among adults	31%	21%	136
Nonwhite, among adults	62%	47%	22
Females, among adults	53%	39%	23

Top ZIP Codes

	1	2	3	4	5
Gay and lesbian	33305	33304	33301	33138	33334
Gay	33305	33304	33301	33138	33139
Lesbian	33305	33138	33309	33304	33127

NA = not applicable

Ages of Same-Sex Unmarried Partners

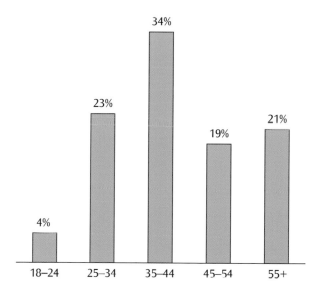

Race/Ethnicity of Householder in Same-Sex Unmarried Partner Households

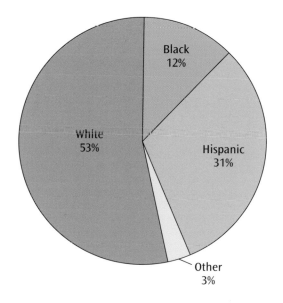

Presence of Children under Age 18 in Same-Sex Unmarried Partner Households

No children 77%

Children 23%

MINNEAPOLIS-ST. PAUL, MINNESOTA

Concentration of Gay/Lesbian Couples (by tract)

Very high concentration
High concentration
Moderate concentration
Low concentration

ZCTA boundary
68506   ZIP Code Tabulation Area
Water

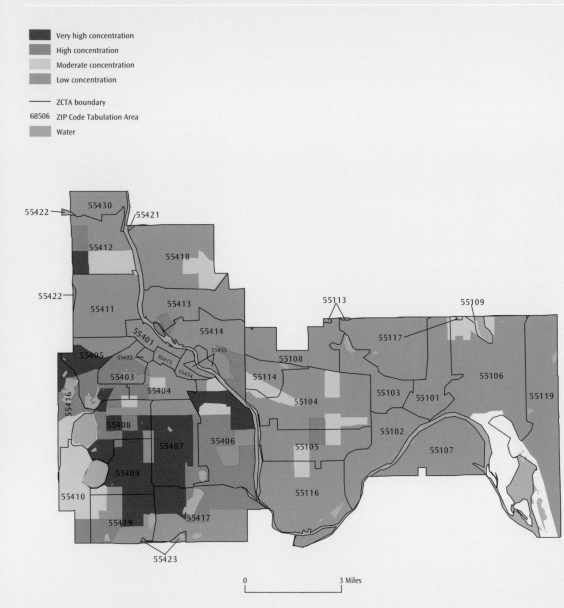

55430
55422
55421
55412
55418
55422
55411
55413
55401
55414
55405
55402
55415
55455
55454
55403
55404
55416
55408
55406
55407
55409
55410
55419
55417
55423
55113
55117
55109
55108
55114
55104
55103
55101
55106
55119
55102
55105
55107
55116

0   3 Miles

Concentration of Gay Male Couples (by tract)

0   3 Miles

Concentration of Lesbian Couples (by tract)

0   3 Miles

MSA Indices

Gay/Lesbian Index	1.08
Gay Male Index	1.00
Lesbian Index	1.16

City Rankings and Indices

	City Index	Rank among top 50 cities	Rank among all communities
(Minneapolis)			
Gay/Lesbian	2.87	5	33
Gay Male	3.09	5	32
Lesbian	2.63	4	37
(St. Paul)			
Gay/Lesbian	1.45	NA	192
Gay Male	1.11	NA	423
Lesbian	1.80	NA	107

Comparative Statistics

(Minneapolis-St. Paul MSA)

	All	GL couples	GL rank
Presence of children, among households	36%	16%	319
Seniors (55+), among adults	23%	11%	321
Nonwhite, among adults	13%	11%	252
Females, among adults	51%	32%	58

Top ZIP Codes

	1	2	3	4	5
Gay and lesbian	55409	55407	55405	55408	55406
Gay	55405	55409	55403	55407	55408
Lesbian	55407	55409	55406	55417	55105

NA = not applicable

Ages of Same-Sex Unmarried Partners

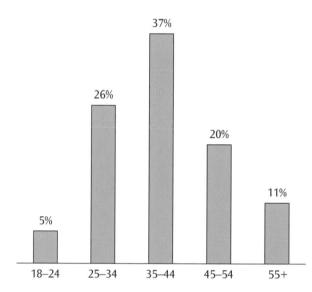

Race/Ethnicity of Householder in Same-Sex Unmarried Partner Households

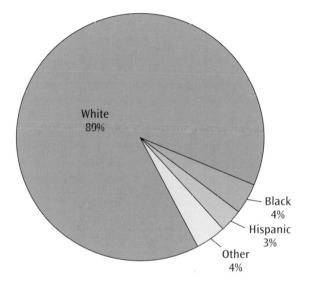

Presence of Children under Age 18 in Same-Sex Unmarried Partner Households

No children 84%   Children 16%

NASHVILLE, TENNESSEE

Concentration of Gay/Lesbian Couples (by tract)

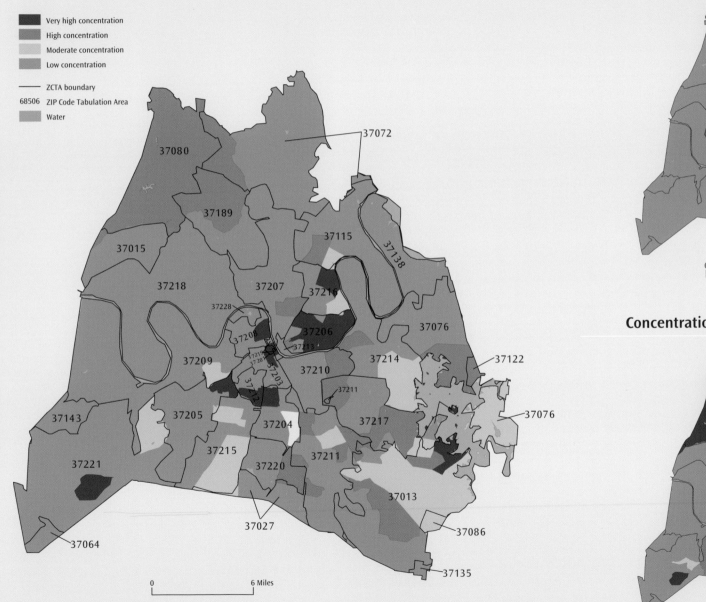

Very high concentration
High concentration
Moderate concentration
Low concentration

ZCTA boundary
68506 ZIP Code Tabulation Area
Water

37080
37072
37189
37015
37115
37138
37218
37207
37216
37228
37206
37076
37209
37213
37208
37214
37122
37210
37211
37076
37205
37204
37217
37143
37212
37203
37221
37215
37211
37220
37013
37027
37086
37064
37135

0   6 Miles

Concentration of Gay Male Couples (by tract)

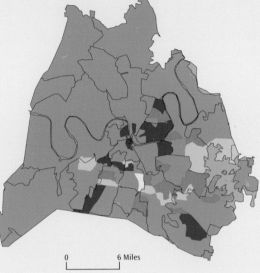

0   6 Miles

Concentration of Lesbian Couples (by tract)

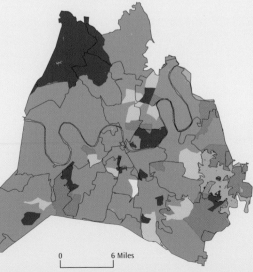

0   6 Miles

196

MSA Indices

Gay/Lesbian Index	0.99
Gay Male Index	1.04
Lesbian Index	0.95

City Rankings and Indices

	City Index	Rank among top 50 cities	Rank among all communities
Gay/Lesbian	1.25	31	323
Gay Male	1.40	27	214
Lesbian	1.11	33	582

Comparative Statistics

(Nashville MSA)

	All	GL couples	GL rank
Presence of children, among households	36%	26%	217
Seniors (55+), among adults	24%	14%	296
Nonwhite, among adults	20%	18%	184
Females, among adults	52%	26%	130

Top ZIP Codes

	1	2	3	4	5
Gay and lesbian	37206	37212	37217	37013	37216
Gay	37206	37212	37217	37216	37013
Lesbian	37206	37013	37212	37207	37072

Ages of Same-Sex Unmarried Partners

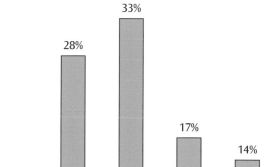

- 18–24: 8%
- 25–34: 28%
- 35–44: 33%
- 45–54: 17%
- 55+: 14%

Race/Ethnicity of Householder in Same-Sex Unmarried Partner Households

- White 82%
- Black 11%
- Hispanic 4%
- Other 3%

Presence of Children under Age 18 in Same-Sex Unmarried Partner Households

- No children 74%
- Children 26%

NEW ORLEANS, LOUISIANA

Concentration of Gay/Lesbian Couples (by tract)

Concentration of Gay Male Couples (by tract)

Concentration of Lesbian Couples (by tract)

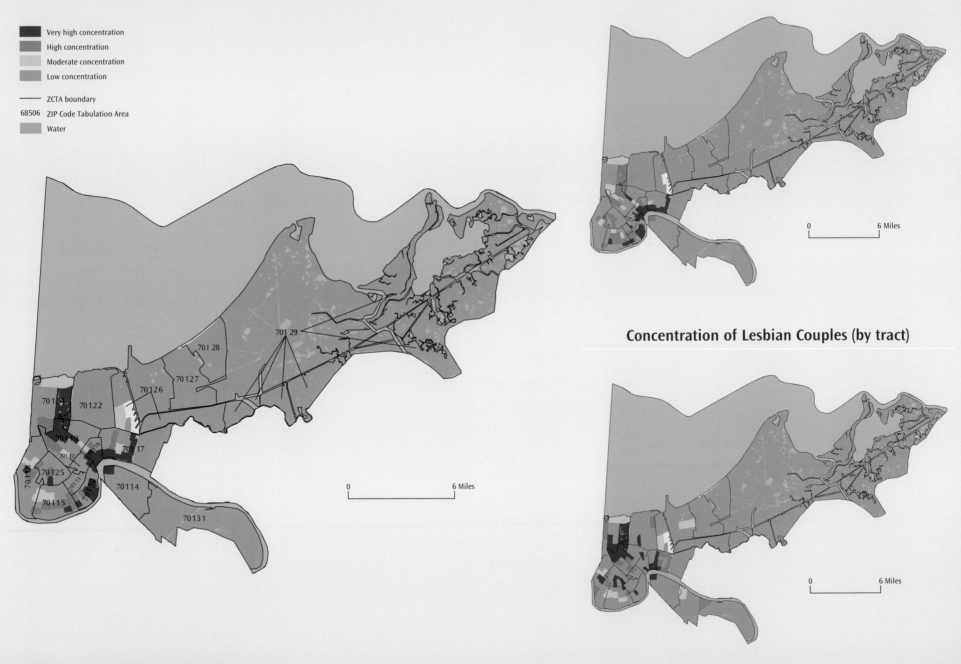

Very high concentration
High concentration
Moderate concentration
Low concentration

——— ZCTA boundary
68506 ZIP Code Tabulation Area
Water

701 29
701 28
70127
70126
701
70122
70119
701 12
70116
701 17
70110
70125
70113
70118
70114
70115
70131

0   6 Miles

0   6 Miles

0   6 Miles

MSA Indices

Gay/Lesbian Index	1.23
Gay Male Index	1.25
Lesbian Index	1.21

City Rankings and Indices

	City Index	Rank among top 50 cities	Rank among all communities
Gay/Lesbian	1.67	16	121
Gay Male	1.99	14	77
Lesbian	1.34	21	304

Comparative Statistics

(New Orleans MSA)

	All	GL couples	GL rank
Presence of children, among households	38%	27%	188
Seniors (55+), among adults	27%	19%	183
Nonwhite, among adults	42%	34%	72
Females, among adults	53%	34%	44

Top ZIP Codes

	1	2	3	4	5
Gay and lesbian	70116	70130	70117	70115	70119
Gay	70116	70130	70117	70115	70119
Lesbian	70119	70117	70125	70124	70115

Ages of Same-Sex Unmarried Partners

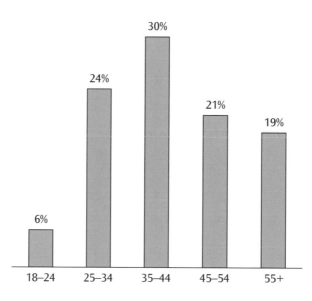

- 18–24: 6%
- 25–34: 24%
- 35–44: 30%
- 45–54: 21%
- 55+: 19%

Race/Ethnicity of Householder in Same-Sex Unmarried Partner Households

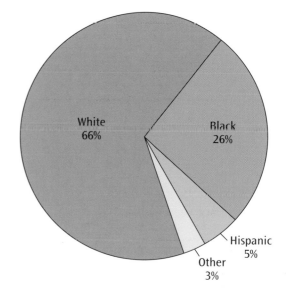

- White 66%
- Black 26%
- Hispanic 5%
- Other 3%

Presence of Children under Age 18 in Same-Sex Unmarried Partner Households

- No children 73%
- Children 27%

NEW YORK CITY, NEW YORK

Concentration of Gay/Lesbian Couples (by tract)

Concentration of Gay Male Couples (by tract)

Concentration of Lesbian Couples (by tract)

Very high concentration
High concentration
Moderate concentration
Low concentration

ZCTA boundary
68506   ZIP Code Tabulation Area
Water

0   2 Miles

MSA Indices

Gay/Lesbian Index	1.47
Gay Male Index	1.65
Lesbian Index	1.28

City Rankings and Indices

	City Index	Rank among top 50 cities	Rank among all communities
Gay/Lesbian	1.52	22	161
Gay Male	1.74	20	121
Lesbian	1.30	24	336

Comparative Statistics

(New York PMSA)

	All	GL couples	GL rank
Presence of children, among households	34%	27%	179
Seniors (55+), among adults	27%	18%	209
Nonwhite, among adults	57%	45%	28
Females, among adults	54%	36%	35

Top ZIP Codes

	1	2	3	4	5
Gay and lesbian	10011	10014	10036	11215	11217
Gay	10011	10014	10036	10001	10003
Lesbian	11215	10014	11217	10011	11238

Ages of Same-Sex Unmarried Partners

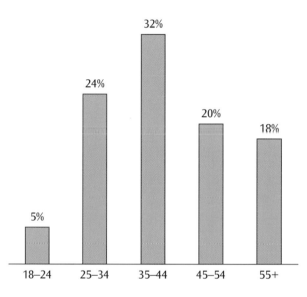

Race/Ethnicity of Householder in Same-Sex Unmarried Partner Households

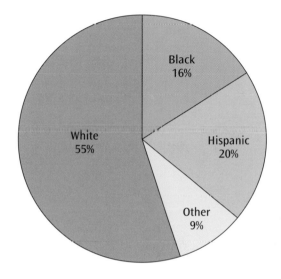

Presence of Children under Age 18 in Same-Sex Unmarried Partner Households

No children 73%   Children 27%

OAKLAND, CALIFORNIA

Concentration of Gay/Lesbian Couples (by tract)

Concentration of Gay Male Couples (by tract)

Concentration of Lesbian Couples (by tract)

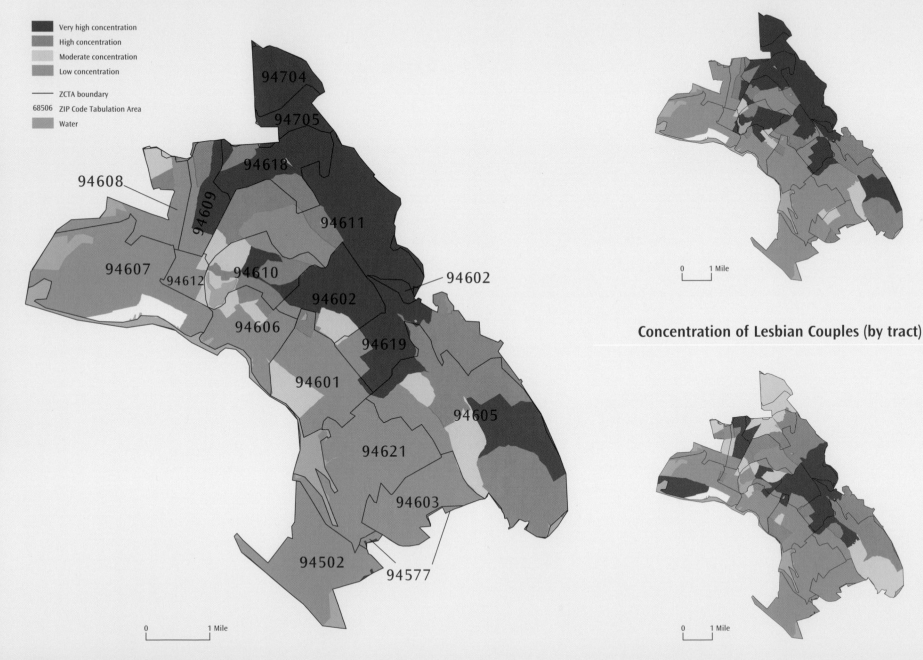

Legend:
- Very high concentration
- High concentration
- Moderate concentration
- Low concentration
- ZCTA boundary
- 68506 ZIP Code Tabulation Area
- Water

94704
94705
94618
94608
94609
94611
94607
94612
94610
94602
94602
94606
94619
94601
94605
94621
94603
94502
94577

0   1 Mile

0   1 Mile

0   1 Mile

MSA Indices

Gay/Lesbian Index	1.76
Gay Male Index	1.58
Lesbian Index	1.94

City Rankings and Indices

	City Index	Rank among top 50 cities	Rank among all communities
Gay/Lesbian	3.12	3	28
Gay Male	2.63	8	41
Lesbian	3.62	1	14

Comparative Statistics

(Oakland PMSA)

	All	GL couples	GL rank
Presence of children, among households	37%	22%	270
Seniors (55+), among adults	25%	14%	290
Nonwhite, among adults	49%	34%	66
Females, among adults	52%	54%	5

Top ZIP Codes

	1	2	3	4	5
Gay and lesbian	94619	94602	94618	94609	94610
Gay	94618	94610	94619	94611	94602
Lesbian	94602	94619	94609	94618	94611

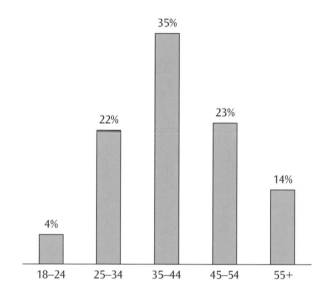

Ages of Same-Sex Unmarried Partners

- 18–24: 4%
- 25–34: 22%
- 35–44: 35%
- 45–54: 23%
- 55+: 14%

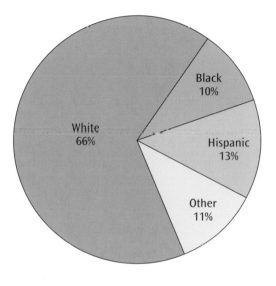

Race/Ethnicity of Householder in Same-Sex Unmarried Partner Households

- White 66%
- Black 10%
- Hispanic 13%
- Other 11%

Presence of Children under Age 18 in Same-Sex Unmarried Partner Households

- No children 78%
- Children 22%

ORLANDO, FLORIDA

Concentration of Gay/Lesbian Couples (by tract)

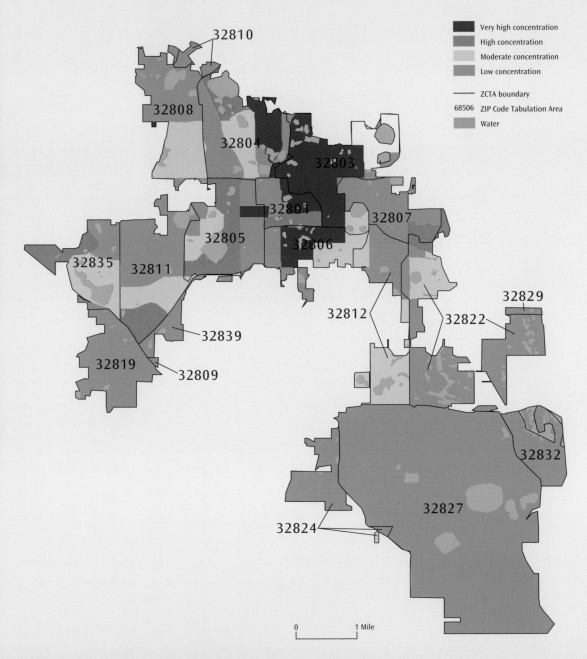

Very high concentration
High concentration
Moderate concentration
Low concentration

ZCTA boundary
68506 ZIP Code Tabulation Area
Water

32810
32808
32804
32803
32801
32805
32807
32806
32835
32811
32812
32822
32829
32839
32819
32809
32824
32827
32832

0   1 Mile

Concentration of Gay Male Couples (by tract)

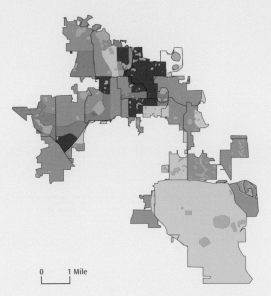

0   1 Mile

Concentration of Lesbian Couples (by tract)

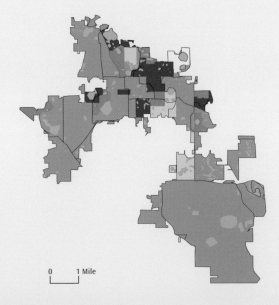

0   1 Mile

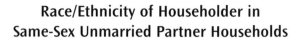

MSA Indices

Gay/Lesbian Index	1.28
Gay Male Index	1.44
Lesbian Index	1.11

City Rankings and Indices

	City Index	Rank among top 50 cities	Rank among all communities
Gay/Lesbian	2.11	NA	61
Gay Male	2.70	NA	39
Lesbian	1.49	NA	195

Comparative Statistics

(Orlando MSA)

	All	GL couples	GL rank
Presence of children, among households	35%	23%	259
Seniors (55+), among adults	28%	15%	274
Nonwhite, among adults	32%	28%	105
Females, among adults	51%	31%	79

Top ZIP Codes

	1	2	3	4	5
Gay and lesbian	32803	32801	32806	32804	32805
Gay	32803	32801	32806	32804	32835
Lesbian	32803	32805	32804	32807	32806

NA = not applicable

Gay Male Index Rank: 15   Lesbian Index Rank: 79

Ages of Same-Sex Unmarried Partners

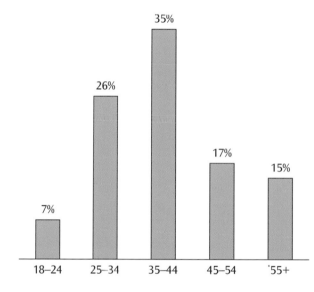

Race/Ethnicity of Householder in Same-Sex Unmarried Partner Households

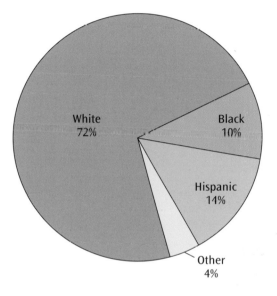

Presence of Children under Age 18 in Same-Sex Unmarried Partner Households

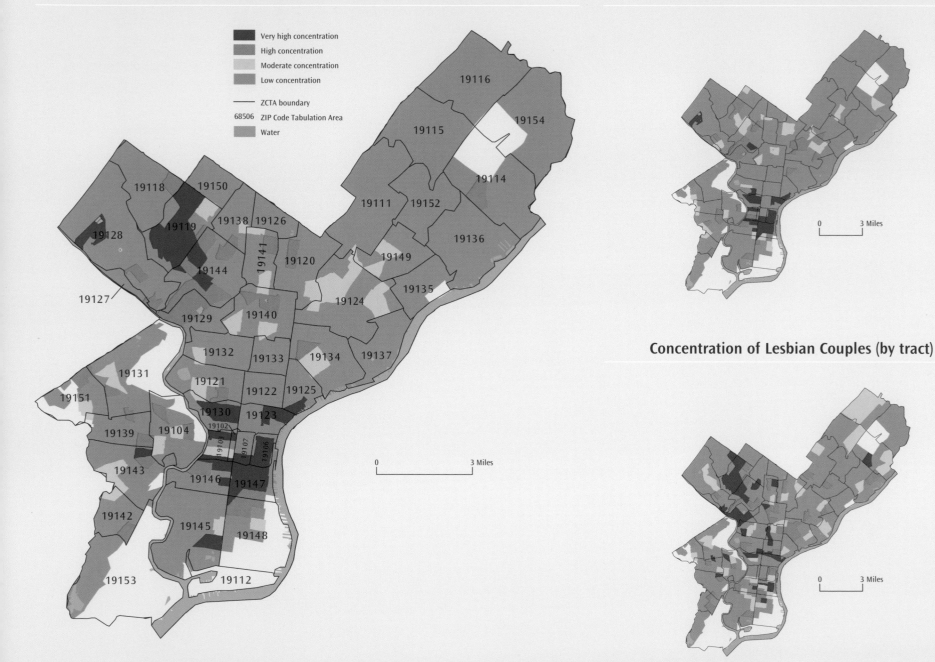

PHILADELPHIA, PENNSYLVANIA

Concentration of Gay/Lesbian Couples (by tract)

Very high concentration
High concentration
Moderate concentration
Low concentration

ZCTA boundary
68506 ZIP Code Tabulation Area
Water

19116
19154
19115
19114
19118
19150
19111 19152
19138 19126
19136
19128
19119
19141
19120
19149
19144
19124
19135
19127
19129
19140
19132 19133 19134 19137
19131
19121
19151
19122 19125
19130 19123
19102
19104
19139
19103 19107 19106
19143
19146 19147
19142
19145
19148
19153
19112

0   3 Miles

Concentration of Gay Male Couples (by tract)

0   3 Miles

Concentration of Lesbian Couples (by tract)

0   3 Miles

MSA Indices

Gay/Lesbian Index	0.99
Gay Male Index	0.99
Lesbian Index	0.98

City Rankings and Indices

	City Index	Rank among top 50 cities	Rank among all communities
Gay/Lesbian	1.30	29	290
Gay Male	1.36	29	233
Lesbian	1.23	29	412

Comparative Statistics

(Philadelphia PMSA)

	All	GL couples	GL rank
Presence of children, among households	35%	26%	208
Seniors (55+), among adults	30%	20%	161
Nonwhite, among adults	27%	29%	99
Females, among adults	53%	27%	119

Top ZIP Codes

	1	2	3	4	5
Gay and lesbian	19147	19107	19106	19119	19130
Gay	19147	19107	19106	19130	19103
Lesbian	19119	19129	19147	19144	19146

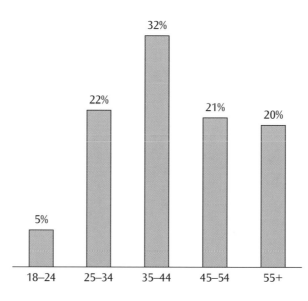

Ages of Same-Sex Unmarried Partners

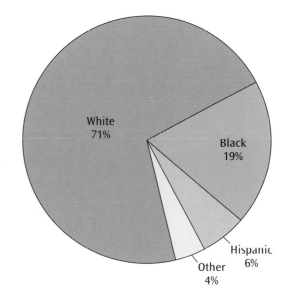

Race/Ethnicity of Householder in Same-Sex Unmarried Partner Households

Presence of Children under Age 18 in Same-Sex Unmarried Partner Households

No children 74%   Children 26%

PHOENIX, ARIZONA

Concentration of Gay/Lesbian Couples (by tract)

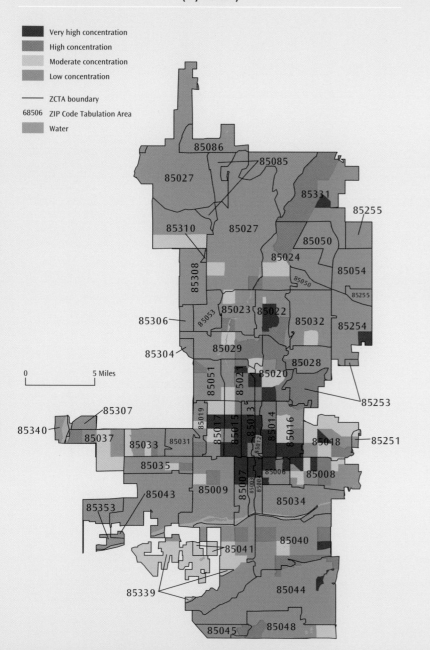

Very high concentration
High concentration
Moderate concentration
Low concentration

—— ZCTA boundary
68506 ZIP Code Tabulation Area
Water

0   5 Miles

85086
85085
85027
85331
85255
85310
85027
85050
85308
85024
85054
85053
85050
85255
85306
85023 85022
85032
85254
85304
85029
85028
85051 85021 85020
85253
85019
85307
85017 85015 85013 85014 85016
85340 85037 85031
85033 85012 85048 85251
85035
85007 85006 85008
85043 85009
85034
85353
85339 85041
85040
85044
85045 85048

Concentration of Gay Male Couples (by tract)

0   5 Miles

Concentration of Lesbian Couples (by tract)

0   5 Miles

208

MSA Indices

Gay/Lesbian Index	1.19
Gay Male Index	1.26
Lesbian Index	1.13

City Rankings and Indices

	City Index	Rank among top 50 cities	Rank among all communities
Gay/Lesbian	1.59	17	138
Gay Male	1.78	18	106
Lesbian	1.40	18	248

Comparative Statistics

(Phoenix-Mesa MSA)

	All	GL couples	GL rank
Presence of children, among households	36%	28%	160
Seniors (55+), among adults	27%	15%	280
Nonwhite, among adults	29%	29%	95
Females, among adults	50%	31%	71

Top ZIP Codes

	1	2	3	4	5
Gay and lesbian	85003	85013	85006	85007	85014
Gay	85003	85013	85006	85007	85014
Lesbian	85006	85013	85015	85017	85007

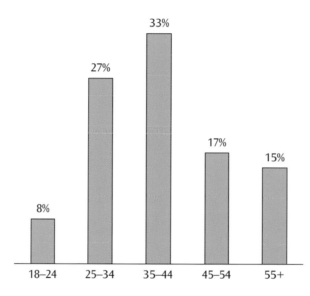

Ages of Same-Sex Unmarried Partners

- 18–24: 8%
- 25–34: 27%
- 35–44: 33%
- 45–54: 17%
- 55+: 15%

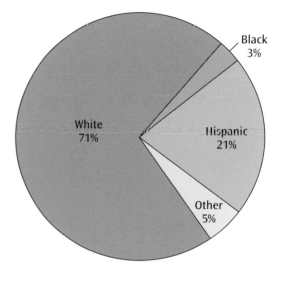

Race/Ethnicity of Householder in Same-Sex Unmarried Partner Households

- White 71%
- Black 3%
- Hispanic 21%
- Other 5%

Presence of Children under Age 18 in Same-Sex Unmarried Partner Households

- No children 72%
- Children 28%

PORTLAND, OREGON

Concentration of Gay/Lesbian Couples (by tract)

Very high concentration
High concentration
Moderate concentration
Low concentration
ZCTA boundary
68506 ZIP Code Tabulation Area
Water

97231
97203
97217
97211
97218
97229
97227
97212
97220
97210
97213
97230
97209
97232
97205
97214
97215
97216
97233
97204
97221
97201
97225
97202
97206
97266
97236
97080
97223
97219
97222
97035 97034

0   3 Miles

Concentration of Gay Male Couples (by tract)

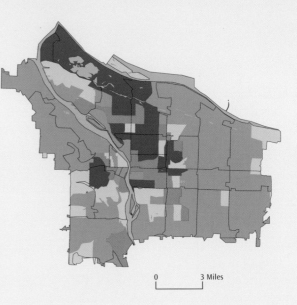

0   3 Miles

Concentration of Lesbian Couples (by tract)

0   3 Miles

MSA Indices

Gay/Lesbian Index	1.38
Gay Male Index	1.20
Lesbian Index	1.56

City Rankings and Indices

	City Index	Rank among top 50 cities	Rank among all communities
Gay/Lesbian	2.39	8	43
Gay Male	2.09	12	69
Lesbian	2.70	3	31

Comparative Statistics

(Portland-Vancouver PMSA)

	All	GL couples	GL rank
Presence of children, among households	35%	19%	306
Seniors (55+), among adults	25%	12%	312
Nonwhite, among adults	16%	13%	240
Females, among adults	51%	43%	19

Top ZIP Codes

	1	2	3	4	5
Gay and lesbian	97211	97212	97214	97215	97213
Gay	97212	97211	97210	97232	97214
Lesbian	97211	97215	97212	97213	97214

Ages of Same-Sex Unmarried Partners

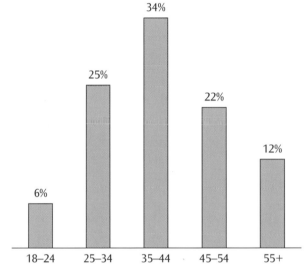

Race/Ethnicity of Householder in Same-Sex Unmarried Partner Households

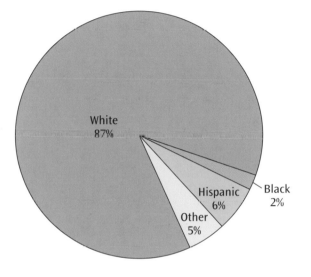

Presence of Children under Age 18 in Same-Sex Unmarried Partner Households

No children 81% Children 19%

SAN DIEGO, CALIFORNIA

Concentration of Gay/Lesbian Couples
(by tract)

Legend:
- Very high concentration
- High concentration
- Moderate concentration
- Low concentration
- ZCTA boundary
- 68506 ZIP Code Tabulation Area
- Water

92027
92025
92065
92128
92067
92127
92014
92130
92129
92121
92126
92131
92040
92122
92037
92117
92124
92071
92111
92119
92109
92123
92120
92110
92108
92116
92115
92107
92103
92104
92105
92101
92102
92114
92106
92118
92113
92139
91911
91932
92154
92173
92154

0   1 Mile

Concentration of Gay Male Couples
(by tract)

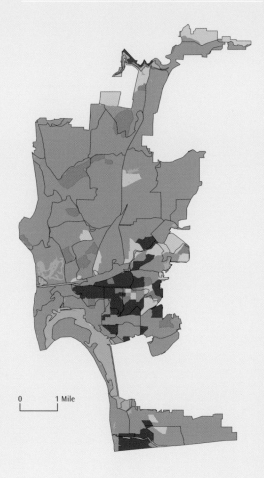

0   1 Mile

Concentration of Lesbian Couples
(by tract)

0   1 Mile

212

MSA Indices

Gay/Lesbian Index	1.36
Gay Male Index	1.52
Lesbian Index	1.21

City Rankings and Indices

	City Index	Rank among top 50 cities	Rank among all communities
Gay/Lesbian	1.86	13	90
Gay Male	2.26	11	57
Lesbian	1.44	14	219

Comparative Statistics

(San Diego MSA)

	All	GL couples	GL rank
Presence of children, among households	37%	21%	290
Seniors (55+), among adults	25%	15%	282
Nonwhite, among adults	40%	30%	93
Females, among adults	50%	34%	47

Top ZIP Codes

	1	2	3	4	5
Gay and lesbian	92103	92104	92116	92115	92102
Gay	92103	92104	92116	92115	92102
Lesbian	92116	92104	92103	92115	92105

Ages of Same-Sex Unmarried Partners

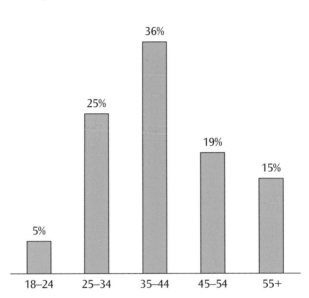

Race/Ethnicity of Householder in Same-Sex Unmarried Partner Households

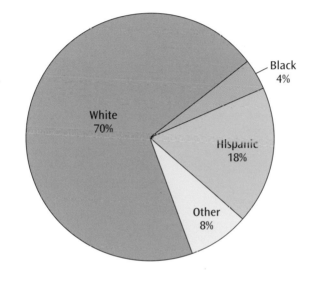

Presence of Children under Age 18 in Same-Sex Unmarried Partner Households

No children 79%   Children 21%

SAN FRANCISCO, CALIFORNIA

Concentration of Gay/Lesbian Couples (by tract)

Concentration of Gay Male Couples (by tract)

Concentration of Lesbian Couples (by tract)

Very high concentration
High concentration
Moderate concentration
Low concentration

ZCTA boundary
68506 ZIP Code Tabulation Area
Water

94111
94104
94133
94123
94129
94108
94109
94105
94115
94118
94102
94121
94103
94117
94107
94122
94114
94110
94116
94127
94131
94124
94132
94112
94134

0   1 Mile

0   1 Mile

0   1 Mile

MSA Indices

Gay/Lesbian Index	3.11
Gay Male Index	4.14
Lesbian Index	2.06

City Rankings and Indices

	City Index	Rank among top 50 cities	Rank among all communities
Gay/Lesbian	4.79	1	11
Gay Male	6.96	1	10
Lesbian	2.57	5	41

Comparative Statistics

(San Francisco PMSA)

	All	GL couples	GL rank
Presence of children, among households	26%	10%	331
Seniors (55+), among adults	27%	14%	300
Nonwhite, among adults	46%	23%	145
Females, among adults	50%	57%	4

Top ZIP Codes

	1	2	3	4	5
Gay and lesbian	94114	94131	94117	94110	94107
Gay	94114	94131	94117	94127	94103
Lesbian	94114	94110	94131	94107	94103

Ages of Same-Sex Unmarried Partners

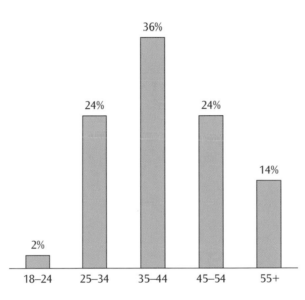

(18–24: 2%; 25–34: 24%; 35–44: 36%; 45–54: 24%; 55+: 14%)

Race/Ethnicity of Householder in Same-Sex Unmarried Partner Households

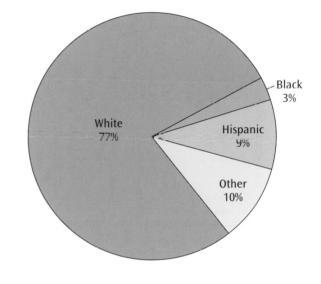

White 77%, Hispanic 9%, Black 3%, Other 10%

Presence of Children under Age 18 in Same-Sex Unmarried Partner Households

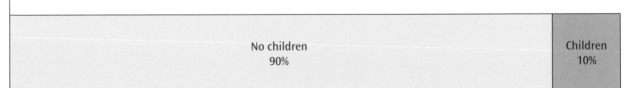

No children 90%   Children 10%

SEATTLE, WASHINGTON

Concentration of Gay/Lesbian Couples
(by tract)

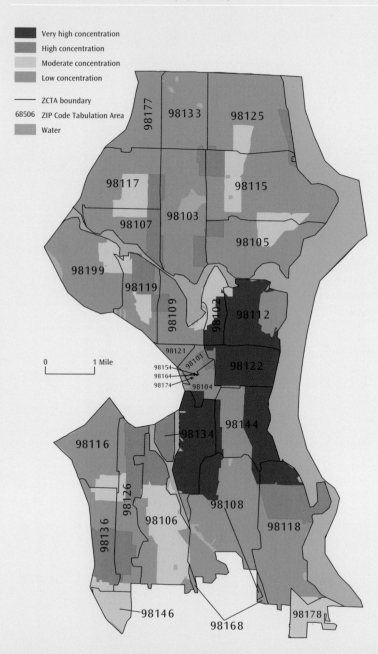

Legend:
- Very high concentration
- High concentration
- Moderate concentration
- Low concentration
- ZCTA boundary
- 68506 ZIP Code Tabulation Area
- Water

98177
98133
98125
98117
98115
98107
98103
98105
98199
98119
98109
98102
98112
98121
98101
98154
98164
98174
98104
98122
98134
98144
98116
98126
98136
98106
98108
98118
98146
98168
98178

0   1 Mile

Concentration of Gay Male Couples
(by tract)

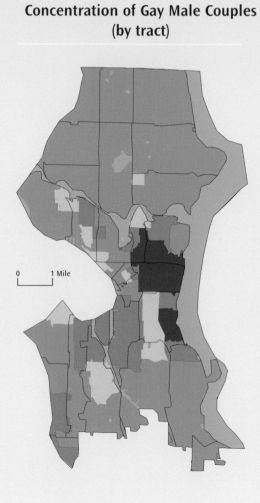

0   1 Mile

Concentration of Lesbian Couples
(by tract)

0   1 Mile

Gay Male Index Rank: 4   Lesbian Index Rank: 15

MSA Indices

Gay/Lesbian Index	1.68
Gay Male Index	1.70
Lesbian Index	1.66

City Rankings and Indices

	City Index	Rank among top 50 cities	Rank among all communities
Gay/Lesbian	3.41	2	25
Gay Male	3.71	4	22
Lesbian	3.10	2	21

Comparative Statistics
(Seattle-Bellevue-Everett PMSA)

	All	GL couples	GL rank
Presence of children, among households	33%	15%	323
Seniors (55+), among adults	24%	12%	319
Nonwhite, among adults	22%	16%	205
Females, among adults	51%	46%	15

Top ZIP Codes

	1	2	3	4	5
Gay and lesbian	98102	98122	98112	98144	98136
Gay	98102	98122	98112	98144	98104
Lesbian	98122	98112	98117	98118	98136

Ages of Same-Sex Unmarried Partners

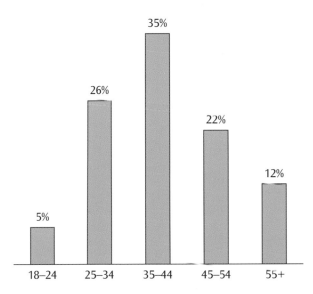

Race/Ethnicity of Householder in Same-Sex Unmarried Partner Households

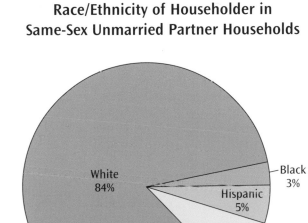

Presence of Children under Age 18 in Same-Sex Unmarried Partner Households

WASHINGTON, D.C.

Concentration of Gay/Lesbian Couples (by tract)

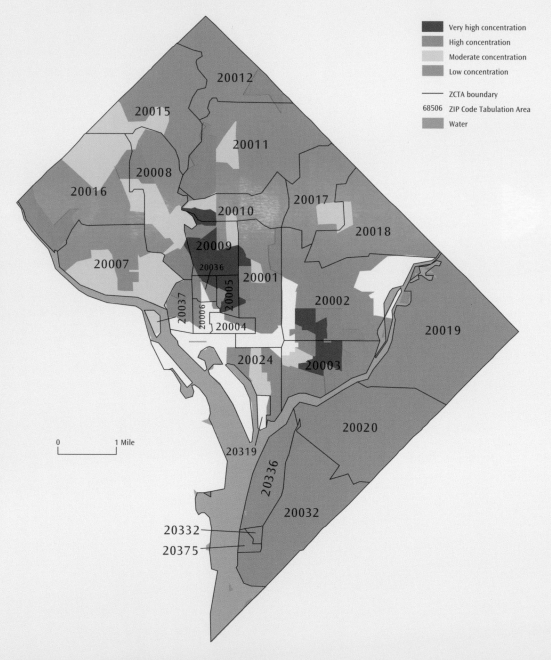

Very high concentration
High concentration
Moderate concentration
Low concentration

— ZCTA boundary
68506 ZIP Code Tabulation Area
Water

20012
20015
20011
20008
20016
20017
20010
20018
20009
20036
20007
20001
20005
20037
20006
20002
20004
20019
20024
20003
20020
20319
20336
20032
20332
20375

0   1 Mile

Concentration of Gay Male Couples (by tract)

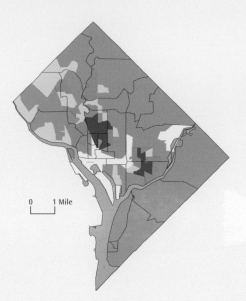

0   1 Mile

Concentration of Lesbian Couples (by tract)

0   1 Mile

MSA Indices

Gay/Lesbian Index	1.33
Gay Male Index	1.51
Lesbian Index	1.13

City Rankings and Indices

	City Index	Rank among top 50 cities	Rank among all communities
Gay/Lesbian	2.63	6	37
Gay Male	3.80	3	21
Lesbian	1.43	16	233

Comparative Statistics

(Washington PMSA)

	All	GL couples	GL rank
Presence of children, among households	37%	19%	308
Seniors (55+), among adults	24%	13%	302
Nonwhite, among adults	42%	31%	90
Females, among adults	52%	32%	66

Top ZIP Codes

	1	2	3	4	5
Gay and lesbian	20036	20009	20005	20003	20010
Gay	20005	20036	20009	20003	20008
Lesbian	20012	20009	20036	20003	20017

Ages of Same-Sex Unmarried Partners

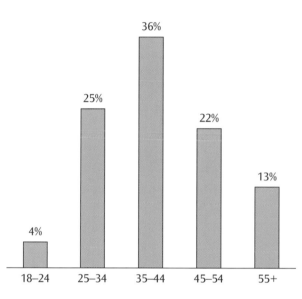

Race/Ethnicity of Householder in Same-Sex Unmarried Partner Households

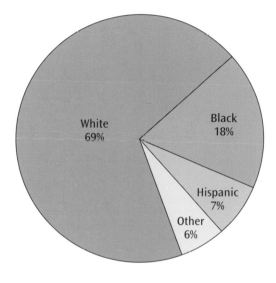

Presence of Children under Age 18 in Same-Sex Unmarried Partner Households

CHAPTER EIGHT

Beyond the *Atlas*

Beyond the *Atlas*

A key motivation for producing this *Atlas* was to demonstrate that census data can dramatically expand our knowledge of the U.S. gay and lesbian population. But these findings are only the beginning. The bulk of the analyses presented rely on only a few questions from the short form, which are answered by someone from every household in the country. One in six households also fill out a long form containing much more detailed information about each member of the household. Analyses of the long-form data can provide insights into patterns of educational attainment, employment and earnings, home ownership, military service, and mobility. These data offer the opportunity for constructing a rich portrait of the lives of gay and lesbian couples in the United States. Such a portrait can better inform nearly every major policy debate affecting the gay and lesbian community. This chapter presents some early findings from analyses of long-form data that have particular cogency to current policy debates.

Civil Marriage for Same-Sex Couples

A recent Massachusetts Supreme Judicial Court decision (*Goodridge et al. v. Department of Public Health*, SJC-98860, decided November 18, 2003) that could compel the state to grant civil marriage licenses to same-sex couples further heightens the most divisive debate about the lives of gay and lesbian Americans. Proponents of civil marriage for same-sex couples argue that since many gay and lesbian couples share such traits as commitment, stability, and child rearing with their married counterparts, denying them the option of marriage amounts to disparate treatment for essentially equal households. Opponents counter that adding same-sex couples to the ranks of the married further erodes a revered institution and potentially undermines its preeminence as the core of family stability and child well-being. So what can census data tell us about this debate?

Many same-sex couples share characteristics with their married counterparts. One in four same-sex couples are raising children, and like their married counterparts, gay and lesbian couples with children have on average two children per household. In the absence of marriage, same-sex couples raising children can face a variety of legal complications in terms of parental rights. When same-sex couples cannot establish dual parental rights through second-parent adoption, the surviving parent and children are left vulnerable if a partner dies. A child without a legal parent may be denied Social Security benefits and health insurance, and parents may not be able to authorize medical treatment for the child in the case of an emergency. Census data show that two-thirds of children being raised by same-sex couples live in states where second-parent adoptions are not a guaranteed option for parents. The lack of second-parent adoption leaves these children at both financial and medical risk.

While the census does not ask specific questions about the stability or commitment of relationships, respondents are asked about home ownership and whether both members of a partnership lived in the same house five years ago. Both measures provide evidence of stability. More than 67 percent of gay and lesbians couples own their home, a figure above the 60 percent rate of U.S. homeownership and below the 78 percent rate among heterosexual couples. Among same-sex couples who have not moved in the last five years, 85 percent have lived in their homes with their partner for at least five years. While that number falls below the rate of 95 percent for heterosexual couples, it still offers evidence that a large portion of same-sex couples live in stable homes and maintain long-term relationships.

Senior gay and lesbian couples represent another group negatively affected by the lack of access to civil marriage. Since they are not married, same-sex senior couples cannot get Social Security survivor benefits when a partner dies. This can result in a sizable reduction of income for the one in 10 gay and lesbian couples that include a partner who is 65 years of age or older. Social Security survivor benefits normally allow a surviving spouse to retain the higher benefit level of the two partners after one dies. The average difference in annual Social Security earnings between two same-sex partners is $5,528 (Bennett and Gates 2004). Marriage would mean that a surviving same-sex partner would retain this income in the event of the death of his or her partner; in the absence of marriage, these survivor benefits are lost. If the same-sex partner with the higher Social Security income dies, the lower-income partner simply retains his or her own benefits, amounting to a loss of more than one-fifth of the average annual gay and lesbian senior income of $25,200.

Workplace Discrimination

Ninety-two of the Fortune 100 companies ban discrimination in the workplace based on sexual orientation, a policy supported by the vast majority of Americans. In contrast, only 14 states and the District of Columbia ban discrimination based on sexual orientation in both public and private employment. Census data provide an outstanding tool to assess both the economic conditions of gay men and lesbians and possible effects of antidiscrimination laws.

Disparities in earnings represent one mechanism often used to document discrimination in a given population. Even when both education and age are taken into account, men in same-sex couples earn less than men partnered with women. For example, a 35- to 44-year-old college-educated man in a same-sex partnership reports median earnings of $53,000 while his counterpart who is either married or partnered with a woman reports median earnings of $60,000. This difference holds across all ages and education levels (Gates 2003b).

Can antidiscrimination laws affect these earnings gaps? Among men with lower education levels, the gap disappears in states with antidiscrimination laws (Gates 2003d). This simple exercise provides some evidence of the policy's effect, but it also demonstrates the utility of census data in exploring these important questions. Measuring the effects of discrimination, especially based on sexual orientation, can be quite complex. A variety of circumstances could explain earnings gaps between gay men and other men. Gay men may choose different occupations and industries in an effort to avoid discrimina-

A 35- to 44-year-old college-educated man in a same-sex partnership reports median earnings of $53,000 while his counterpart who is either married or partnered with a woman reports median earnings of $60,000.

tory environments and accept lower wages in return for more tolerant working conditions, a concept economists call "compensating wage differentials." Since the census provides information on both occupation and industry, the data could be an important tool in informing this much-debated civil rights issue.

Gays in the Military

The so-called "don't ask, don't tell" policy codifies a procedure of silence and invisibility for gay men and lesbians who wish to serve in the American military. The policy prohibits gay men and lesbians from acknowledging who they are in exchange for their military service. Issues of visibility, silence, and recognition are crucial in the debate about the service of gay and lesbian military personnel, as those most affected cannot self-identify to reporters, judges, or their political representatives and actively participate in that debate. In this sense, they cannot exercise the same rights afforded their heterosexual counterparts. At a very basic level, part of the difficulty in analyzing and debating the merits of the "don't ask, don't tell" policy has been proving that forced invisibility is discriminatory toward gay and lesbian military personnel.

Census data for the first time provide a mechanism for estimating the prevalence of gay men and lesbians among America's military personnel. Using a variety of sources including Census 2000, Gates (2003a) estimates that there are one million gay and lesbian veterans in the United States. Further, military service rates among same-sex coupled women exceed those of other women by a factor or five (Gates 2003c). Census estimates demonstrate that gay men and lesbians have and continue to serve in the military. Such estimates mark an important step toward increasing the visibility of gay and lesbian service personnel and question the logic of a policy that forces invisibility among a sizable portion of the American armed forces.

Conclusion

For centuries, cultural and legal prohibitions of homosexuality obscured and often completely hid the lives of gay men and lesbians. While attitudes toward homosexuality are changing, incidents like the tragic murder of Matthew Shepard provide a stark reminder of the risks faced when gay men and lesbians choose to live their lives openly and honestly. Every same-sex couple that checked the box on the census form marked "Unmarried partner" took such a risk and offered a powerful witness to dramatic changes occurring in American society. Their openness provides an opportunity to better understand who they are and how they live.

The myriad maps, charts, and tables contained in this volume will hopefully inform policy debates, help service organizations provide better outreach, and encourage social scientists to explore the changing dynamics of the American family. But the *Atlas* only begins this process. Ongoing analyses offer the promise of constructing a rich and compelling portrait of same-sex couples and their families. Such efforts honor and respect the important decision of more than half a million gay and lesbian couples simply to be counted.

References

Badgett, M.V. Lee. 1995. "The Wage Effects of Sexual Orientation Discrimination." *Industrial and Labor Relations Review* 48: 729–39.

———. 2001. *Money, Myths, and Change: The Economic Lives of Lesbians and Gay Men*. Chicago: University of Chicago Press.

Badgett, M.V. Lee, and Marc A. Rogers. 2003. "Left Out of the Count: Missing Same-Sex Couples in Census 2000." Amherst, MA: Institute for Gay and Lesbian Strategic Studies.

Bennett, Lisa, and Gary J. Gates. 2004. "The Cost of Marriage Inequality to Gay, Lesbian, and Bisexual Seniors." Human Rights Foundation Report. Washington, DC: Human Rights Foundation.

Black, Dan, Gary J. Gates, Seth G. Sanders, and Lowell Taylor. 2000. "Demographics of the Gay and Lesbian Population in the United States: Evidence from Available Systematic Data Sources." *Demography* 37(2): 139–54.

———. 2002. "Why Do Gay Men Live in San Francisco?" *Journal of Urban Economics* 51(1): 54–76.

Brown, Robert, Ruth Washton, and Robert Witeck. 2002. "The Gay and Lesbian Market: New Trends, New Opportunities." http://www.Market Research.com.

Cahill, Sean, Ken South, and Jane Spade. 2000. "Outing Age: Public Policy Issues Affecting Gay, Lesbian, Bisexual and Transgender Elders." New York: Policy Institute of the National Gay and Lesbian Task Force Foundation.

Catania, Joseph A., Dennis Osmond, Ronald D. Stall, Lance Pollack, Jay P. Paul, Sally Blower, Diane Binson, Jesse A. Canchola, Thomas C. Mills, Lawrence Fisher, Kyung-Hee Choi, Travis Porco, Charles Turner, Johnny Blair, Jeffrey Henne, Larry L. Bye, and Thomas J. Coates. 2001. "The Continuing HIV Epidemic among Men Who Have Sex with Men." *American Journal of Public Health* 91(6): 907–14.

Cole, Wendy. 2003. "Being Out at 65: Gay Retirement Communities Are Catching on Fast." *TIME*, 30 June.

Florida, Richard. 2002. *The Rise of the Creative Class*. New York: Basic Books.

Florida, Richard, and Gary J. Gates. 2002. "Technology and Tolerance: Diversity and High Tech Growth." *The Brookings Review* 20(1): 32–35.

Gates, Gary J. 2003a. "Gay Veterans Top One Million." Washington, DC: The Urban Institute.

———. 2003b. "Income of Gay Men Lags Behind That of Men Partnered with Women." Washington, DC: The Urban Institute.

———. 2003c. "Lesbians More Likely to Have Served in the Military." Washington, DC: The Urban Institute.

———. 2003d. "Workplace Protection Linked to Higher Earnings for Less-Educated Gay Men." Washington, DC: The Urban Institute.

Kinsey, Alfred. 1948. *Sexual Behavior in the Human Male*. Bloomington, IN: Indiana University Press.

Laumann, Edward O, John H. Gagnon, and Robert T. Michael. 1994. *The Social Organization of Sexuality: Sexual Practices in the United States*. Chicago: University of Chicago Press.

Lieb, Spencer, Sam Friedman, M. Zeni, D. Chitwood, Tom Liberti, Gary J. Gates, Lorene Maddox, and T. Kuper. 2003. "An HIV

Prevalence-Based Model for Estimating Risk Populations of Men Who Have Sex with Men and Injection Drug Users." Working paper.

National Public Radio. 2003. *All Things Considered,* May 1.

Sell, Randall L., and Christian Petrulio. 1996. "Defining Homosexuals, Bisexuals, Gays, and Lesbians for Public Health Research: A Review of the Literature from 1990 to 1992." *Journal of Homosexuality* 30: 31–47.

Simmons, Tavia, and Martin O'Connell. 2003. "Married-Couple and Unmarried-Partner Households: 2000." Census 2000 Special Reports. Washington, DC: U.S. Census Bureau.

Smith, David, and Gary J. Gates. 2001. "Gay and Lesbian Families in the United States: Same-Sex Unmarried Partner Households." Washington, DC: Human Rights Campaign Foundation.

U.S. Census Bureau. 1975. "Accuracy of Data for Selected Population Characteristics as Measured by the 1970 CPS-Census Match." 1970 Census of Population and Housing, Evaluation and Research Program Report. Washington, DC: U.S. Government Printing Office.

———. 2002. "Census 2000 Basics." Washington, DC: U.S. Government Printing Office.

About the Authors

Gary J. Gates serves as a research associate in the Center on Labor, Human Services, and Population at the Urban Institute. A native of Johnstown, Pennsylvania, Dr. Gates holds a PhD from the H. John Heinz III School of Public Policy and Management at Carnegie Mellon University. His doctoral dissertation included the first research study of the demography of the gay and lesbian population using U.S. Census data; his ongoing work on that subject has been featured in many national media outlets. Dr. Gates cowrote a study examining the interplay of diversity and the location and growth of the technology sector, and facilitated development and implementation of Pennsylvania's first statewide HIV prevention plan. In addition to his PhD, Dr. Gates holds a Master of Divinity degree from St. Vincent Seminary and a BS in Computer Science from the University of Pittsburgh at Johnstown.

Jason Ost is a research associate in the Center on Labor, Human Services, and Population at the Urban Institute. Originally from Lincoln, Nebraska, Mr. Ost received a bachelor's degree from Georgetown University in 1999. He is currently pursuing a master's degree in geography to complement his professional interest in demography and public health.

Index

5988